KENT RUSSELL

IN THE LAND OF GOOD LIVING

Kent Russell's essays have appeared in *The New Republic*, *Harper's Magazine*, *GQ*, *n+1*, *The Believer*, and *Grantland*. He is the author of *I Am Sorry to Think I Have Raised a Timid Son*. He lives in Brooklyn, New York.

IN THE LAND OF GOOD LIVING

IN THE LAND OF GOOD LIVING

A Journey to the Heart of Florida

KENT RUSSELL

VINTAGE BOOKS
A Division of Penguin Random House LLC
New York

FIRST VINTAGE BOOKS EDITION, MAY 2021

Copyright © 2020 by Kent Russell

All rights reserved. Published in the United States by Vintage Books,
a division of Penguin Random House LLC, New York, and distributed in Canada
by Penguin Random House Canada Limited, Toronto. Originally published
in hardcover in the United States by Alfred A. Knopf, a division
of Penguin Random House LLC, New York, in 2020.

Vintage and colophon are registered
trademarks of Penguin Random House LLC.

Grateful acknowledgment is made to HarperCollins Publishers for permission
to reprint an excerpt of "The Florida Poem" from *Florida Poems* by Campbell
McGrath. Copyright © 2002 by Campbell McGrath. Reprinted by
permission of HarperCollins Publishers.

The Library of Congress has cataloged the Knopf edition as follows:
Names: Russell, Kent, author.
Title: In the land of good living : a journey to the heart of Florida / Kent Russell.
Description: First edition. | New York : Alfred A. Knopf, 2020.
Identifiers: LCCN 2019045678 (print) | LCCN 2019045679 (ebook)
Subjects: LCSH: Russell, Kent—Travel—Florida. | Florida—Description and travel.
Classification: LCC F316.2 .R87 2020 (print) | LCC F316.2 (ebook) |
DDC 917.5904—dc23
LC record available at https://lccn.loc.gov/2019045678
LC ebook record available at https://lccn.loc.gov/2019045679

Vintage Books Trade Paperback ISBN: 978-0-525-56319-8
eBook ISBN: 978-0-525-52139-6

Author photograph © Benjamin Travers
Book design by Soonyoung Kwon

www.vintagebooks.com

For Florida, and Ders

Even if Florida does not believe in history
it cannot help but believe
in the tide, and the tide for its part is
a compelling historian.

—CAMPBELL McGRATH, POET

We went there to serve God, and also to get rich.

—BERNAL DÍAZ DEL CASTILLO, CONQUISTADOR

IN THE LAND OF GOOD LIVING

EXT. U.S. ROUTE 98—HIGH NOON

Three friends—GLENN, NOAH, and KENT—walk a SHOPPING CART loaded with hiking packs and film gear along the shoulder of a beachside highway. Occasionally, one or another steals a glance at the backward-facing CAMERA mounted atop their cart.

Trudging rightmost in its wide shot is GLENN, a blond, blue-eyed, dad-bodied man in his early thirties. Were it not a contradiction in terms, UNAPOLOGETICALLY CANADIAN is a phrase one might use to describe him. The puzzled smile permafrosted across Glenn's face shows him to be too alive to nuance and contradiction to be American. He often fusses with the camera's framing, as he is the only one with experience in documentary film.

Pushing the cart next to Glenn is NOAH, a short, scowling IRAQ WAR VETERAN. Noah's formerly bulging muscles are swaddled with a layer of fat, as if the action figure of his past life has been packed away under Bubble Wrap. He would be more intimidating if the tattoos sleeving his limbs were related to anything other than DUNGEONS & DRAGONS. Written in two rows across the knuckles gripping the handlebar is the phrase *I CRY OUT / FOR MAGIC.*

Limping closest to the westbound lane is KENT, a PAUNCHY NEBBISH and the youngest of the three. Because he once contributed essays and reviews to magazines, Kent considers himself something of an ARTISTE and/ or INTELLECTUAL. He grew a long and flowing mullet in anticipation of this return to his home state.

> GLENN
> (adjusting camera)

Okay, so. We open on us walking like this, only we're arguing over what the tagline of the doc should be.

> NOAH

Dudes, where's our car.

KENT

We could riff on a real one. State's tagline.

KENT (CONT'D)

(scrolling through smartphone browser)

We've got: *The Sunshine State,* obviously. *The Orange State. The Peninsula State.*

Inches away, an eighteen-wheeler barrels past the men, SHATTERING the stillness of the sun-dazed landscape beyond their shoulders. They don't flinch, but the lovebugs hovering about their faces scatter with the displaced air.

GLENN

We have to consider tone. What is the tone we wish to convey?

KENT

Elegiac. We want this to be the state's swan song. The last, most comprehensive postcards from Florida as we know her. Before she takes the waters.

GLENN

What about a riff on that sign from Waffle House? "You had a choice, and you chose us."

NOAH

Every buddy movie should begin at the Waffle House.

GLENN

Only it's *Florida: You had a choice, and you chose this.*

KENT

Florida: Would we lie to you?

NOAH

Florida: Where America goes to die.

    The friends fall silent for a few dozen paces. They pass tacky condos and T-shirt shops. The lovebugs return.

GLENN

What a saltwater-taffy shithole this is.

NOAH

(pensive)

What we *should* do . . . is draw an *n* at the end of that Ramada sign. At the end of every Ramada sign we pass. And then film what happens.

KENT

Florida: If it weren't true, we'd have to invent it.

NOAH

Then we'd get to the *real*-real about this place.

GLENN

(lifting camera from cart)

Hold up. Say that again?

NOAH

This has already gotten old, my dude.

GLENN (O.S.)

So, okay, I'll film you two—

NOAH

Fuck outta here with that. We need to stop and eat first.

KENT

Then we'll come back and set it up. Yelp says that that auto shop over there's got good Mexican in the back.

GLENN (O.S.)
(resignedly)

Our heroes steel themselves with four-pound plates of chimichangas. Just like in the other grand adventure narratives.

FADE OUT

MILE 73 ——— DESTIN

TO ARRIVE WHERE WE STARTED,
AND TO KNOW THE PLACE
FOR THE FIRST TIME

We've been lying here—on drainage swales, mostly, but also in the beds of pickup trucks—for nigh on four hours now. We'll be lying here when Ocean Drive is returned to its namesake, feels like.

Noah and I have grown stiff as marks in this mini-mall parking lot, where we're waiting for Glenn to conclude his business with the Geek Squad. It appears as though Glenn's laptop broiled inside his pack yesterday while we walked the seventeen miles from Wynnehaven Beach to the resort town of Destin. Or maybe these seventeen miles were the last straw, who knows. We've walked (and filmed) seventy-three sweltering miles during this first week of our journey.

If Glenn's computer is toast, we are well and truly boned. Lose that hard drive, and we lose what we've shot, sure. But we lose future footage, too, because what are we going to process it on? We have not the wiggle room in our budget for a new MacBook.

So to calm my nerves, I jot this while huddling in the shade of a decorative sapling. I'm a freelance writer in my civilian life. This means, firstly, that I am a failure in the practice of ordinary existence. Secondly, it means that I get by on my wits. I make my living inside of language. What I can't control out there, I refashion in here.

But writing's not *writing* unless it's got a figure of address. An other, real or imagined, at the opposite end of the bargain. *O Muse,* it used to be. Then *O Lord.* I think I'll go with "friend." *O friend,* since friendship starts with invitation. It begins at the point where it offers itself, be it with an extended hand or a once-in-a-lifetime proposition. Therefore, friend: I propose you join us as we sit here praying that our angle isn't botched before it's had the chance to get off the ground.

Speaking of which—the blacktop in this plaza is rippling like a runway post-takeoff. Not a car or shopper is stirring, nor has one been for a minute now. Things are still as a tableau in this commercial garden, where we've got, what: a liquor outlet, cigar store, fitness franchise. A beach-supply warehouse with an array of rafts and limp flags out front, along with neon poster board promises of *Free Hermit Crab with Every Purchase.* The usual. A Chinese buffet. A Big Lots! Bibs of evaporated oil in each empty parking spot. Itchy air, thick with humidity as well as biotic chaff. Chain pharmacy, cell phone service provider, real estate office deigning not to advertise. Between this and the few rags of cloud above are power lines like musical staves. The thrum I feel seeping into me—couldn't tell you if it was from the coursing of grounded electricity or the buzzing, writhing, germinating plainsong of Florida under the late-summer sun.

And, as if summoned by this thrum—out from under the dumpster behind the Sonic Drive-In a snake came writhing. A flaking snake, in the midst of shedding. It undulated across the asphalt, slithered onto a swale parallel to mine. Then it slipped into a sluice pipe. As soon as the snake had disappeared, it's like a switch flipped—cars turned in off the highway and shoppers pushed carts down storefront aprons.

"Hey, Noah," I called out. "Kind of snake was that?"

"What snake?" Noah responded. I twisted my head and saw his hot-weather combat boots poking toes-up from a lowered tailgate. "Is it a coral snake?" he deadpanned. "Is it coming directly this way?"

After a minute or two, I asked: "You think Glenn's getting his computer fixed in there?"

"I don't care if that computer is dead and buried," Noah said. "We're walking. We're shooting on goddamned iPhones if we have to."

"I hear you," I replied. "The sunk costs are very great. And it'd be humiliating as hell, calling my uncle to come back and get us one week in."

"Hell, man," Noah said. "This guy's not even a real videographer. Who even knows if he's been hitting record half the time."

He's not wrong, I thought. But what I said was: "Glenn's legit, man. Everything's gonna work out."

Ten years ago, Noah was fresh out of the Marine Corps and I was his college-boy neighbor at a run-down apartment complex near the University of Florida named, what else, the Ritz. The Ritz was a favorite haunt of junkies and armed robbers. It also was dirt cheap and had rooms to rent month to month. Most importantly, it's where Noah and I became fast friends. Though seemingly different as different can be, the two of us discovered we were complementary. Noah was a standoffish loner and a tough guy, a legitimate one, having finished more bar fights than he'd started. I was less dweeby bookworm than incautious Kerouac wannabe; this half observer, half shit-stirrer who hovered between worlds while dwelling for the most part in the one of my own fashioning.

Noah grew fond of me in the manner of a big brother. Whereas he to me represented this original source I'd been too long and too far removed from. We fit together and dangerously so, like a motorcycle and its sidecar. What kept us connected was the ability to articulate self- and world-loathing in a way that made the other laugh. So we'd crack wise over old horror movies or while tossing around a football. Some nights, we'd have what you might call "adventures." Other nights, we'd sit in silence in front of the Xbox as Noah cultivated the remote and private air of a man who had *seen some shit*. Midweek, we'd suffer through our "Wednesday Night Throwdown," wherein we housed suitcases of beers before squaring off in the courtyard and charging one another like rival rams, shouting *"Defend yourself!"* all the while, Noah slap-boxing as if hoping to knock the timidity out of me like dust from a rug.

Fast-forward to 2014, when I was hosting Noah in my Brooklyn apartment. "Hosting" being maybe too euphemistic a word.

Noah was deep in student-loan debt and without a place to stay after (1) graduating from a criminal-justice master's program in Manhattan, but (2) breaking up with the girlfriend he'd moved to New York to be with. He had sold his pickup truck to fund the initial relocation, so he couldn't even live out of that. Owing to our history at the Ritz, I offered Noah an air mattress on the floor of my "home office." Temporary, like. After he'd stabbed that Coleman GuestRest to death—in his sleep, with his Ka-Bar knife, during some kind of PTSD-inflected night terror—Noah received a cot. Months later, jobless still, he got his own bed.

Noah spent his days applying to jobs online. His nights he spent drinking hard while blasting Poison's *Open Up and Say . . . Ahh!* from my stereo. His employment history read as such: dishwasher, fry cook, USMC artilleryman, apprentice carpenter, assistant medical examiner, security guard at an Alabama island for millionaires. Lots of jobs, yet Noah lacked a coherent skill set. He could bench-press three-hundred-plus pounds but could not touch-type. I asked him what his ideal job would be, and he said, "Hasn't changed since I was thirteen years old. Front man in a cock-rock band. Failing that— professional wrestler."

Thus did we find ourselves one evening in my apartment: Noah was unemployed, I was between freelance assignments, and together we were whiling away the hours watching a Little League World Series doubleheader on TV. It was serendipity, perhaps, that we were many Coorses deep by the time a commercial for the film adaptation of Cheryl Strayed's *Wild* came on.

"Dude," Noah said. "There it is."

"Only if you're buying the tickets," I drolled.

"The answer, dude." He placed his beer on the coffee table, knuckled himself upright on the couch. "You need to find something to write about, right? *I* need to find something to occupy my time, lest I blast myself and others. We *both* need to get rich, and quick."

"Agreed on all counts," I said after emptying my beer.

"So . . . ?"

"So?"

Now, once he'd worked out of his . . . funk, let's call it . . . post-Iraq, Noah used his G.I. Bill benefits to study history at his local University of West Florida. At UWF, he became enamored of Walkin'

Lawton Chiles, our former governor and senator, the cornpone "He-Coon" who is remembered as one of Florida's favoritest sons. In my apartment that evening, Noah muted the TV and explained it: In 1970, Chiles was an electoral nobody—only 12 percent of Florida voters recognized his name—so he decided to canvass the state on foot, county by county, town by town, on a "walking-talking and listening campaign." Some 1,003 miles later, Chiles had captured the imagination of the state and launched a high-profile political career that lasted until his sudden death in 1998. "No one's sure if Lawton really, actually did it," Noah said, "or if he took rides in the support trailer behind him. All we have to go on is his journal, which spends about a third of the time describing the meals he ate."

"Huh," I said. "So you're saying—*try it again fifty years later*." I hopped off the couch, began to pace the apartment. I got a little worked up, I must admit. I pattered aloud about how Florida is absolutely bereft of mythic infrastructure. How it is symbolically impoverished, how it has no hallowed grounds besides golf courses and no great cathedrals outside of adventure parks.

Florida, I said, is the only megastate in this union—is in fact the most important place in *America*—that has never defined itself. Florida has always been construed by outsiders, has been typecast by those with allegiances to elsewhere. "Imagine New York without its media or literary champions," I said. "Or California without Hollywood."

Florida is spiritually unclaimed, was my point. It's never had a hero of history like the cowboy or frontiersman for its people to rally around.

That night, Noah and I resolved to become those heroes. We'd be the native sons who created the grandest, funniest, most far-ranging, depth-plumbing, tear-jerking, je-ne-sais-quoi-capturing work of art ever to emerge from the rank morasses and mirage metropolises of our beloved home!

"*Vanishing* home," Noah pointed out. "Climate change. Rising tides. Place is sinking back into the water, don't forget. There's our timeliness peg."

It was decided. We'd give Florida the elegy she deserved. We toasted ourselves.

Of course, we toasted ourselves many times more that night.

When we came to the next afternoon, our plan had curdled somewhat. Spoiling our excitement was the sour taste of real-life exigency. (For one thing: the lactic acid we would have to expend.) Over the course of days, then weeks, then months, our plan fell out of focus. We hadn't consciously rejected it so much as recognized it as fantasy. We'd love to see it through, yet it was practically impossible for us to imagine taking the time necessary not only to plan such a trip but to carry it out.

Noah found a job—at JPMorgan Chase, of all places. Something about billions of dollars in fines levied by the U.S. government, and Chase needing to hire more veterans as part of their penance. Noah settled in as a client investigator. He found and promptly married a young bride, whose extended, very Polish family understood four or five syllables of my best-man speech. He moved to Queens and climbed slowly out of debt.

I, meanwhile, puttered apace. I adjunct-instructed a handful of undergraduate courses at Columbia University, where the six grand they paid me in no way remunerated my efforts. I authored several hacky magazine features, for which the dwindling cents-per-word rates were no better. In lieu of updating my résumé, I revised my bio whenever a publication I had written for folded. Day jobs—I had a few. But traditional employ does not agree with me. Mostly what I did during this period was worry that my shallow wellspring of story ideas had been exhausted by my first book, which was a commercial catastrophe.

Nevertheless, while Noah thrived, I kept on keeping on, at least in terms of being a moody, difficult, irresolute fellow plagued by tensions and contradictions. My hypos got the upper hand of me, as they say. I drank deeper and deeper of the bottles of Old Overholt I bought every week. Then every five days. Then every two. I put on records by that good Catholic boy Ronnie James Dio and staggered about my apartment, medicine in hand held steady as a gyroscope. Without Noah there, I was free to kick about my piles of remaindered hardcovers like a stinko dragon circling the worthless ingots in its den. I ordered delivery nonstop. I lost weekends to actions that felt newly taken but were in truth the original action acted out over and over again. I went to Sunday Masses trashed, so that I might meet my maker while buoyed with Dutch courage.

Here I will cop to the fact that I had no mortgage payments and no outstanding student loans. No health crises, car accidents, run-ins with the law. Nor parents, siblings, or children in dire financial straits. Yes. Seemingly blessed in most respects.

And forasmuch as I would like to wax pedantic about how it takes greater virtue to bear good fortune than bad—don't worry. In due time, fate's fickle hand shot me the bird, which arrived in the form of a letter from the government. According to this certified letter, I *was* beholden to something. Ho ho. I owed $37,000 in back taxes to the Internal Revenue Service. For you see, when you are granted an advance on a book prior to its publication, the check you receive has none of your federal, state, or city taxes deducted from it. It's one big lump sum, like the number stamped on an oversized game-show check. And cashing such a ludicrous check, I can assure you—it induces a kind of stupor. Witnessing your ATM balance wink from three integers to six, you can't help but shush the small inner voice that warns: *You know that check was worth about half of what it said it's worth, right?*

So if one were to, say, blow through all of one's advance? After improperly reporting said advance on one's tax return? One might discover that one owes Uncle Sam the dregs of one's savings account. And then some. And then *then* some, garnished wages and all (if one had wages to garnish), since Uncle Sam had been attempting to bill one at one's old address back in Manhattan, compounding interest as he went.

I *had* to go on Noah's walk now. Hastily I educated myself, reading every walking narrative I could find. But in absorbing walking narrative after walking narrative, I came to realize that I *loathed* walking narratives. I loathed their epiphanies. Their treacly sentimentality. Most especially, I loathed their tropes. Like, the walk-as-exorcism. The walk-as-self-sanctification. The walk as fast shuffle of stale experiences. As through line between me-as-I-was and me-as-I-am.

Walking and confessional writing have been convoluted for centuries, basically since the time of Rousseau, who noted: "Never did I think so much, exist so vividly, and experience so much, never have I been so much myself . . . as in the journeys I have taken alone and on foot." What Rousseau started, the Romantics popularized. Their peripatetic heroes walked and pondered, walked and pondered.

They jotted down the discursive links between their thinking and their strolling in "nature" (some footpaths around a country estate, usually). By turns maudlin and peevish, these fancy boys sounded out their selves with each step. Like the Sierra Club after them, they sought to repair their sense of lost unity by hiking through pretty scenery.

And, Christ—bourgeois origins notwithstanding, America *loves* this hero.

Why should this be? Maybe it's because "the soul of the [pedestrian] journey is liberty, perfect liberty . . . to think, feel, do just as one pleases," as Hazlitt wrote. Maybe it's because "Afoot and lighthearted I take to the open road, / Healthy, free, the world before me . . . Henceforth I ask not good fortune, I myself am good fortune," as Whitman wrote.

Maybe it's because the road is supposed to be the American's home, and movement his means of expression. The only way I can truly *pursue* happiness is if I take off after it down that American Way. And so on.

Yeah, I wanted to write about none of that. Neither self nor scenery nor old, dusty trail. The only state I wished to chronicle was Florida. Understanding and then making credible my birthplace—the peninsula that stupefies, sickens, infuriates, and finally embarrasses the rest of the nation—was task enough for me. But how best to capture it?

I marinated on that. Wily as I judged myself to be writing-wise, I felt I lacked the chops to match up against my home. Almost daily it tossed up villains and tragedies that were the envy of any novelist, to say nothing of a reality artist in desperate need of quick bucks.

Then I asked myself: Wait a minute, does one *describe* an advertisement? A franchise? A souvenir store, gated subdivision, drive-in church? Of course not! These are all signs, and one does not describe signs. Words slip from these as though they are Teflon-coated. No, signs you take pictures of. Dreamscapes, you film.

So we'd make a gonzo documentary! Duh! We'd go it alone, sleep anywhere, interview anybody, live on almost nothing, eat and drink whatever, befriend strangers rich or poor, sane or not. We'd brave the worst that heat and sun, mishap and blister, officialdom, prejudice, and politics could do to us. Most crucially, we'd film nonstop. Altogether *sui generis*, behaving just as we pleased, we would do what the Chamber of Commerce has always encouraged: *Come on down to Florida, and exploit her! Use* her *resources to satisfy* your *wants*.

I pitched Noah. He thought the idea excellent. What especially excited him, he told me, was the prospect of quitting his corporate-greed-enabling gig at Chase. "I felt less bad shooting at people during the siege of Fallujah," he said. Problem was, neither of us knew anything about documentary filmmaking. So the plan stalled again.

A couple of weeks later, out of the blue, I received a Google Chat message from a guy I'd studied writing with—Glenn. From our limited time together in New York City, I'd known Glenn to be an affable Ottawan, a genuinely sympathetic guy who had been socialized within a functioning family in a functioning democracy. An excellent youth tennis player and camp counselor, like. The kind of progressive international who betrays no anguish over, say, a God-shaped hole. Who believes the best lack all conviction. That's the Glenn I palled around with: the near-ideal product of a tolerant society.

We were as much fascinated by each other as we were repulsed. While we studied "cultural reporting and criticism," whatever that could possibly mean, Glenn and I engaged in epic weekly drinking bouts. Friday nights at dive bars across the city, we two contraries roared like men who had carried a confrontation with each other to its distressing limits before suddenly safely passing those limits. Bit by bit, I learned that Glenn had been born in Malawi to a diplomat father and an accountant mother. At age four he returned with his parents to Canada, where he was treated to the aforementioned idyll in suburban Ottawa. Nothing much to report, Glenn contended. He wasn't even that rebellious of a teen, since the idea of rebelling in order to gain identity requires that you have something to rebel *against*. Canada is . . . post-liberally humane. To a fault.

Mostly there was the basilisking glare of television, of mall movie theaters. That's where Glenn's filmmaking enthusiasm was stoked. The screen gave him something to crane his neck toward, like a plant in a hothouse with a single bulb above.

After receiving his English degree from McGill University in Montreal, Glenn spent a few gap years tramping around Africa with the woman who would become his wife. He freelanced news stories to Canadian outlets. When those didn't kick-start a whirlwind career, he became the tiniest bit depressed. Depressed enough to consider entering the field of nonprofit development, I should clarify. Traveling around the continent, Glenn became fascinated by the ways in which systems break down, noble intentions go awry. He decided to involve himself in some real white-savior stuff: water purification projects, mobile financial networks for informal economies—you know the type. Then he realized he had no future in any of that. Aimless and listless, Glenn made the mistake of applying to a writing program in New York City. Which was where "our destinies became commingled," as he put it.

On Google Chat, Glenn caught me up with his life. Turned out, he had abandoned the writing thing four years ago, when he moved to Toronto. Turned out, he was working in documentary film—first as an assistant, now as a producer. Mere days ago, in fact, he'd finished shooting a couple episodes of a Vice Media television show.

But he was having something of a thirty-three-and-a-third life crisis, he told me. "I'm tired of being a do-boy for tattooed chefs getting drunk in Copenhagen" was how he phrased it. What he wanted to do, he confessed, was *direct*.

"So," Glenn typed. "I need a project. And I thought maybe it'd be fun to come up with something together."

"Boy," I replied. *"Wouldn't it."*

~~~~~~~

First I had to enlighten Glenn. Which was easy enough, since every native Floridian regardless of occupation happens also to be a psychoanalyst of our state. This is because people, when they find out one of us is actually *from* the place (and they see that our eyes are clear, and we do not twitch involuntarily like a sleeping pack animal), tend to take us by the arm and wonder earnestly: Just what is the *deal* with Florida?

The deal with Florida, I told Glenn, is the charlatans and lunatics and Snapchat-famous plastic surgeons. It is the Ponzi schemes, the Byzantine corruption, the evangelical fervor, and the consenting-adult depravity. It is the seasonless climate. The lack of historical consciousness. The way in which this nation's unctuous elements tend to trickle down as though Florida were the grease trap under

America's George Foreman Grill. It is the bath salts. It is all of the above, and more on top of that.

Its name means "feast of flowers," I explained, but what "Florida" has come to connote is: hucksters, boosters, and fly-by-night mountebanks. Carpetbaggers, chicanerers, and salesfellows who grafted the American Dream onto strange roots in sandy soil. These rule breakers and rainmakers constructed modern Florida within the last seventy-odd years. They were able to do this because, unlike those of Hawaii and California, Florida's plots were bog-cheap, its taxes nonexistent, and the flat, empty canvas of its peninsula allowed for the projection of any and all fantasies. Every single day since 1950, about a thousand people have been lured to Florida by its chimerical promise. (Several hundred recent arrivals also *flee* every day, repelled or disillusioned by what they've found, but we needn't trouble ourselves with them.)

In an astonishingly brief span of time, Florida has grown from a backwater of 955,000 mostly white, mostly rural, mostly Southern-born inhabitants to our third most crowded state. Its population of newcomers is more ethnically, racially, and religiously diverse than the United States itself. As a result, Florida is now the petri dish whence things like Stand Your Ground laws, core curricula, and majority-minority city governments spring. It is where fabulous wealth, natural splendor, and unfettered desire intermingle with systemic poverty, inequality, violence, and addiction. Growth here is pegged to housing and defense industries, the largesse of corporate giants, the fairy tale of expansion-in-perpetuity—and yet, for all of the rhetoric about entrepreneurship, global convergence, and affordable mortgages for all, everyday life in Florida is *still* tied to the service sector, is *still* a perilous, debt-ridden existence stitched together from the shreds of part-time shifts. Oh, also: The rising seas caused by global climate change will wash over this state within a hundred years—and we're *still* selling the dream, *still* hawking waterfront condos as fast as we can build them.

"This is vulgar and despair-inducing," Glenn offered in reply.

"Yes, fine, whatever!" I said. "But know that the vulgarity and despair exist only *because of* the rest of the country." Florida is a pure creation of others' demand. It is a reflection of the hopes and wants of America at large. Florida's retirees, its vacationing families, its arriviste millionaires looking for second homes and tax havens—to say nothing of the losers and dreamers and petty criminals who drive down the map in search of orange groves, smoking rivers, and third chances—these people are *us*.

There was a simpler way to put it, I said. *"Florida: America Concentrate*™.*"*

Glenn was aboard. Noah—aboard. They made peace with their wives; I found a subletter. Together we emptied our savings accounts, rainy-day funds, and IRAs. We applied for new credit cards. We Skyped to plan, ostensibly, but mostly we giggled. Finally, in late August 2016, grinning as though expecting our bluff to be called *any moment now!*, the three of us convened in Atlanta, where my uncle lives. He'd agreed to drive us to the Florida-Alabama border. My uncle was in fact a little disappointed that we hadn't invited him along, for my uncle is something of an adventurer himself, albeit a real one. Guy used to compete in Ironman Triathlons and has through-hiked the likes of the Pacific Crest *and* Appalachian trails. When he got his first look at the three of us, though—at the Dunwoody MARTA station snapping our fingers at one another's crotches while wearing basketball shorts and shower slides—the guy wires supporting his smile snapped.

He insisted on taking us to REI posthaste. There, he perched upon a hunting stool and tried to slacken his cramp of disgust. We'd need *these* kinds of underwear, he said, and actual packs (not camera bags, which Glenn had brought along). "We gotta get this," I said, extending and collapsing a retractable baton in the self-defense aisle. "You try to use that against a criminal," Noah responded, "and it for sure is going to end up in your butt."

My uncle ordered us to march a few laps around the store while wearing our loaded packs. Doing so, I caught a glimpse of myself in a full-length mirror. Friend, let me tell you—I am built for the sartorial generosities of sweater weather. My training regimen leading up to this trip had been: mash out thirty minutes on the elliptical machine; hit the bar; use customer rewards points for Papa John's on the way home. Like a functionally alcoholic baseball player rolling into spring training twenty pounds overweight, I figured I'd play myself into shape. Honestly, I'd put more effort into my lustrous, shoulder-length mullet.

The next day, we piled into my uncle's SUV and drove to Florida's westernmost border. Along the way, Noah and Glenn took the opportunity to size each other up IRL. I'm sure they also took note of the different versions of my self I presented when addressing one guy and then the other. But since I cannot abide being an interpersonal go-between (sink or swim, my dogs), I turned our attention to a paper map of Florida whenever possible.

"What's your budget per day, gents?" my uncle asked from the driver's seat.

We stared at him blankly. "What about per week?" he tried again. "Per month?"

We didn't have an answer for him.

"How many miles do you have to walk per day to meet your deadline?"

The three of us turned to one another, shook our heads, shrugged.

Midafternoon, we pulled up to the Flora-Bama Lounge, a debaucherous indoor/outdoor Hooverville that straddles both states. We sat down, had a beer. "I'll be staying the night in Gulf Shores," my uncle said. "So if you change your mind . . . you know . . . there's no shame in that."

We cinched our packs and said our goodbyes. We clomped through a deckside bingo game on our way to the beach. Dropping onto the fine grain, we took our first small steps as effortlessly as astronauts on the moon. For one hundred paces, we were away and floating. Then Glenn said, "I suppose I should be filming this." We turned back. By the time we'd made it a hundred feet past *that,* we had concluded that walking on shifting sands with forty-five-pound packs on our shoulders was the worst possible introduction to our odyssey.

We moved to the two-lane highway running east-west through Perdido Key. We plodded past grim hotels and fried fish shacks. Noah tried scooching over to the weedy, sloping, safer turf abutting the road's narrow shoulder. Thrice in the span of a mile, he shrieked when his foot sank through the soft detonating pad of a red-ant land mine. The third time this happened, he jogged into the scrub, kicked like a chorus girl, fell over, and needed help returning to his feet.

Quickly did we learn that it was impossible for us to lower our heads and trudge mulishly. We simply *needed* to look into windshields.

A watched pot never boils; likewise, a motorist-made-eye-contact-with won't knock my lungs out of my mouth. Or so it seemed.

"How many drivers do you think have passed wondering if this is a gun in my hand," Glenn asked, scanning the horizon with his 4k camera.

We cut across parking lots where many pairs of warblers were chasing one another in dipping synchronicity, like fine tango dancers. We spanned several bridges and reached mainland Florida just as the sun extinguished itself offshore. Our taffied shadows stretched farther and farther away from us until they dissolved into the mauve dusk. We turned down an unlighted stretch of highway.

Our knees creaked until they'd locked our legs straight. We tottered on if only to keep from pitching over. At last, a small Baptist church emerged from the timbered darkness.

We'd tromped eight miles, all told, and we could tromp no more. We lurched toward the teens fellowshipping in the playground. Before we got within twenty yards of them, one of the young women sprinted into the church. Out came three burly men, striding at us with purpose.

Long story short: Noah was able to disarm them with Panhandle candor. We dropped our packs. Under arc lights in the parking lot, we stretched, shuddered, and yowled like men undergoing werewolf transformations. One of the pastors noticed Glenn's wedding band. Glenn told him what he'd told us: Upon being asked what she thought of his going on this trip, Glenn's wife had responded in the affirmative with such enthusiasm that Glenn had wondered, briefly, if she was having an affair. But then his wife pointed out that this trip was a world-class learning experience. Rather than collecting another useless diploma at film school, Glenn would "invest" his money in this. He'd learn on the fly how to be a director, cinematographer, casting agent, key grip.

The pastor placed a hand on Glenn's shoulder, walked him a few steps away from the group. In a low voice, he told him: "If you need marriage counseling, son . . ."

Try as we might, we could not convince these Baptists that the three of us were a danger to none but ourselves. They informed us that sleeping in the church was out of the question, though we were welcome to camp in the woods behind it so long as we watched out for coyotes. They wished us good luck. Then they hesitated before leaving. They asked if we believed in Jesus Christ. I bugged my eyes at Glenn and Noah until they nodded their assent. The men prayed over us, earnestly beseeching our blessing in Christ's name.

"Don't see how it could hurt," Noah said after. He half-assembled his tent with the indifference of a guy who's slept in places far, far worse. "Gentlemen," he added with a nod of his head before ducking under his flap.

Glenn and I had decided to share a two-man tent. Mostly for logistical reasons; Glenn's pack was filled with film gear, so he hadn't the room for a sleeping pad, much less a tent. In his most condescending camp-counselor voice, he explained how I was supposed to stake the tent poles and attach the rain fly. I followed along as best I could.

We'd been punchy on the road, but now we were too drained for yuks. The tent grew hot, close, and thick with masculine reek. A smell not necessarily *bad,* no, just piquant, like a crumbly blue cheese. I dozed to the intermittent *thwap* of hissing things searching for ingress.

That was one day down. Six later, here we were in a parking lot strewn with shopping carts rolling about like ghost ships. I glanced from them to our packs. "We are fools," I announced.

"What now?" Noah asked from his truck bed.

Hobblingly, I went and cased the parking lot. The hiking boots thrust upon me by my uncle, unyielding and German and vaguely cocoonish, have been painfully metamorphosing my flat feet since, oh, mile three. Raw, pink, and throbbing now, they are nothing like the feet I remember. They are becoming something else.

My Quasimodo gait attracted attention, but oh well. I searched out the trustiest steed. The carts from Michaels appeared weak, sheltered; their plastic wheels had no rubber on them. The PetSmart ones were promising, but their carriages proved too flimsy for the amount of pricey electronics we had. In time, I limped my way to a wide, red, heavy-duty Office Depot cart. I pushed her up and down as many rows of cars as I thought prudent. The old girl clattered so vigorously that my hands went numb against her bar. She pulled hard to port, too, causing what little muscle I had to rise to the surface of my forearms. I'd no choice but to name her Rolling Thunder.

Glenn was standing next to our bags by the time I returned. Noah was still resting his eyes in the truck bed.

"You jackasses leave seven thousand dollars' worth of gear sitting here, with no one to watch it?" Glenn asked.

"Yes," I said. "But look what I got!" I spun the cart while smiling like a Showcase Showdown beauty.

Noah clambered out of the truck, yawning. "You get your computer fixed?"

"The Geek Squad guys said it'll be a few more hours. So we're sidetracked here another day at least."

"Fine by me," I said. "My dogs have lost the ability to bark."

With that, we shoved off. A teen in a red smock watched disinterestedly as I guided the cart out of the parking lot, Glenn and Noah flanking me. "We need two poles and a tarp," Noah said. "Turn this mother into a highway schooner." We doubled back to last night's beach campground.

FADE IN:

EXT. U.S. ROUTE 98—MIDMORNING

The men are on the shoulder, using Rolling Thunder to pierce the knit of humidity. All three sport unique limps, though Kent's is particularly exaggerated. He lags a few paces behind Noah and Glenn. Beyond them, the walls of gray slash pines seem to be closing in.

> NOAH
> (over his shoulder)

How many synonyms for "trudge" you got?

> GLENN

You'll be like Eskimos with "snow" by the end of this.

> KENT
> (huffing)

My feet are monkeys' paws that've run out of wishes.

None laugh. All nod.

> GLENN

I don't know what I was expecting at the start of this trip. Or even before this trip. But I know it was not sharing a motel bed with you every third night.

> KENT

You should be so lucky.

> NOAH

I'll trade with you next time. You can sleep on the hard-ass pullout.

GLENN

I don't actually mind a hard pullout.

KENT

Oh, yeah?

NOAH

Is that so!

GLENN

You guys don't make honesty a rewarding experience.

Glenn is torquing his lower body in order to keep the cart's considerable payload upright along the sloping road shoulder. His movements are reminiscent of the way a surfer travels along the face of a wave—little elliptical humps. He is grimacing.

NOAH

Having to watch these trucks coming at us, I haven't felt this . . .

KENT

Clenched?

NOAH

Not since the military. *That's* what's fucking exhausting.

KENT

Never hear the one that kills you.

Cars whoosh by in groups of three to five, swerving away from the men as though afraid their cart might suddenly detonate. From a nearby Air Force base comes the rip-roaring sound of F-22s banking, landing, taking off.

KENT

(reading from phone)

You guys get this push notification? "New poll suggests that Mr. Trump is keeping his hopes alive in Florida, the largest and most diverse of the crucial battleground states. The reason: White voters favor him by a large margin."

NOAH

Yeah. Dead heat between them, right?

GLENN

That is absolutely terrifying.

NOAH

Guarantee you Trump's winning everything north of Gainesville. Handily. Guarantee.

A convoy of flatbed trucks hauling bundles of pine trunks blasts the men with an evergreen-scented slipstream, mussing their hair.

GLENN

Are "scared shitless" and "scared the shit out of" the same reaction?

NOAH

Say what?

GLENN

Do the phrases "It scared me shitless" and "It scared the shit out of me" refer to the same thing?

NOAH

Huh.

KENT

They don't have those in Canada?

> GLENN

I am pretty sure we didn't come up with them.

> NOAH

They're both *involuntary,* right? Just involuntary reactions to fear. So I'd say: the same.

> GLENN

So when I see those poll results, or I see a Mack truck drifting across the shoulder line, I am free to say either "It scares me shitless" or "It scares the shit out of me."

> KENT

Correct.

Glenn, nodding, pushes Rolling Thunder up the shoulder onto the level, empty lane.

CUT TO:

EXT. U.S. ROUTE 98—HOURS LATER

> GLENN

When do you suppose we will reach the parts of Florida that recharge our souls?

> NOAH

Ehhh . . .

Traffic thins, and the men take the opportunity to lower their heads. Conversation stalls as they pass a cluster of small white crosses planted next to the shoulder. Bouquets of fresh-cut perennials have been laid around them.

NOAH (CONT'D)
(eyes averted, talking with hands)

I've been to Iraq. The Middle East, and shit. This is not a new take.
I know that. But to me, going back to those poll results . . . These
places are almost the same. Like—an old, backwards culture forced
to confront, like, Twitter and shit. A more advanced civilization is
surrounding them that they don't like and can't ever hope to beat.
So they reject that civilization, you know, violently if they have to.
They have a sense of past greatness that's been lost. And there's a
shitload of resentment at how weak they've become in comparison.
They are who they think they are *because of* the rage they direct at
that civilization.

NOAH (CONT'D)
(looking up)

If that makes any sense.

Noah nudges Glenn off the handlebar, taking over the cart. Behind them,
Kent pants heavily, his mouth gaping as though a magician were pulling a
string of knotted handkerchiefs out of him.

GLENN

I think I am about done with this cart, guys. The torquing is killing
my tendons.

KENT
(gulping air)

Look like . . . Soviet realist painting . . . opening valve with a
wrench.

Over Kent's shoulder, a GREEN JEEP comes speeding down the
tunnel of bare pines. It passes the three men, cuts across the highway, and
SCREECHES TO A HALT on the shoulder some fifty feet ahead of them. The
men stop in their tracks.

GLENN

Hmm.

KENT

(hands on knees)

This time, if they offer us money, we're taking it.

Offscreen, a thirty-something CONCERNED CITIZEN wearing a trilby hat, chef pants, and a camouflage tank top emerges from her Jeep smoking a Black & Mild. She opens the rear passenger door, removes the constituent parts of a wheelchair, and hurls them into the nearby drainage ditch. The men register this with souring expressions.

CONCERNED CITIZEN (O.S.)

(shouting)

Get in!

GLENN

(voice raised)

Come again?

CONCERNED CITIZEN (O.S.)

Get in the car!

GLENN

Ahhh. Do you at least want to know where we're going?

Offscreen, the Concerned Citizen takes a few steps toward the men. The three friends lean back in their stances.

CONCERNED CITIZEN (O.S.)

The car! Get in it!

GLENN

Sorry! We're on a walking trip!

NOAH

Yeah, sorry, lady. No cheating.

Unseen by the camera, the Concerned Citizen begins to tear up. She kneads her hands, brings them to her face, kisses them while kneading them. She begins to MOAN AUDIBLY.

KENT

Thank you, though! That's very kind of you!

Glenn retrieves the camera from the cart and aims it at the Concerned Citizen. Seeing this, she sprints back to her Jeep. Its rear tires spew sod as the vehicle ACCELERATES across the oncoming lane, SWERVES into the eastbound one, and DISAPPEARS from the men's sight.

KENT (O.S.)

Jesus H. Christ.

NOAH (O.S.)

I didn't want to say anything. But I think I saw what looked like a rifle on that woman's dashboard.

GLENN (O.S.)

Phenomenal.

KENT (O.S.)

Let's, ah, take a break in these woods for a bit.

HACKLES UP IN FORTRESS FLORIDA

We're currently stalled in a neck of the woods known as Fortress Florida. Here be the greatest concentration of military installations in a state that historically has been dependent upon them. For example— some distance ahead of us is Tyndall Air Force Base, while behind us beyond layers of high fences is Eglin Air Force Base. Known as the "largest air base in the free world," Eglin covers about 640 square miles across three counties, encompassing nearly half a million acres.

No other section of Florida is as tied to military spending as this stretch of Panhandle; no other section is as contingent upon federal funds. Generations of politicians have ensured that the pump stays primed: Claude Pepper, Spessard Holland, George Smathers, Dante Fascell, Bill Young. Come the Cold War, these politicians gave over an area equal to that of Rhode Island in order to combat the Red Menace. By the time the Berlin Wall fell, only California had more defense and defense-related establishments than Florida. And only tourism brought in more money for the state.

Though it's not just Northwest Florida that owes its existence to war. War in general has been a tremendous boon for Florida. The three bitter guerrilla wars waged against the Seminoles in the 1800s (mirroring the Indian wars raging across the western frontier) brought waves of troops and support personnel to the mostly vacant state. In order to move these troops and supplies, the army had to build roads and set up a communications network. Eventually, the outposts in Fort Myers, Fort Meade, Fort Pierce, and Fort Lauderdale became towns. Fort Gatlin turned into proto-Orlando. Fort Brooke—it became Tampa. Fort Dallas is now Miami.

The Civil War, the Spanish-American War, and World War I—these, too, brought swarms of people into Florida to train, ship out, or, in the case of barkeeps and brothel runners, extract cash. Many of these people decided to stay or else return once the fighting was done. I cannot overstate how important this development is to understanding modern Florida. The expansion of the military-industrial complex explains in large part how Florida went from the least populated state in the South on the eve of World War II to the third largest state in the union following it.

Between 1941 and 1945, Florida was converted into an ever-larger army/navy garrison. There sprang up a new air station at Jacksonville; an army training center near Starke; the reactivated naval base at Key West; Drew and MacDill airfields at Tampa; as well as Eglin in the Panhandle. Millions of young people from every demographic group across this fruited plain poured into and around these bases. One out of every seven servicepersons, in fact. They marveled at the untamed peninsula, which resembled nothing they'd known before.

Or so my maternal grandfather told me. He was a squat Slav who'd come of age on a western Pennsylvania farm. At eighteen, he passed through Miami on his way to the European theater. Like so many others, my grandfather came back to Florida with his wife after the war. They bought a new tract house, pumped out children. Their daughter—my mother—would go on to marry the son of an Ohioan minesweeper who'd done *his* training on the *west* coast of Florida. Some time after that, I hit the scene, a direct outgrowth of Fortress Florida's buildup.

The very moment the United States became a superpower, modern Florida blinked into being. Born of the Pax Americana, begotten by the American Century, New Eden from First Eden, consubstantial with the fatherland, amen. The transformations that swept the country in the decades after World War II weren't so much transformations for Florida; they were first principles. The economy was humming along at wartime speed. Millions of veterans, laborers, immigrants, and children of immigrants were being launched into wide-scale material comfort the likes of which the world had never seen. Workers were granted two-week vacations and *pensions,* even. Advertising, marketing, and public relations firms were busy transforming "leisure" into "consumption." The large, impersonal forces of technology that had been summoned in order to deal out death were now offering themselves as palliatives for the fear of death they had aroused.

This—history's most spectacular burst of economic expansion and upward mobility—this was what modern Florida was born of, and into, like a Baby Boomer. And, like a Baby Boomer, modern Florida knew *only* this, so in the most important respects, modern Florida took it for granted.

While actual Boomers were populating this state, America's rudder-steering cultural classes were teaching them to care naught for anything but the project of liberation. That is to say: If the Boomers wished to be free, *truly* free, they had to unmask and discredit every last form of inherited authority that placed demands on the resources of the self. Parents, priests, cops, Boy Scout troop leaders, elected officials, anyone over thirty—rightly or wrongly, these were denounced.

As Boomers came of age, they were schooled to search after a "unity" and "wholeness" of self. They were to reclaim "feeling" from the one-sided preeminence of "reason." They were to rescue the body and its pleasures from the inferior and guilt-ridden place to which these things had been relegated. With the help of analysts and gurus, they were to exorcise all haunting memories of severe upbringings, restrictive churches, repressed traumas, prohibitive norms. Free from internalized oppression, they were to finally find *their* truth. They were to assign themselves identities which, because they were self-assigned, could be donned or doffed at any time, like dollar-store Halloween costumes.

Moose Lodge members and Chamber of Commerce types reacted as if they had a problem with this, but they didn't. Not really. After all, the self—the self unencumbered of family, history, and custom—was supposed to be the ideal actor in the free market. Therefore, honchos left and right had found common ground here (even if they'd never admit it): a dawning neoliberal order in which the market and the wider culture were free to quietly work their solvent action on all impediments to the chooser within.

These braided Boomer ideals of (a) unfettered choice and (b) the authority of individual experience were the closest thing to a polestar that postwar Florida ever had. Clear the way for uncontested personal and economic growth! No superego stricture or top-down regulation here! Don't forget, corporations are people, too! And anybody wishing to champion ecological, aesthetic, or moral criteria as factors in Florida's development—go screw, fascist!

Florida: No value higher than whatever the will wills. Freedom here is understood as formless potential. The sole truth? That each individual fashions his or her own unimpeachable truth. In good conscience. And with a whiff of progress about it. *Florida: No judge but one's own.*

Do *you,* friend! Because I'm certainly gonna do me.

CUT TO:

EXT. U.S. ROUTE 98—ONE HOUR LATER

The men walk between the pines.

> GLENN
> (to Noah)

No offense, but I have to ask. What's the deal with the Dungeons &
Dragons?

> NOAH

None taken. Hurricane Opal destroyed my home in Fort Walton
Beach in 1995, all right? I had to move to Navarre. I tried to hang out
with the Air Force kids, but they didn't want to hang out with me.
So I hung out alone after school all day. I was by myself all the time.
I had to make my own worlds.

> NOAH (CONT'D)

I got good at making my own worlds. People at the comic book
store would want me to DM. Be the dungeon master. It's basically
cooperative storytelling. You control a character, and then I
describe the situations your characters get into. "You enter the
dank dungeon and are confronted with a band of orcs. What do you
choose to do?"

> GLENN

And people win?

> NOAH

Nah. You make up stories with your friends, and you stay sane.

The men snicker. Then they seize up. Offscreen, the CONCERNED
CITIZEN'S JEEP is barreling down the piney alley.

GLENN

Oh, God.

The Concerned Citizen emerges from her vehicle, a cigarillo in her mouth and the RIFLE in her hands. She works the bolt action while striding toward the men.

KENT

(staring ahead)

Just—just know that I love you.

NOAH

What's up!

CONCERNED CITIZEN (O.S.)

Don't you question me.

She flicks away her cigarillo. She stops. She aims her rifle at the men. They raise their hands.

CONCERNED CITIZEN (O.S.)

WHAT'S IN THE CART?

GLENN

FILM STUFF!

CONCERNED CITIZEN (O.S.)

WHAT. DO YOU HAVE. IN THE CART!

NOAH

(calmly)

Cameras. Microphones. Tents. We are making a documentary.

The Concerned Citizen lowers the rifle from her sighting eye.

CONCERNED CITIZEN (O.S.)

A documentary?

NOAH
(calmly)

A documentary. We're walking the entire state.

CONCERNED CITIZEN (O.S.)

WHAT'S YOUR CAUSE?

KENT

HUH?

CONCERNED CITIZEN (O.S.)

YOUR CAUSE. CANCER?

GLENN

WE DON'T REALLY HAVE A CAUSE.

The Concerned Citizen takes aim again. She approaches the cart.

CONCERNED CITIZEN (O.S.)

KEEP YOUR HANDS UP. BACK AWAY FROM THE CART.

The Concerned Citizen proceeds to dig through the men's packs. The framing of the scene abruptly shifts, shifts, and then settles on the gravel below Thunder's handlebar.

CONCERNED CITIZEN (O.S.)

COME HERE AND TURN THIS CAMERA OFF.

CUT TO:

EXT. U.S. ROUTE 98—MINUTES LATER

> CONCERNED CITIZEN
> (laughing)

That's *my* bad!

Glenn is holding the camera, filming the scene. The Concerned Citizen has propped her rifle against Rolling Thunder. She stands with her hands on her hips, shaking her head.

> CONCERNED CITIZEN

I called the MPs, and I told them some guys with beards were pushing some IED-looking thing right by the base. They never stopped you?

> NOAH

They must have missed us.

> CONCERNED CITIZEN

I really am sorry.

> KENT

Hey, better safe than sorry, am I right?

The Concerned Citizen picks up her gun.

> CONCERNED CITIZEN
> (looking into the camera)

I want you boys to have this.

NOAH

Thanks, but no—

CONCERNED CITIZEN

(to the camera)

Take it. Don't worry, I got more. Take it, or I'm leaving it by the side of the road. It's for keeping the bad ones off.

KENT

(under his breath to Glenn)

Does not appear to be working.

CONCERNED CITIZEN

You boys have any salt?

NOAH

Like, for hydrat—

While holding the gun in one hand, the Concerned Citizen takes Noah's arm with the other. She licks it.

CONCERNED CITIZEN

You can lick me up and down if you want. I've been in the ocean.

KENT

Aha, thank you, but I think we're good.

The Concerned Citizen lays her rifle atop Thunder. Once again, she begins to tear up. She hugs each of the men in turn.

CONCERNED CITIZEN
(to the camera)

Travel safe, boys. Shalom. Think of me.

After the Concerned Citizen has driven off, the three men COLLAPSE onto the grass next to the shoulder.

GLENN (O.S.)
Anybody else still shaking?

NOAH
Balls currently under chin.

KENT
How did nobody driving by *stop*?

GLENN (O.S.)
We absolutely cannot keep that firearm.

NOAH
We keep this thing, and we're getting shot before the cop car has even rolled to a stop.

Noah pushes himself to his feet. He checks to see if the rifle is loaded. Then he walks it to the drainage ditch, where he underhand-tosses the gun into the black water.

GLENN (O.S.)
So, she was schizophrenic, right?

KENT
At the very least.

Glenn returns the camera to its perch on the cart. The men press on.

NOAH

Probably for the best we didn't go around writing RAMADAN after all.

The friends' straight faces begin to unravel. They look at each other. They laugh. Then they laugh harder.

FADE TO BLACK

NOSTALGIA IS A FORM OF WILLFUL FORGETTING

It's been pouring rain for two days straight. Waylaid thus, I'm writing you on letterhead from the *one* motel in Seaside, Florida. It's quite nice. The paper, I mean. Card stock. Premium matte. The concierge also gifted us a bottle of Robert Mondavi white wine and a Seaside-branded wine key upon check-in.

Naturally, we have strung our porch with dripping vines of hand-washed underpants.

Despite the weather, Glenn is in high cotton. He can't *stop* filming out there. Seaside is an entirely planned community. Pristine, manicured, and as unnatural-seeming as the rest, Seaside is nevertheless unique in all of Florida in that it was laid out as a *pedestrian community*. No cars allowed in off the highway, except on select thoroughfares. Seaside's eighty acres were formerly a wealthy family's beach retreat; now, they constitute a conscious rebuke to the helter-skelter development and peckerwood debauchery of the rest of the "Redneck Riviera."

Upon arrival the other evening, we rolled toward the town square on sidewalks lit by gas lamps. The streets were busy with red-faced couples riding beach cruisers, their bottles of prosecco clinking in handlebar baskets. "This is the first time I have truly felt transient," Glenn said.

We wandered the scene in town, filmed it. The structures were built in styles that called for wood, that *appeared to be wood*, but . . . were not wood. They were coated in brunch colors—pink, mauve, periwinkle—that complemented nothing better than baseline white. Homes had been bedecked with verandas and tin roofs and were situated as if in relation to cross breezes, yet . . . all had clattering Rheems affixed to their sides like insulin pumps.

There was much dread here. Dread in the bottom of the lungs, dread occasioned by the uncanny. I mean, each home had its own official name on a sign out front of it, along with a roll of who's inside.

"Yo man, how long you thinking of spending in this Lilly Pulitzer village of the damned?" Noah had asked Glenn. "I'm getting strong vibes of a sacrifice-the-outsiders scenario here."

"I sympathize," Glenn said. "I'm getting the sense that the people milling around the soda fountain are plants meant to keep tabs on us."

Dread because we're being commanded—not asked—to recall something fondly, I noted in my notebook.

"Lotta Trump bumper stickers," Noah noticed as we walked the winding lanes under tupelo trees.

"Probably can't post signs in their yards," Glenn said. "Otherwise, we'd be seeing those, too, I bet."

We shot streetside interviews with visitors. The takeaways were more or less the same: They liked it here because here they were reunited with something they had feared was irretrievable. Here, the present made a kind of sense. The limited system had an artificial coherence.

Great, we said. Cool. We grew tired of filming; we looked for a place to rest. The beach—no. The beach is everything we spend our days dealing with: heat, abrasion. We wanted to keep from that insidious dust. Instead, we stretched out on one of the small green spaces that dot Seaside. We alarmed passing families when we attempted to charge our gear via the landscape lighting's electrical grid. Enough of them stopped to gawk that we were goaded into moving on. Their staring eyes gave us the bum's rush.

"You begin to understand why public libraries are so popular with the indigent," I said.

"A comfortable space where you don't have to literally *buy time* just to sit there?" Glenn agreed. "Sign me up."

The moon rose above the stars. The center of town was honeyed with the light of Edison bulbs. Blond women in white linen pants browsed boutiques. Robust men with dewlaps and tucked-in polos held palaver, like-minded, in front of several converted Airstream trailers dishing out artisanal barbeque. We sat at a picnic table not far from them. They halted their business jibber and sauntered toward us, hands tucked under their hips' gut spillage. They lit up when Glenn pointed the camera at them.

"What're y'all doing?" one asked.

"You see, we're from *Mississ*ippi," another clarified.

We gave them our shpiel; they were delighted by it. They kept asking, via slightly different phrasings: "Y'all doing this for charity?" "No, but what's y'all's cause, though, for real?"

Eventually, Noah barked: "It's *us*. Our cause is us."

"Y'all got some huge-ass balls," one concluded. "Yessir," another assented. "Heavy testes."

We demurred. The man went on: "But what you *really* need, you know . . ." Whereupon this man withdrew from his rear waistband a compact pistola. Glenn and I yelped while dropping into half crouches, our hands aflutter at the sides of our faces.

"Are there vending machines throughout the Panhandle or something?" Glenn asked rhetorically as he straightened. "Are they handed out as door prizes?"

"Y'all ain't know where you was going," the men told us when we asked where we should camp for the night. "Y'all walked into Palm-Beach-on-the-Gulf. Redneck Palm Beach." They suggested we push further inland and camp in an under-construction lot.

As it was not yet late enough for prowling, we parked Thunder under an awning—"None of these magnolia charmers are a flight risk," Noah assured us—and sat ourselves at the bar portion of a beachside bar and grill. The lights were down; the screens showing pro football cast a pallid, undersea glow across the patio. A nondescript young guy in salmon shorts plus oxford shirt did not look away from the game when he said, "Hey there, cats. Seen y'all on the highway."

His name was Damon. He was from southern Louisiana. He and Noah sniffed each other out fairly quickly; Damon was also a vet. He'd been an armed escort for bomb-removal teams in Iraq. Presently, he was using the revamped G.I. Bill to study at Louisiana State University. "Also to indulge my alcoholism, here on my honeymoon," he said.

"Where's, uh, your wife, bro?" Noah asked.

"Aww, hell, she says she's got a UTI, so she's back in the room." Damon finished his drink, ordered four shots of Fireball whiskey. "You cats don't go together at all, you know," he said. "It doesn't look like there's a world where y'all fit together."

Damon spent twenty minutes trying to entice us into wagers on the plays unfolding onscreen. He was an inveterate gambler as well as an alcoholic, he declared to the camera. Unbidden, he proceeded to tell it his goals and aspirations. Foremost, he said, was the investment service he wanted to start for guys just getting out of the service. "Me," he said, "I've got some sharps to me. I knew what to do with my money. My daddy planted a pine stand for me when I was a kid. Come back home, that shit is mature and ready to be cut and milled."

"Is that what you're studying?" I asked. "Finance?"

"Were that I was a sharper man, I'd be looking into real estate. Selling the shit is always more profitable than trying to grow things on it. That's how you make a lot of money in not a lot of time, boy."

Noah, I could tell, had had enough of this inveigle. He was no longer athwart his stool but on his feet, pushing his weight away from the bar. Damon was a little too unctuous for his taste.

"Aww," Damon said. "Y'all are all right. You guys are fucking *drifters*. Y'all are ready for the apocalypse to*night*. Now, in the event of the apocalypse, I would kill my wife and then myself very quickly. That's it. She's on board, she just don't know it yet."

With that, Noah began to pack up the sound gear. Damon took this personally. "You—drink your fucking drink. C'mon, now." He turned to me. "And *you—you* look like Weird Al Yankovic."

We found Thunder where we left her, unmolested, and we walked her down the middle of the street in the pellucid moonlight. The night was voluptuous, round, and perfumed. Silent but for the boom of the surf. "That guy with the gun negated the point he was making," Glenn said. "I don't want to be pushing this cart onto some guy's property, then see a light come on, and then have to take cover."

Reluctantly we made our way to the beach after tethering Thunder to a bicycle rack. Seaside's beach *was* a marvel: a seventy-five-foot-wide sweep of fine powder, fishbelly white. The only blotches on the pristine moonscape were the listing lifeguard chairs.

We spread our rain tarp in the lee of a dune, directly behind the large receptacle where beach chaises sleep at night. With our arms pillowing our heads, we stared into the bath of stars. "Noah," Glenn said. "I've been meaning to ask. Every couple of minutes, when we're walking or not, I notice you expel breath from the side of your mouth. Like you're exhaling secondhand smoke conscientiously. What's going on there? If I can ask."

"An IED," Noah said. "In Iraq. The compression of the air when it went off—it fucked with my respiratory system."

A breeze tickled over us on its way out to sea. Noah shifted on the tarp. Without a word, his body language communicated: *Oh, what the hell.* He opened up to Glenn.

"When I was nineteen, I signed up with the Marines. I was very high. This was immediately after I'd rewatched a DVD of *Starship Troopers,* so you understand. That movie, it's a little fascist. It gets you pumped. September Eleventh had happened not too long ago at this point.

"The Marines are a department of the U.S. Navy—the *men's* department. That's an old joke. Anyway, I'm nineteen, I'm a pretty big fuckup. I'm from a military town, as you've seen. I was around the stuff a lot. I guess I loved America. A lot of guys I knew, they came back, and they were like, 'I decided to give my life to my country, you know, because I had faith that my country would use my life well.' And there's some truth to that. When I was nineteen, the United States Marine Corps had better ideas about what I should be doing than I did.

"But—if I'm being honest. My mother was a nurse. One day, she explained death to me. That you get old, you get weak, and then you succumb. Me, as a five-year-old—I said that I'd prefer to go to Africa. Try to fight a big cat. Get killed by a lion. Rather than just wait to get old and die. And *that's* probably why I signed up. If I'm being honest."

"What was it like?" Glenn wondered. "I know that that's a hackneyed question. But I'm from Canada. I don't know anyone who served in any capacity."

"You want a war story?"

"Sure."

"OK, here's a war story: I'm back from Iraq. I head over to some buddies' place, to play Call of Duty. We're playing, and one of them turns to me and goes, 'I thought you were supposed to be good at this.' So, I get up, I wrap the controller cord around his neck, and I garrote him half to death."

"Jesus."

"They wanted to charge me with assault, but I convinced them to drop the charges. I can be very convincing, Glenn."

"That's not quite what I was expecting," Glenn said.

"Whatever you think war stories are, they're not," Noah said. "They're not, like, tales of valor, most of them. If some guy says he's a veteran and then tells you a 'war story' that has a moral—don't believe a fucking word that guy says."

Here Noah turned to me. "Kent knows," he said. "Your dad ever tell you any glorious tales of battle in Vietnam?"

"They were pretty embarrassing, yeah. Nobody acting particularly heroic. Most of them funny, and pretty obscene, I guess. What he *would* say was that anybody who loves sappy war movies and all that—'Watch how they vote.'"

"But what about feeling a part of something greater than yourself?" Glenn asked. "I thought that was the whole thing. Even with a volunteer army, and nobody in the country cares, you're still fighting for the guy who's got your back, right?"

"You want to believe that what you're doing has a purpose, sure," Noah said. "You don't want to think your friends are dying for nothing. But—I've been a civilian for more than a decade now. And the fact that America has more or less forgotten about Iraq only makes me feel worse. If anyone even bothers to ask—anybody but you, Glenn, I mean—bothers to ask, *What was it like over there?* all I wanna do is scream as loudly as I can while shooting around their silhouette with a handgun. Then I'd say, 'Exactly like that.'"

"Fuck, man," Noah continued. "Like, teenagers today, a lot of them don't even have memories of 9/11. Eighteen-year-olds enlisting now—they might know that it was *some*thing. They might not know what it *was,* what *led up to it,* what *happened because of it.* They might know, like, 'It was bad.' That's it.

"I endured hellish, block-by-block urban warfare during the siege of Fallujah. I'm not trying to brag here. That's just the truth. I remember a lot of it. Or, like, I *think* I do. It's just hard to separate *what happened* from *what seemed to.* Like, what happened when that IED went off? I'll be fucked if I know. But I can tell you what it felt like, to me, when it went off. I've told the story of what it felt like when it went off so many times that it's become *what happened.* You know what I mean? Does that make sense?"

The strengthening wind was pushing clouds like watered ink across the gibbous moon. If I didn't know any better, I'd never guess we were right in the middle of hurricane season. Mean Season, as we natives have christened it. Glenn had drifted off to sleep by this point, but I mentioned nothing. Noah was feeling pensive. That was rare enough to let ride.

"My exit interview was administered by one of the surviving men in my company. He goes, 'You're gonna give the right answers, right?' Then he asked me: 'Do you feel suicidal? Do you feel homicidal? Yes? No? Indifferent?'

"Again, no offense. But how do I tell you or some eighteen-year-old stories about that, that you'd understand?"

Noah fell silent. "Should've bought a quart of something to help us get to sleep," he said after some time. This was his way of indicating that his expressiveness was spent.

Not mine. I was too flooded with esprit de corps, lying there between my friends, the moonlight on the sand foaming like peroxide, to fall asleep. And that, I thought, may be the best definition of male friendship I can muster: sharing the same space, purpose, and perspective while moving shoulder to shoulder in the same direction, drawing however much nearer to the horizon line.

In this moment, I felt my heart fall open like a clam with a severed adductor muscle.

HELL IS TRUTH SEEN TOO LATE

Greetings, friend! I am on a shrimp boat, and I understand now that we're all going to die.

The three of us are seated in the galley of the good ship *Cracker Style,* a vessel manned by Captain Gabriel and his younger first mate, Wesley. In fact, Wesley has just strode into this galley to microwave another frozen hamburger. Judging from the humid mists floating in his eyes, he and Captain Gabriel have gotten quite high in the pilot-house. I am digressing. What I mean to tell you is that we are doomed.

Glenn, Noah, and I got here by trudging twenty miles through the Box-R Wildlife Management Area yesterday. Box-R is a chute of bare pines, laser-straight and continuing as far as the eye can see. The thin trunks were like beds of nails on either side of the road. Between that road and the trees: moats of stagnant water. Here, a man was at a loss to understand how or even *why* the Spaniards persisted in pushing deeper into the *La Florida* quagmire some 450 years ago. They, like the three of us, thought they were making a go of it, alive and sinning. They, like the three of us, were set upon by carnivorous bugs the instant they stopped forcing their shadows through the vegetable siss. I wonder now whether *this* wasn't the force impelling the conquistadores: not God or country or even wealth and renown—it was biting flies.

Box-R was hell. Technically the first day of fall, yet what we got was: popsicle-blue skies, no cloud cover, 120 degrees at pavement level, total humidity. We took turns waving a sweat-rusted hand towel at one another's ankles and knees. The flies especially liked to settle into and bite through my socks. There was little there to stop them, for I wasn't wearing my hiking boots; I was wearing the shower sandals I'd brought along. (The night before, in the sopping tent in the pitch dark, I'd accidentally degloved my pinkie toe while attempting to change a "second skin" blister bandage, leaving this little piggy with "zero skin.") The flies also covered our gear, our damp clothes laid out to dry, our fogged Gatorade bottles half-filled with spigot water—they covered every square inch of Rolling Thunder. I felt bad about this. I wished I could give her a tail.

Late in the day, we crossed into Apalachicola, a still-charming town on Florida's Gulf Coast. There we found long lanes of wooden homes overhung with Spanish moss; wrought-iron balconies; a cemetery on a mound; a few pioneering retirees walking with their hands clasped behind their backs, inspecting For Sale signs. That weepy sort of Old South haunt that is just *glimmering* with dappled sunlight, and idle bigotry.

Apalachicola is also where America's best oysters come from. *Came* from, I should say. There was a period between the 1880s and 1980s when Apalach was exporting fifty thousand cans of the plump, slightly sweet bivalves per day. But in 1989, Georgia rerouted the flow of one of the tributaries that feed Apalachicola Bay in order to water Atlanta. Now, the bay is more saline, and there are new predators feeding on the smaller, nutrient-starved oysters. Apalach is hurting, and has been for decades. Time was, you could find four hundred oystermen out on the water any given day; presently, you'd be lucky to spot eighty or ninety. Many of them have done like Captain Gabriel and first mate Wesley and traded in their oyster tongs for shrimp nets.

Perfect, Glenn decided. A down-on-his-luck oysterman turned shrimper would make for a compelling character study. So, after a night spent camped behind a burned-out Quonset hut, we went down to the Apalach docks. We ambled among the trawlers and seiners moored a few dozen paces from the gift shops, bars, and boutique hotels across Water Street. We knocked on hulls, saw if anyone would oblige.

A shriveled redhead from some Melvillian fish town explained that he would love nothing more than to give us a harrowing experience at sea. However, his trip tonight had to be all business. "Got no time except for making money, fellas" is how he put it, one foot on the gunwale, hands in the rigging. "No time to fart around."

We asked why that was. He said it's because your average fisherman can't really hang around Apalach, much less operate out of here. "It's all tourists now," he said. "It's like what happened to Key West. Key West used to be a real fishing village." But then came the tourists. "And they wanted it to look like a fishing village, only without guys like me there."

The redhead tossed us two beers each, waved us on our way, wished us well. "There's no place to even buy supplies here anymore," he added. "I gotta do that in Panama City before I come." He told us to try the packinghouse on the docks. They're the ones who buy ships' catches, set prices, and control the local market.

We moved down the waterfront to Buddy Ward & Sons Seafood. Inside, we met the scion of the business, one T. J. Ward. T.J. was a fifth-generation fishmonger, a strapping lad in his late twenties who at that moment was more concerned with the Florida State football game on the small television than he was with our questions. Still, he humored us.

It's extremely unlikely to find Apalachicola Bay oysters outside of a few restaurants in Franklin County, T.J. said, his eyes on the screen. And even if the restaurants *do* say they have them, you should make sure and ask for them special, since a lot of the restaurants supplement Apalach oysters with oysters from Louisiana or Texas. "I just came back from a trucking run delivering oysters to a restaurant in Indian Pass," he told us. "Hardly had anything to give them. We got a problem with overfishing now."

If we could go back in time ten years, we'd find this wholesaler teeming with thirty or forty trucks loaded with product, T.J. said. Back then, Buddy Ward and sons delivered to businesses in Florida, Alabama, Georgia—as far away as South Carolina. "We get maybe two oystermen a day now," T.J. said. "And they average maybe three to five bags a day."

What was also a problem, though maybe not in the way you'd expect, was the 2010 *Deepwater Horizon* oil spill. Apalachicola Bay didn't see a single drop of oil—yet the fear of contamination led state officials to recommend the preemptive harvest of everything in the waters. Scheduled harvests were months away, yet the oyster beds were cleared. A whole generation of juveniles was completely wiped out.

T.J. said that his father has lobbied to have Apalachicola Bay closed for a year, and for the state's $6.4 million subsidy from British Petroleum to be earmarked for the unemployed oystermen—but to no avail. "You gotta replenish the substrate," T.J. said. "You have to shell it, you have to nurse it. You gotta let the oysters do their thing."

Onscreen, Florida State's soon-to-be-pro tailback broke off a thirteen-yard touchdown run. All else was expunged from T.J.'s consciousness. We returned to the dock.

That's where we found Captain Gabriel and Wesley loading up the *Cracker Style*. They needed little convincing as to letting us aboard. Suspiciously little convincing. We went out with the tide on cobalt water just before sundown. We puttered past collapsed processing plants adjacent to waterfront hotels under construction. Birds crowded the exposed boughs of sunken trees near tawny stands of high grass. The bay was glassy, hot, and treacherously shallow. Southwesterly waited marauding storms.

When we'd hit deeper water, Captain Gabriel left the pilothouse and joined us at the stern. He's a thin, hard man wearing a graying ponytail and a T-shirt with motorcycles on it that read *Ride Free*. He smiled a picket smile at us and said: "Time to get to work." He and Wesley removed their rubber boots and clambered barefoot up the rigging like a couple of ring-tailed lemurs. They dropped the boat's trawling nets, asking Noah and me to hit that switch or flip that lever at the winch. Glenn ducked between the swaying parti-color nets, scrambling to film the scene.

"I make all these nets myself," Gabriel said, turning from on high to drip his accent into the camera. "I do shrimping, crabbing. I'm a third-generation net maker. Logging. All depending on the season."

Wesley dropped to the deck, ran into the pilothouse to correct course. His stout, shirtless torso was slabbed with work-related muscle as well as carceral-looking tattoos. He returned with a lit Marlboro, which he smoked to the butt in five puffs. He said to the camera: "I'm a little glad the oysters are going. I've seen the old oystermen. They have strong backs but weak minds."

"Idiot sticks!" Gabriel called down. "An oysterman used to could make two hundred dollars before lunchtime just playing with his idiot sticks. But with this here," he said, clinging to the rigging with his legs while gesturing with his arms, "with this here a guy in Georgia owns this boat, takes half the catch right off top. That's why we don't deal with no wholesalers on the dock. [The Wards] pay out only three dollars per pound of shrimp. And if you want to sell to restaurants, you need a license for that. But we can charge five or six dollars per just peddling to friends and individuals."

Gabriel flipped down the rigging, dismounted. "Where'd you boys say you was walking to again?"

"Key Largo, maybe," Noah answered.

"Where that at?" Wesley wondered.

"South Florida?" I said.

"That ain't *real* Florida," Gabriel said. "Anyway, c'mon then, you said you wanted to do an interview." He led us into the pilothouse. He sat in his captain's chair, steering now and then with his bare feet. He produced a small jar of marijuana from the console cabinet. "You know how you know I've been at this longer than him?" Gabriel asked, nodding at Wesley. He swiveled his chair, pointed to the back of his neck. It was scaly with sun-charred skin. "I promise you it's still red deep down, though," he amended.

Noah and I set up the microphones, Glenn hit record. We started with some basic biographical questions. The story Gabriel and Wesley told was the opposite of the transient Floridian story. They were part of Old Florida, North Florida, had roots sunk deep into this part of the earth. "Some people think *beaches*," Gabriel said. "But I think pine trees, palmetto ridges, and shrimping—that's Florida to me."

"This life," Wesley added, "it's definitely something you grow into. It's not something you show up and decide to do."

Outside, a pod of dolphins escorted us toward the molten cylinder of setting sun. The boat slowed appreciably as its nets filled.

Noah, holding a boom, asked why they'd taken us on such short notice. "Because I want people to know," Gabriel said. "I want people to know what's happening to hardworking American people."

He and Wesley were caught in a trap, he explained. On one side, they had the one-percenters who owned the packing plants, who did their damnedest to rip them off on the distribution. On the other, they had cheap, farm-raised Chinese imports flooding the seafood market.

"Don't nobody know the kind of shit we go through to get you New Yorkers your seafood cocktail," Gabriel said.

"I'm actually from Miami," I corrected.

"Same difference," Gabriel shot back.

"We're getting it in both ends," Wesley solemnly affirmed.

"We want to draw attention to this," Gabriel said. He fretted his feet over the wheel.

"We're American people," Wesley said, sweeping his gaze to take in the three of us. "And we can't live like this anymore."

"There's an election coming up . . ." Glenn ventured.

"And there's the one man in it who can do something about all this," Gabriel agreed.

Glenn laughed. Then he said, "But surely you don't think . . ."

Gabriel and Wesley looked to one another, and then back to us. Gabriel said: "I think the Donald knows the American people, and cares about them, unlike some other people."

"He eats KFC on his plane," Wesley solemnly affirmed.

"You guys watch the debate?" Noah asked. "You think he did good?"

"Better than her!" Gabriel said. He put his hands on his shoulders, pantomiming shoulder pads, I guess, and crudely impersonated Hillary Clinton. He said: "Every answer was a straight lie. Every answer was some bullshit like *'Back when I was sucking pussy in Africa . . .'*"

Wesley did a spit take of the Mountain Dew he was drinking.

And that was the moment, friend. That was when it clicked for me: Donald Trump is going to win North Florida, and then Florida at large, which'll give him a more-than-fighting chance at the presidency. All those Trump signs that had been canyoning the highwayside? The many ramshackle homes we'd passed on which owners had painted messages like Lock Her Up and No to One World Government? The latrinalia in the construction site Porta Potties we frequented—"UR going back to Mexico" and the like? It'd all seemed incidental, just more examples of how, shall we say, *suboptimal* the Panhandle could be. But whenever I'd try to joke the clues away, Noah would shake his head and say: "I don't know, dude. This place is the canary in the coal mine."

The news videos we'd watch on our phones at day's end—they were always about this elusive beast, *demos*. *Just who are these white, working-class voters driving the poll numbers?* one pencil neck would ask another pencil neck. Then, before bedding down, I'd read long articles penned by pencil necks about the irrational anxiety of factory workers in Ohio and auto mechanics in West Virginia and, yes, commercial fishermen in Florida—but the *demos* they described, did these geeks ever actually *interact* with them? Outside of press junkets at town diners, I mean. Did they ever actually meet with them on their own terms? Hop aboard their trawlers? Or did they just condescend to these people, who had to listen to themselves be argued over like children caught between feuding parents at the dinner table?

In parking lots and gas stations, in churchyards and high school football stadiums, we've met with *demos*. Who are they? They are a class that has been told time and again that they are exceptionally free. Free to fashion their social and economic identities howsoever they choose. Free to master their fates and captain their souls. Yet everywhere they turn, these individuals are stymied by political and financial powers from whose vantage they appear to be as abstract and insignificant as remainders on a spreadsheet. There is a growing discrepancy between *demos'* right to self-assertion and *demos'* capacity to control the forces that might make such self-assertion feasible. And this growing discrepancy is getting to be too much for many to bear.

So they are a class disabused of everything, even of their privileges, to which they cling by reflex. In spite of that they are polite, for the most part, and eager to explain themselves—especially so when Glenn takes out his camera (and I hide my notebook). But they are also resentful, and the resentful are, of their nature, coarse and ponderous. (The resentful can destroy, but they cannot create.) Most of all, they are scared and angry. Talking to them, we've seen terror and rage pass from person to person the way a leaf in the wind passes its shudder to its neighbor.

And *demos* want us to be led by a bunko man. Donald Trump is a swindler and a demagogue in the sense that Ahab is a swindler and a demagogue: He draws his strength from his oratorical ability to sweep away an individual's fear that her sufferings are meaningless. He convinces her instead that there exists a gloating, external consciousness that has arrayed the world against her. He has replaced her sense of life as a series of random defeats with the sense that life is a righteous struggle against a huntable enemy. Mexicans, Muslims, tax-evading financiers, free traders, blacks, Jews, the Chinese and their farm-raised prawns—the enemies are innumerable, interchangeable. All that matters is their names be recited in Ahab's high raised voice that drops into an animal sob. All that matters is this litany never, ever include the one true adversary: pride.

Donald Trump is from New York City, but he operates out of Palm Beach. I think it's more than safe to say that this real estate tycoon turned reality-television star will make for our first Floridian president. This development would tickle me greatly if it didn't also frost my marrow. What can you say, though? Guy's got the better pitch. He tells the better story. He's figured out what people want to believe, and he's giving it to them. People don't need to be *persuaded* to believe, you know. People want an excuse—*any* excuse—to believe. That's why there is no limit to the damage the best rhetorician—the best storyteller—can do.

"Riiiiiiiight," Glenn finally answered Gabriel.

The ensuing silence was given definition by the cackling gulls pacing the boat.

"Well," Gabriel said, plucking a couple of nuggets from his weed jar. "Just like your seafood is fresh, this was grown right here in these woods. You liberals are welcome to partake in our little powwow. You're gonna need *something* to dull the pain come November."

"You guys got any opioids?" I asked, not entirely joshing.

"We don't play around with those," Wesley stated.

"It's why we're extra careful on the boat," Gabriel added. "You get hurt out here, they'll give you scrips. But you get hurt out here, might as well be a death sentence. That's *it*. You start taking them so you can get back to work. Then you keep taking them so you can keep working. Next you know, you're hooked on them."

"Next you know, they're putting you in the ground," Wesley said.

⁓

The nets swung heavy, studded with shells. Wesley uncinched one and then the other over a table affixed to the end of the stern. Horseshoe crabs, eels, electric skates, juvenile catfish, shovelnose sharks—a slapping gawping pile of bycatch was spilled onto the table as "Runnin' with the Devil" poured from the ship's hi-fi. Glenn, crouched and scrabbling against the roll of the Gulf, stepped on a stray fish and nearly lost the camera overboard.

"Y'all watch for them rays," Gabriel said. "You step on one of them and you will bust your heinie." He turned and kicked the fish overboard. The gulls flurrying around the spotlights screamed hideously, frothed after it in the wake.

"We've dumped nets three times already," Noah asked, hoisting the mike over me as I tried to pluck a shrimp from the spasming mound. "How many more we gotta do?"

"We do this till the sun comes up," Wesley said. He and his captain were using a tool like a craps rake to sift the bycatch. Gabriel was hoping for a large haul so he could buy Christmas bikes for his grandkids as well as the children he's got with his new girlfriend. Wesley needed money for the solar-powered houseboat he was building. "Then we sleep for six hours," Wesley said, "and have the privilege of doing it again."

Glenn drew nearer to the table, zoomed in on a convulsing fish. Its eyes were wide; its fins were propellering; its parted beak vibrated with a silent death rattle. "I think, ah, this guy's having a hard time over here," Glenn said. Neither Gabriel nor Wesley heard him, or chose not to. For reasons too existential to get into, I began to laugh hard.

"That poor goddamned fish," Glenn continued, strafing with his camera. "Sacrificed at the altar of redundancy." He checked the footage in the flip-out LCD screen. A shallow smile spread across his lips.

Gabriel removed his cap to wipe a slime streak across his brow. He said, "We do this two nights a week, and then the other five we hustle something else. Ain't no such thing as a full-time shrimper no more. But maybe once Trump starts whupping Chinese ass, that all gonna change."

He and Wesley proceeded to fulminate at length against globalism, the Chinese, and Hillary Clinton's Satanism. They presented a critique of contemporary liberalism that was, I thought, remarkably cogent. To them, contemporary liberalism was the ideology of imperial academia funneled through the media into governmental bureaucracies. (In so many words.) Why they hated it, they explained, was it was ultimately responsible to nothing but itself. Contemporary liberalism had overlooked or downplayed their grievances, derided their identity, dismissed their worldview as the product of poor education and congenital ignorance if not outright moral deficiency—and this was a big part of why the men were voting for Trump. As much out of spite as conviction.

We pulled thirty pounds of jumbo shrimp from the hundreds and hundreds of pounds of dead and dying bycatch. Gabriel and Wesley's working rapport was an easy one—though it was less buddy-buddy than current-cellmates. Partners in a particular kind of suffering and survival, like. We three didn't have much to add to their back-and-forth. But they enjoyed our presence, I think, because they believed we were there only to *document*. They could ease their pain in the certitude of our muteness, if not our sympathy.

Wesley pushed the suffocated fish over the side of the boat with his craps rake. Their bodies did not sink and evanesce; sharks snapped them up just below the surface. "Couple more hauls, fellas," Gabriel announced. "Then we'll have ourselves a thousand-dollar night. Cut in half and split two ways, of course."

The two of them returned to the pilothouse for another powwow. Glenn, Noah, and I stayed on deck, leaning against the gunwale and staring into the blackness. "One thing Florida is *not*," Glenn stated, "is short on anecdotal metaphors for human nature." I thought it'd started to rain, but the plosive little plops hitting the deck were gobs of seagull shit.

GOOD, BAD—DALE'S THE GUY WITH THE BANG STICK

A rosy twig of dawn widened into a crow's-foot of dawn. We of the *Cracker Style* made one last haul before dropping anchor. Punctuating the mass of blacktip sharks, jellyfish, skates, and grunts were twenty-five pounds of shrimp. Removing these pink commas from the hodgepodge spilled onto the table—it was as if we were diagramming a sentence, editing out all punctuation so as to hasten its conclusion.

As the sun rose, it reflected brightly off the Gulf, casting our tired faces into high relief. "Captain Dale'll be along shortly for you boys," Gabriel told us, wiping his hands with a rag. "Your sea Uber approaches, never you fret." He and Wesley chuckled to themselves as they shook our hands. Then they retreated into the cabin, to sleep till late afternoon.

"We really do draw deeply on the kindness of others," Glenn remarked.

"It's not easy to like yourself, leeching like this," Noah agreed.

"The moral cost of ambition," I said with a shrug. "Also: journalism."

A speck appeared on the horizon. Within a few minutes, an aluminum fishing skiff was puttering up to us. "I woulda come met you yesterday, but I had contact bridge until eight p.m.!" called out

Captain Dale, a wiry, white-haired, deeply tanned codger. The most immediately striking things about Dale were his blue eyes, which glowed as though wicked up to some unadulterated fuel. How I imagine a prospector's or a frontiersman's eyes to shine—with a steady, all-illuminating rapacity—that's what Dale's did. While his skiff drifted to the *Cracker Style,* he flitted about with the jumpy excitement of a sourdough mustered out of bed while still in his union suit. He stowed this, threw that overboard. He was a-grinnin' and a-gigglin' as if on the verge of striking the mother lode.

We dropped our gear and then ourselves into Captain Dale's craft. We motored toward Carrabelle, a fishing village down the road from Apalachicola where Dale works as a nuisance-alligator wrangler.

"Uh-huh, yessir, you boys aren't the first come out here trying to film me," Dale said as Glenn kneed his way around the skiff, camera in hand. Deftly, Noah fitted Dale with a remote mike. "I got all kinds of TV people coming here, trying to do a reality show about me, or about Carrabelle. I guess gator hunters are a category now. I tell 'em no. I don't feel comfortable speaking on behalf of this region. I only been here twenty-two years, you know. So I chase 'em off."

"Then why let us film you?" Glenn asked.

"Well, I seen you boys camping by the side of the highway a few days ago. And then I saw you walking into town. I figured you weren't like the other documentary fellas. Yessir, you boys need all the help you can get."

Dale's boat skipped across the placid Gulf. "I'm seventy-seven years old," he told the camera. "Lived in Florida for all of 'em. Been all over both coasts. This here is the most unique place in all the rest of Florida. This stretch of coastline. Yessir, hands down."

Prior to 1992, Dale had lived on the southwestern outskirts of Miami (which he pronounced "My-ammuh"). But then came Hurricane Andrew. The Category 5 storm wiped out his home, and the homes of his family, so they decided to up and move to the "Forgotten Coast" as a unit. "Was like going back in time," Dale said, which was his way of complimenting the area and the few isolatoes populating it.

"Yessir, it's real living out here," he continued. "We're all from the earth, you follow? And we're all going back to the earth. We used to be able to live with the earth like this in My-ammuh. But they got away from it. And when you get away from the earth, that's when you're lost."

Dale steered us to the dock at the end of his property. There, a rolling lawn led to a modest one-story house and adjoining workshop. "Bought this house twenty-two years ago, uh-huh. See them pines there? See how they're all scarred up along the trunks? No, look there. Point the camera at that. You call that 'catfacing.' You scar the trunk of the longleaf pine like that, and it causes the gum, or the 'resin,' they call it, to run. Then you attach gutters like those there to direct the resin into a cup like that one. The resin you distill into what you call 'pitch.'

"Now, the reason that this industry here is referred to as *naval stores* has its origins in that the majority of the resin that they distilled was distilled to create *pitch,* you follow? Then fellas would use this pitch to caulk holes in their boats and coat their rigging. Of course, boats aren't made of wood no more. Except the one I'm building in here . . ."

Captain Dale led the way to his workshop, waving hurriedly at Glenn to follow. It struck me, then, how sorcerous the camera is—like a dowsing rod that cannot fail at finding water. Having never worked with one prior to this trip, I kind of can't believe how much easier it makes things. Not only does the camera mediate the complex demands of face-to-face interaction—it also makes plain the compromise inherent to any reportorial venture. We're splitting off what we need from you, what we can use. And you, you're gaining a platform, a force multiplier. Maybe even legitimacy.

As opposed to the pen and pad (or even the voice recorder), the camera practically *compels* the words and actions out of a subject. It's so simple, my God! We might as well be pointing a gun at them the way we get whatever we want, whatever we demand. Get—and *get away with*. We don't even need the credentialing of a respected outlet. In our case, it's probably *better* that we don't have the imprimatur of some studio. No, the Nikon's all the justification we need: Have camera, will travel. It's as if a subject sees the void in the lens, decides it's *his fault* it's vacant, and tries as hard as he can to fill it up.

In his workshop, Captain Dale showed off the boat he was building out of juniper and cypress. "An oyster boat," he said, running his wrinkled hand along the smoothly planed wood. "Not a fast boat.

Though I used to race those. Airboats. Race and build them. Used to have a place out there in the Everglades, but actually the government took it."

"Hey, my dad used to race boats," Glenn said, bringing the camera nearer to Dale's face.

"Yessir, I could get those suckers up to eighty-six miles per hour," he said. "Not this one, though. This one, I'm gonna patch up with the resin from that catfaced tree. You know, turpentiners, they came down from North Carolina. Scarred up all the trees there, so they came down to Florida for its pines. Uh-huh, ain't no more but three million acres of old-growth longleaf left in the state. Hike through the St. Marks Forest, you might find some old Herty cups left over from the crackers. That's what they called the pioneers of the Florida backwoods, you know. The Florida cracker, he ain't like your Georgia cracker. The Georgia cracker gets his name from corn cracking, but the Florida cracker, he gets his name from the crack of his whip. Rawhide whip, what would drive the oxen carrying his timber and his turpentine. Sounded like someone shooting a pistol in the barrens. I don't know how it come to designate a shiftless man. But, yessir, as I was saying, I got a big family here . . ."

Captain Dale exhibited his bear traps, his many tools, his considerable arsenal of weapons. His property, taken altogether, was a shrine to autosufficiency. And—look. I get that masculinity does not inhere in one single guy. That it is shared. That it is a code of conduct that requires men to maintain certain attitudes and postures, often to the detriment of themselves and others. That it can exist only with the cooperation and complicity of everyone on the boys' team. It's a group activity. It's something that, as you practice it, you are accompanied by and critiqued by an invisible chorus of all the other guys. Who hiss or cheer as you attempt to approximate some arbitrary ideal. Who push you to sacrifice more of your humanity for the sake of said arbitrary ideal. And who ridicule and shame you when you hold back. This chorus is made up of all your friends and bitter rivals, your drinking buddies and bosses, your ancestors and putative heroes—and, above all, your old man, who may have been a real person or who may have existed only as the myth of the man who got away. Masculinity is a prison, they say. The world's only true panopticon.

Sure. But in this place, with Captain Dale explaining to us just *how* one stalks an alligator, sidles up to it, and shoots it in the brain— explaining this while wearing (on a thick, Cuban-link gold chain) the tooth of one nine-footer he bagged *right here, in his backyard, and look, there's its skull mounted on the hood of his RV*—in this place, I could not help but feel inadequate. Did we know how to butcher an alligator? Dale asked. How about constructing a smokehouse for the meat? What kind of wood would we use for the fire, and why? Where would we find this wood? How do you *build* a fire, even, much less a boat?

I might attribute this feeling of inadequacy to a kind of Aristotelian sensibility deep within me. Some dim awareness that a man cannot have practical knowledge of the useful and the good unless he himself is conformed to the useful and the good. "The Grandpa-ean Ethics," we could term it. And Dale, I sensed, knew well the instruction manual for the human machine. Glenn did not. Noah—not really. *I* certainly don't.

Dale's eldest son pulled into the driveway. He carried with him a string of fish—mullet, for that night's spaghetti-and-mullet feast. He waved at us with his free hand, nonchalant as you like, as though three grimy dinguses filming his dad was par for the course. Bounding out of the house to greet this man was a young boy.

"That's my grandson, who I adopted," Dale said, nodding at the boy. "Dale McDonald the Third. Poor kid, he was born with cocaine in his system. My boy, he and his wife was on drugs. He's the one who named him Dale McDonald the Third. Because he knew I'd take care of him, I figure. I built that tree house there for him. You boys ever seen a bear go up a tree? When they go up the tree, the bark just flies. It's un*real* how agile they are . . ."

Which, now that I think about it, is probably why Dale turned down the other documentary crews—the real "reality" TV folks—but not us. Men like Dale would sooner embrace the heathen than the degenerate. And *degenerate* is no doubt how Dale sees the real "reality" folks. "Folks from L.A. wanting to show the country how they already think we are back in L.A." was how he'd summed them up earlier. "Fake news," he'd added.

What he meant, I believe, is this: The real "reality" folks would've come and shot Carrabelle, yes. But then they would have selectively edited their footage so as to serve their vision of "reality." Perhaps they would have portrayed Dale as a bloodthirsty rube, and his fellow townsfolk as swamp louts preoccupied with humping cypress knotholes when not criminally neglecting their children. Perhaps the "reality" folks wouldn't have done this. Either way, whatever they chose to stitch together in the editing bay—*that* would've become the "reality" of Carrabelle for people not from or familiar with it.

These folks have power, real power, to fabricate narratives about the world. And Dale with his practical knowledge—his *common sense*— will forever be at odds with the malleable "reality" encoded and presented by television, social media, all of it. This malleable "reality" (which, let's be honest, is displacing Dale's reality via every screen in the land) is largely a rhetorical achievement. "Reality" no longer refers to the natural world and its limits. "Reality" rejects preconditions. "Reality" is whatever people want it to be, and then say it is, individually and en masse, making it so.

In this sense, the real "reality" folks and the stars they have produced really *are* a breed of artist. Credit where credit is due. What they fashion is their particular "reality," crafted less out of verifiable truth than sheer, dogged will. On the Bravo TV network, on Instagram—on the campaign trail!—these artists work tirelessly on the details. The whole world beyond their heads becomes instrumental to their creation(s), self- and otherwise. All becomes material. And material can be altered as needed, can be worked over like clay, can be molded into artifice, can be transfigured into an artifact indistinguishable from what it is meant to represent.

These artists, they *act natural*. And that is their art. The real "reality" artist is his own best fiction. His best fiction is his true self. One thing you could say about him—he'll never be found guilty of insincerity! Or, for that matter, sincerity. In the end, "Kent" can no more be separated from Kent (were I one of these cretins) than lightning could be separated from its flashing.

"You're from My-ammuh, you said, ain't that right?" Captain Dale asked me with a smile.

"Yessir, that's right," I said.

"I know you. I know what you'll like." Dale jogged into his house and returned with a plate piled high with golden-brown fritters.

"This one, they didn't want him by the school," he said. "An old, old, old gator."

"You get to keep the meat off the nuisance ones?" Noah wondered. "The skins? No regulations on that?"

"The easy way to do it—and they let me do it—I work with the Fish and Wildlife Commission, I gotta be careful"—Dale scarfed a fritter, then continued through his padded mouth—"the easy way to do it, they let me bait a hook, and hang a hook for 'em. Bait with fish, chicken—they like it rank. The worse it smells, the better off you are. And once you get 'em on a line, then they're easy. Well, most of 'em are easy. Then I have a bang stick."

"And it never bothers you that you work for the *government*?" Glenn teased.

"Bang stick's a shotgun shell at the end of a stick, correct?" Noah asked, crossing his arms.

"I use a .223," Dale said. "See, with a shotgun, you get a big ol' gator with a head *that* thick, you can blow a bone into your leg."

"Ahhhh," Glenn and I said, as if that made perfect sense to us.

"A .223, it'll penetrate, since it's a small projectile."

"And the skins, the meat . . . ?" Glenn reminded.

"My wife, she makes jewelry out of the gator scoops. The bumps on their back. Necklaces, earrings. Yessir, uh-huh, I get to keep 'em."

Dale shook his bang stick at us. He told us to check its heft and balance.

"Don't need a license for that!" he gloated while we handled it inexpertly.

"We could absolutely use one of these on the road," Glenn said, waving and thrusting the rod.

"Whoever's pushing Thunder could hold it like a lance," Noah agreed.

"I used to be a gun dealer," Dale continued. "Believe me, I know. Frankly, I was surprised the government conceded on this, of all things.

"Anyway, et up. *You* know, My-ammuh, that you can't get this down where you're from!" Dale turned to the camera. "Can't eat any gator that comes out of a canal in Miami-Dade or Broward County, because of the lead poisoning. So, enjoy. I got an idea where to take you boys next."

We tried to make a perceptible dent in the pyramid of fritters. Dale brought his truck around. Glenn set up the camera stabilizer in the front seat; Dale poured the remaining fritters into four red Solo cups, which he placed in holders around the cab. He pulled us away from his property, and the four of us waved to his grandson-cum-adopted-son as he tear-assed up a tree like the bear Dale had described.

"So, Dale," Glenn said, squinting into his viewfinder, throttling the focus. "You never did tell us how you got into alligator wrangling."

"Saw an ad in the paper!" he exclaimed. "Now, I'd poached some gators, back when I was frogging. I'd poached a tail or two, uh-huh. They know, when they hire you, that if you don't mind messing with gators, that means you've messed with 'em before."

This led Dale to exposit on the history of the alligator in Florida. "Used to be an endangered species, you know," he told the camera. "They were hunted in Florida just the same as the bison on the Great Plains. Yessir. In the late 1800s, what they'd do is, tens of thousands of alligator hides, they'd roll 'em up and pack 'em in wooden barrels, you know, send 'em to tanneries in the Northeast or even Japan. Then the skins'd ship back to Florida and get solt to tourists."

"Talk about free trade!" Glenn said.

"Yessir!" Dale agreed, plucking a fritter from the cup in the center console. He winked at the camera. "They put up hunting restrictions in the 1900s, but that hardly did nothing. By the 1960s, you couldn't see a gator by day. It was like they were *terrified,* holed up. State finally banned hunting 'em in '62. Then of course the federal government came in and protected them in the early '70s, uh-huh. The population rebounded re-*markably*. I believe it was '87 when they took 'em off the endangered species list. But, you know, they track that by alligator *density*. Not by total numbers. Nobody knows how many alligators there used to be. From what I've heard, you couldn't swing a dead cat without hitting one."

Dale turned off at a break in the piney bulwark. He parked next to a dredged pond. "There's a little one that's still in there," Dale warned. "Worst he'll do is probably bite a toe. Little ones got puppy teeth, you understand. The big one, though—it hissed at the gentleman owns this property. Which means he wants it gone. Which means, because he's over four feet, he'll have to be destroyed."

"How do you know he's a nuisance gator?" Glenn asked on behalf of the camera.

"Because the gentleman reported him!" Dale smiled. "And that makes him a nuisance. If you got an alligator in your yard and you don't want him there? Then he's a nuisance, and you can have him removed." He popped a fritter, winked again.

"How'd that sound?" Dale wondered. "That sound all right?"

"Sounded great, Dale," I said.

We hopped out onto the sodden grass surrounding the pond. A larger man in overalls came running up to us. "They won't let the people—they hissin' at people!" he pleaded. This man gestured toward the jet-black water dotted with lily pads. "Baby's still in there somewhere," he said. He showed us to a dry culvert at the edge of the property. "Big momma's in there."

Dale nodded, rubbed his chin. He got down on one knee, slapped the side of the culvert. He listened to the alligator shifting inside.

"*Semper fi,*" Dale addressed Noah, "go get me my catch pole, and my gaff hook, and the lines out of my truck. We're gonna try for the baby first."

We gathered round the pond. Glenn orbited it like a satellite, recording. "It's no different than fishing," Dale said, tying a large metal hook to a line. "You don't always get them when you go."

He slid the nick of the hook through the white flesh of a marshmallow. Anticipating our question, he said: "I use marshmallows because they float good. And I guarantee you somebody been feeding this baby human food in this pond. He's gonna come for this mallow, yessir, just you watch." Dale handed the line to Noah. "Spin it over your head like a lasso, *Semper fi,* and let 'er rip. But don't pull on the first tug, now. Alligator this small, he's got puppy teeth, real sharp. Let him sink those in there."

After a minute or two, the baby surfaced. It floated toward the marshmallow, seemingly without propelling itself. It hesitated. Then in one fluid motion, it bit into the mallow and dove for the bottom of the pond. Noah emitted a noise I did not know he was capable of emitting: a half-delighted, half-terrified castrato shriek.

"Now pull on 'im!" Dale ordered. Noah gripped the line in two fists, spun his considerable bulk, and yanked with all of his strength. The juvenile alligator came flying out of the water, pinioning its legs as it sailed directly at us. We three amateurs dove out of its way.

When I looked up, I saw Dale scrambling after the line as the gator beat its way across the property. He pulled up short, made an "awww, phooey" gesture. "You boys owe me a hook and some line," he said.

Dale returned to his truck, withdrew his bang stick from the bed, fitted it with a .223 round. "You did good, though. Little guy was under four foot, which means we'd've had to tape him up and release him anyway. You just hurried him along his way. Uh-huh."

Dale tried to give the bang stick to me, but I backed away. "I'm taking notes," I explained, and withdrew my pen and pad from my pocket. "Guess it's you again, *Semper fi,*" Dale concluded.

He walked us to the culvert. "See, that's where they'll winter," Dale said. "Like a cave."

The dusk had siphoned the last of the daylight. Glenn handed me a small spotlight, which I aimed into the pipe. A husky growl resounded in the black hole.

"The fella wanted to wait until tomorrow," Dale relayed with a snicker, "but I said, 'Well, I got three fellas here, and they wanna film this!'"

"How, uh, big would you say this one is, Dale?" Noah wondered, holding the bang stick across his chest.

"This one? Only about six, seven foot," Dale said.

"Ah, ha, yes," Noah said. "Only."

"You ever get nervous?" I asked Dale.

He dropped to his haunches and curled a hand around the lip of the culvert. "I told you boys I only been doing this about ten years, didn't I?" He laughed.

"Guhhh . . ." Noah groaned, his gutturality almost harmonizing with what was rippling out of the pipe. He got into an athletic crouch, steadied the bang stick atop his right shoulder.

"Now, My-ammuh, shine that light right in her eyes," Dale ordered.

I did as the man said. Two glowing ember-orbs appeared in the darkness. I thought that the pipe should be emanating heat, but the black was clammy. I withdrew my free hand from Noah's other shoulder. I took out my notepad and pressed it against my thigh. Retreating into it, I scrawled *eyes like struck matches at the bottom of a grave.*

"Steady, now, *Semper fi,*" Dale said. "Steady as she goes."

Noah slid the stick deeper into the culvert while turning his face oblique to it. "Oh, *Jeez*us," he muttered.

"That's it!" Dale said, anticipation rising in his voice. "Little more now! Right there! Get ready to jab her! Both hands!"

The alligator's growl deepened. Noah's *"Guhhh"* returned, and intensified. "Finish 'er!" Dale said.

There was a flash, and a crack, and a sibilance like leaking air.

~~~~~~~~

MILE 260 — Tallahassee

A GROTESQUE PLACE

We had to ditch Rolling Thunder. There was just no getting around it—Route 319 didn't have a shoulder, and try as we might, we could not force shopping cart wheels through the roadside underbrush. So we found a relatively quiet thicket wherein we made Thunder comfortable. We laid her on her side, we draped her in mini American flags we'd bought at Walmart. We thanked her for her service. We played taps on our phones. And I, at least, had to keep from looking over my shoulder as we left her behind.

Inside of three thousand feet, I knew I couldn't hump my pack. A party blower's honk of agony unfurled up my legs with every step. These roads are so *hard,* man, and my feet remain shredded. Anguish tickled my purple toenails like a master pianist.

"I'm feeling the romance again!" Glenn announced. "Feeling like I'm taking ownership of my awful decisions. It's more *mature* this way. Having my awful decisions yoked to me."

Noah stopped to tighten his stomach harness. He burped something up.

Thanks to the heat, a skim of sweat coated my body before the first mile was out. Each minute felt as if it had been spread thin against a rough surface, like butter on toast. I tried to think Bruce Chatwin-y thoughts, but I couldn't strike one spark within the wet nest of my hair. Everything was given over to pain, the first and queenliest of sensations.

We were still deep in the Panhandle. The wet-pulp odor of nearby paper mills weighted the air with the flavor of human grease. Refreshing scythe swooshes of passing traffic were rare. Much more common were high fences and Keep Out signs that fronted compounds set into the pines. The best way to describe the look of these boondock fortresses: *Nouveau Dark Ages.*

"The universal thump," Noah wheezed. "Lord hits serf. Serf hits wife. Wife slaps boy. Boy kicks dog. Round it fucking goes. Anybody we encounter here is gonna be just *itching* to pass that thump on to us."

By the time we reached a suitably remote spot to camp, I was too tired to wonder at the spilt salt stars above us. Nor could I contort my body into a position that quieted the pain in my feet and shins. Sitting up, I gingerly removed the hiking boots that I insisted on wearing for whatever reason. Archipelagoes of grub-white blisters ringed both feet. The blood under my big toenails had drained, but now those toenails appeared to be unmoored from their nail beds. They were opaque keratin plates. I pressed down on the right one, and clear amber discharge splurted out. I decided to see the operation through. The nail slid out like PEZ from a dispenser. It'd have to be shower sandals from here on, I decided.

"We're running up against the problem of not being able to spend any time in these places," Glenn said the next day. He was checking his phone to see if Sopchoppy's renowned worm grunters had responded to his Facebook message. "If people don't get back to us immediately, it's not like we can hang around waiting a day or two for them."

"Right," Noah said. "We had a choice, and we chose this."

By the time we reached the Sopchoppy general store, I had taken to leaning forward and wrapping my arms around myself, so as to transpose the burden of the bag. "You guys wait here," I said. I entered the dilapidated concrete market. Very few supplies there— certainly no eggs, as chickens roamed freely about town. An elderly woman sweating through her Canadian tuxedo gaped at me from behind the register. "Please," I asked her, "do you have any shopping carts you don't want? Or that you'd sell?"

"Ren!" the woman sang out, tilting an ear toward the back door. "We got any carts back there? Or you give 'em all away to your cousin last month?"

An underdeveloped man shuffled in and affirmed that his cousin got the carts. He looked me up and down. Pity clouded his non-strabismic eye. "Sorry, we need the ones we got," he said. "We got one out back with hoses in it, but it don't move." He bit his lip, dropped his gaze.

"Well," I sighed. "We all gotta die sometime, huh?" I moped out of the store, joined Glenn and Noah at the bench in front. The sudden flash of hope had left me more in darkness.

After three minutes of silence, Noah said: "C'mon, man. You gotta do it."

We pulled ourselves to our feet. Bursting through the shop doors came the cashier. "We got an antique baby buggy, I forgot!" she announced. "If you want it!"

"Oh, no," Glenn said. "Oh, no no no."

The underdeveloped man wheeled the buggy around the corner. Thing looked as if it'd rolled unpushed out of an Edward Gorey panel. Four tall, thin, white wheels, dry and cracked, supported a scissor-frame chassis upon which a tapered box sat. The box was suggestive of an open coffin. Plush blue velvet covered its exterior; its interior was bare particleboard. It had a sinister velvet hood, too, and a white plastic handlebar with molded finger grooves.

"This is either a new low or a new high," Noah said.

"This is perverse," Glenn said.

Into the pram I dropped my bag like a weighted sack into a lake. I took it for a test jog, giggling deliriously. Unlike those of a shopping cart, its wheels were fixed, so there was no torquing. The buggy was also light enough to pilot it with one hand.

"It's got shocks and everything!" the underdeveloped man called out.

"You're goddamned right it does!" I cried.

Pain could not reach me as I ran the stroller through several donuts. The carriage swung rhythmically on its springs, rocking my pack to sleep. "Glenn! Noah!" I said. "There's room enough to stack one of your bags here! Rock-a-bye Thunder!"

"No," Glenn said. "Absolutely not. This is what's going to get us messed with. We're talking about people who . . . *literacy* is provocative to these people. Their line of thinking will go: *Why do you have that? Where did you get it? Who are you? Are you people who are better off dead?*"

"It's on the nose," Noah said of the buggy. "But, hell, I'm down."

He slung his bag into the pram. I held my breath as the springs squealed. They strained, they settled, they supported the box at an uncanny depth, like that of a full diaper.

"So what's y'all's cause?" the cashier asked. "Where can I put some money towards your cause?"

"We're actually collecting for our cause," Noah said, turning to her.

"But what's the cause?" she pressed.

"Uh." I stepped in for Noah. "We're making Florida great again. For the first time."

"Wonderful!" the cashier said. She handed Noah a fiver. "God bless you boys."

Glenn started down the road at a rapid clip. Noah and I hurried to catch up. "I am a malingerer and a pussy," I said. "Fine. But this trip is not about putting on hair shirt. You know? We gotta be able to *think* if we're ever going to see that money?"

Glenn said nothing. He leveled his chin at the road, raked a hand through his wet hair.

"Hey," Noah said, looking at his phone. "According to eBay, this brand of buggy goes for a hundred and fifty dollars, plus a hundred dollars for shipping."

Glenn kept to his brisk estrangement. But I was euphoric. I babbled on and on during this honeymoon period, my sweat streaking the insides of my glasses lenses like obverse tears. I paid no mind to the burning drill bit of postmeridian sun. I sweltered under it happily, remaining outside with my new filly while Glenn and Noah entered a gas station to get Gatorades.

To be honest, I no longer *want* to step inside a gas station, CVS, Publix when we're out on the road. I can't abide the air-conditioning. My body balks at it, seemingly cannot process it, as if it were lactose or something. I cross the threshold into a frigid Tom Thumb, and boom—I evince all the symptoms of shock.

It feels *good* to be perspiring, especially come evening. No longer do I get the sense that I am covered in the day's expectorate. It's almost as if the sweat is evidence of a skill.

I've grown acclimatized, is my point. And I've realized something. Being sweaty is a self-fulfilling circuit.

Now, I am a torrential sweater. This I chalk up to my childhood bedroom not having air-conditioning. In retrospect, this seems patently *insane,* considering that every other room, building, automobile, and enclosed space in South Florida is chilled to a bracing sixty degrees. My bedroom, however, was exposed to the elements. And according to the research, the intensity of one's sweating gets "set" during one's earliest years. Though everybody is born with virtually the same number of sweat glands, they'll be "activated" only if they are exercised in youth. Hence, those who grow up in hot or even moderately warm places will have more active sweat glands. *If* those places aren't intensely climate-controlled, that is.

And therein lies the self-fulfilling circuit. If you don't sweat when you're young, you won't sweat when you're older. If your formative years took place in a conurbation that is laid out like an ore-extracting colony on an inhospitable planet—if you hold your breath and run from one air lock to the next—then of course you're going to feel like you might die when you have to spend time outside. If you never get sweaty, you're going to loathe that little amount you do sweat. You're going to go to greater and greater lengths to avoid it.

It was not always this way. As recently as one generation ago, Floridians were attuned to the rhythms of their environment. They lived in tin-roofed bungalows built to capture crosscurrents. They planted shady, fast-growing chinaberry trees alongside their homes. They closed the windows and shut the blinds at midmorning, to keep the cool inside. They made rituals out of sitting on the front porch in the evening, or going for twilit strolls. They met the place halfway. The contemporary mind recoils at the thought. Dormers, screened windows, wide verandas, high ceilings, sleeping porches, paddle fans, louvered jalousies, terra-cotta tile, classical porticoes, dogtrot breezeways, canvas awnings, iced tea brewed in pickle jars. Even sleep—sleep was induced by the sounds of hooting owls, croaking frogs, fish flashing out of water. Air-conditioning changed all that.

The road to hell is paved with good intentions, and the birth of air-conditioning does not contravene this fact. John Gorrie, a physician in (where else?) Apalachicola, wanted to lower the body temperatures of his malaria and yellow fever patients, so he began experimenting with crude forms of mechanical cooling. He developed an apparatus that blew air over buckets of ice suspended from the ceiling of his hospital. The results were mixed, but Gorrie became obsessed with the idea of chilled-air-as-cure-all. He tried using a steam-driven compressor to cool air; this led to his patenting the world's first "Machine for the Artificial Production of Ice" in 1851. His pioneering work would become the foundation for modern air-conditioning.

Willis Haviland Carrier perfected the mechanical air-conditioning system in 1902. Problem was, mechanical air-conditioning was incredibly costly. Only a few movie theaters, department stores, and wealthy residences could afford it. Motels and hotels charged an extra dollar for rooms with it. "The return on this investment has proven to be quite phenomenal," admitted the owner of the Raleigh Hotel in Miami back then. "Our summer trade has increased considerably."

In 1922, Willis Carrier had a breakthrough: He ditched the large and inefficient piston-driven compressor and coupled a centrifugal compressor to the air conditioner in its place. (He also came up with his own refrigerant, Carrene, which was a good deal safer than the *deadly ammonia gas* his old ACs ran on.) Not too long after, air-conditioning could be found in banks, government buildings, hospitals.

The biseasonal culture of Florida—half the year: inferno, other half: paradiso—was never to be the same. No longer a six-month industry, tourism became a year-round engine of growth. Air-conditioned factories and offices meant that businesses could relocate from the Northeast and Midwest. New Floridians bought new houses built with concrete block instead of wood. Efficient, inexpensive window units fit these tract houses perfectly. Or, rather, the houses were built around the units. Then came the shopping malls and chain restaurants which were built around the sprawl built around the AC in microwavable insta-metropolises like Port St. Lucie, Cape Coral, Port Charlotte, Pompano Beach . . .

The unintended consequence of this-all was the slow death of Old Florida. Agrarianism, cultural isolation, historical conscious-ness, an orientation toward folk culture, a preoccupation with kin-ship, neighborliness, a strong sense of place, a relatively slow pace of life—the lot of it went the way of vernacular architecture. Regional distinctiveness was reduced to culinary habits and tics of speech. Previously enculturated lives were reoriented toward . . . what? The TV room?

So goes technological determinism. The air conditioner, the TV, the automobile—these supposed tools are remarkably good at creat-ing demand for themselves. People decide they cannot live without them; they restructure their lives around them; they work to serve them rather than the other way around. It comes as absolutely zero surprise that the single greatest source of energy expended by Flo-ridians today is: air-conditioning. Virtually every problem associated with the present-day state, from urban sprawl to highway congestion to contaminated drinking water to antisocial atomization, has been exacerbated by its spread.

But, hey—climate control. Modern Florida couldn't exist without it. If you look past the social and cultural costs, why, we purchased our existence for the low, low price of shifting the surplus heat some-where else. Onto surrounding streets, and ultimately into the planet's atmosphere. Just wait till rural India and China get a taste of this!

In the late afternoon, Glenn finally said, "I haven't seen you this happy since the last time we got a cart."

"Yeah," I said. "My mind is free! My gaze is outward and upward."

"Roadkill," Noah interjected. "Watch out for the roadkill there."

"Think of how good it'll be for *you*, though, in a couple weeks," I said. "Joy is the feeling of your power increasing, right? By then, you should be a bag-carrying *machine*!"

"It is amazing for someone to have so much privilege and yet choose to waste it in this way," Glenn deadpanned.

"Whatever, man," I said. "What would you rather us be doing?"

"No, no. I look *forward* to this profoundly self-destructive, self-critical *Sherman's March* we're doing here. In which no behavior is ever justified. And the endeavor itself is a mark of shame."

We three laughed.

"That was really good!" I said.

"Even your praise is patronizing."

"*Especially* the praise," Noah clarified.

"Please," I said. "That was purposefully ironic patronizing."

"So many layers," Glenn said. "All of them toxic."

"I think we have the blurb for the Blu-ray case," Noah said.

We three laughed.

"If you're not carrying your bag," Glenn concluded, "you'll still have to do some kind of labor. You're going to have to do the emotional labor of supporting me. Providing me with diversion and moral support."

We stopped for supper. We made some phone calls. Glenn arranged an interview with a veteran newspaperman who'd written his PhD dissertation on Walkin' Lawton Chiles. I thought this idea a boring one—but, you know, emotional support. I labored to keep my mouth shut.

At Tallahassee's outskirts, we checked into a motor lodge. We filmed B-roll the next morning while killing time before our meeting with newspaperman Jim. Tallahassee, friend reader, blows, so I won't waste time telling you just how much. It's the capital, of course. It's the capital because it is equidistant from Pensacola and St. Augustine, the two biggest Florida cities back in 1821. That's it. That's the reason. The overland journey between those cities was fraught with peril, plus it took too long to sail around the peninsula. Tallahassee was the compromise.

Tallahassee also happened to be located upon the only significant portion of the state *not* undergirded by a thick honeycomb of highly porous limestone. It's that rarest of things in Florida: terra firma. This made Tallahassee's rolling hills and vales the one spot suitable to cultivating cotton—and importing plantation culture (and slaves) en masse. Yet Tallahassee's aristocratic pretensions were not enough to impress Ralph Waldo Emerson when he visited in 1827. Our eternal poet laureate took one look around and adjudged Tally "a grotesque place" populated entirely by "public officers, land speculators, and desperadoes."

Aside from bureaucracy, Tallahassee also accommodates Florida State University, our densest concentration of staggeringly beautiful, rock-dumb youths. FSU is a research university, yes, but its greatest endowment to this state, bar none, has been its ongoing contribution to comedy. To wit: Q. Why do Florida State graduates put their diplomas on their dashboards? A. So they can park in the handicapped spots. Or how about: Guy walks into a store and says, "I want a garnet hat, gold pants, a garnet shirt, and gold shoes." Clerk goes, "You must be a Florida State man!" Guy asks, "How did you guess? By the colors?" "No," the clerk goes. "This is a hardware store."

We saw few students and zilch in the way of tourists as we ambled around the empty, brutalist spaces downtown. "I like that they're not giving up on the paradise vibe here," Glenn said, his eye in his viewfinder. "Even the striped awnings on the capitol building look like they're made out of parasol fabric. Nothing in this state appears to have been built for any serious attempt to govern itself according to reason."

Not yet sufficiently bored, we walked to the Museum of Florida History. The docents were startled; then they were overjoyed. Abso-*lutely* we could film in here, they said. After all, we had the museum to ourselves.

Glenn particularly liked the thousand-yard stares painted onto every mannequin in the place, native and colonist alike. They looked defeated, dismayed. The Indians, well—the cause of their dismay was obvious. There were about 40,000 Timucu, 7,000 Tocobaga, 20,000 Calusa, 25,000 Apalachee, 5,000 Tequesta, and 2,000 Jeaga when the Spanish first waded ashore in the sixteenth century. Two hundred and fifty years later, these natives were gone, wiped out by imported pathogens, cycles of warfare, slavery. The most famous of them, the patchwork tribe who came to be known as Seminoles, weren't even *from* here. They showed up in the early eighteenth century, migrating into sparsely populated Florida in order to escape pressure from white settlers in Alabama and Georgia. When settlers began to pour into Florida as well, the Seminoles were forced down "the long frontier" of the peninsula during three wars of removal. Along the way, they intermarried with the Miccosukee. They welcomed runaway slaves into their ranks. They fought bravely. In the end, all but 200 were killed or forced to relocate to Oklahoma. Those 200, though—

they beat a strategic retreat into the furthest reaches of the Everglades. There, amid a saw grass prairie stinging with life, they held out. Never did they surrender to the United States government. They call themselves, rightly, "the unconquered."

The Spaniards' thousand-yard stare, however—the reasons behind that one are a little less immediate. I'll let T. D. Allman explain: "People are constantly ruining Florida; Florida is constantly ruining them back," he wrote in his fine book *Finding Florida*. "Florida's history has been dominated precisely by those kinds of people who do not rationally consider the consequences of what they do. For five hundred years successive waves of conquerors, ignoring the reality of Florida, have tried to re-create, in Florida's alien clime, a more perfect—sometimes outright hallucinatory—version of the society they left behind. A new Castile, where every Spaniard is a gentleman on horseback, his saddlebags bulging with gold doubloons! A new Ohio, where every house is located in a crime-free suburb, only with a swimming pool, and it never snows!"

The thousand-yard stare of the Spaniard is the thousand-yard stare of the subprime mortgage holder. It is the thousand-yard stare of the man who stepped out of his car into ankle-deep water at the property he'd bought sight unseen. It is the expression Ponce de León wore when he played out a protracted and excruciating deathbed scene after a poisoned arrowhead was fired into him by a Calusa warrior.

Ponce did *not,* I am sorry to report, give a shit about any fountain of youth. What he was looking for was the island chain of Bimini. He'd been sailing around the Bahamas for twenty-five days, trying to locate one particular island, when he sighted a much larger landmass. He came ashore near the St. Johns River in 1513. Natives attacked, injuring three of his crewmen. When Ponce reached his second landing site, at Jupiter Inlet, he was attacked again. Then, while sailing around the Keys and up the west coast, he was attacked twice more. Still, he took possession of *La Florida* in the name of Spain's king. The king then granted Ponce the patent to conquer, govern, and colonize the land.

Seven years later, Ponce returned to Florida with two ships, two hundred colonists, fifty horses, livestock, farm implements, all of it.

They landed on the west coast near Charlotte Harbor. They were constructing houses and public shelters when the natives attacked, wounding Ponce with a manchineel-poisoned arrow. He and the other survivors fled to Cuba, where Ponce died. None of his heirs showed any interest whatsoever in settling Florida.

A few other noblemen would try and fail to set up colonies on the peninsula. Fortunes and reputations were squandered. Somewhere around two thousand lives were lost, too, in the futility. But just as King Philip II and his advisers were deciding to wash their hands of the whole enterprise . . . they caught wind of a French settlement—a *Protestant* settlement, no less—near present-day Jacksonville. If they couldn't have these "accursed lands," as the Spanish called Florida, then no one could. In 1565, King Philip dispatched Pedro Menéndez de Avilés to destroy the French settlement. Menéndez sailed with three hundred soldiers to the mouth of the St. Johns River, where he found five French ships blocking the entrance. Menéndez backed off. He set up a field base that would become St. Augustine, the first permanent European settlement in North America. Seeing this, the French moved to attack the encampment before the Spanish could muster their strength and attack them. But lo! A hurricane intervened, pushing the French ships past the Spanish and wrecking them upon an inlet. Menéndez rounded up the survivors, bound their hands, slit their throats. After that, the Spanish were free to control *La Florida* for the next two hundred years. All praise to God's *huracán*.

Even so, Florida was considered the bottom rung of Spain's empire. Anyone interested in wealth or renown did well to avoid it. Not once did the colony turn a profit. It was floated by the lucre and natural resources of Spain's other New World holdings, Cuba most of all.

Spain was finally relieved of Florida in 1763, following the French and Indian War. In winning that conflict, Britain had captured the crown jewel of Spain's empire—Havana. To ransom Havana, Spain gave Florida to the Brits. And although *La Florida* extended way up the Eastern Seaboard at that time, only a few thousand Spanish colonists inhabited it. They walked away without much of a fuss. The British then split Florida into two colonies—West Florida and East Florida, with capitals in Pensacola and St. Augustine. Almost instantly, they learned that Florida was a money pit. They ran the two territories as cheaply as possible.

And the territories remained loyal to King George throughout the American Revolution. That's why you never hear East or West Florida mentioned with the original thirteen colonies. When they sent delegates to the Continental Congress in Philadelphia, the Floridas declined. When the other colonies rallied around John Hancock and Sam Adams, Floridians in St. Augustine burned effigies of the two patriots. When fighting broke out in earnest, British Loyalists fled north to Canada—and south to Florida.

Which made for awkward times when Florida was returned to Spain after the war. Rather than submit to the Spanish, many Loyalists relocated to Jamaica or the Bahamas. For those who remained, it was as if the intervening decades of British rule had never happened. Florida once again regressed into a semilawless haven for brigands and freebooters. Runaway slaves took up the Spanish on their offer of freedom in exchange for conversion to Catholicism and service in the militia. Indian raids launched from Florida into U.S. territory became more frequent and brazen.

In 1821, Secretary of State John Quincy Adams purchased Florida from Spain for $5 million. The United States simply wanted Spain— and the gangrenous stench of her moribund empire—the hell off the continent. Practically no American official thought this territory would ever amount to much. There were only three towns of significance in Florida at the time: Pensacola, St. Augustine, and Key West. And statehood was not exactly a priority for these few Floridians, since the federal government picked up almost all of the territory's administrative costs. Joining the union as a full member would mean a greater voice in government . . . but *ehhhhhh* it'd also mean higher taxes.

The Indian wars of the 1800s brought more settlers to Florida. They also left roads and a communications network in their wake. The hastily built forts? Foundations for new cities. The blank spots on the map? Finally filling in. Make no mistake, though: Florida was frontier, no less wild than the West. In 1843, one visitor wrote that Florida "is the tip of the top for rascality and knavery. Nowhere this side of Texas can you find so many rascals who live by their wits."

In 1845, Florida became our twenty-seventh state. It would be a long time yet before it resembled anything more than a quaggy offshoot of the western frontier spliced onto the South. "More than any other force, the frontier shaped Florida for most of its history," the historian Gary Mormino has written. "Frontier values—fierce individualism, gun violence, a weak state government, and rapacious attitudes toward the environment—defined and continue to define Florida."

Indeed, from the granting of statehood till the mid-twentieth century, Florida was a national afterthought. Nothing much going on beyond some land booms and hurricanes. In spite of herself, Florida had escaped the fate of a Caribbean sugar colony; she'd also dodged the "curse of cotton" that continues to plague her Dixie neighbors. Florida was just . . . there. It was as if the Peter Principle had been applied to geography.

Then, in the second half of the American Century, while the populations of California and Texas were tripling—Florida's increased sixfold. All of a sudden that green vacuum became very enticing. Air-conditioned tabula rasa for those who'd been scarred by the Great Depression and forged by the Good War. They came not in Conestoga wagons but in coupes and tin-can trailers. Millions of individual migrations: factory workers leaving Detroit, Akron, and Toledo; old Jews fleeing New York winters; retirees uprooting themselves from Rust Belt ethnic enclaves; Canadians trekking south and Central Americans trekking north. Franchisees brought McDonald's and Holiday Inns to new markets. Their accountants and bankruptcy lawyers followed them. Cubans fled Castro. Jamaicans came to cut the sugarcane. Space-age engineers and other white-collar functionaries relocated because the boss preferred the tax breaks in sunny F-L-A.

For these people, Florida held the promise of dignified endings and new beginnings. It appeared to be that much nearer to the fabled "state of nature," that condition of absolute liberty in which the autonomous self can achieve its desires without obstacle. No longer need anyone be constrained by the restrictive traditions of "back home." Anything that felt unchosen or inegalitarian could be sloughed off like snakeskin. Here, social and familial bonds could be made anew. All relationships—permanently revisable. Here, there'd be nothing immutable, no impositions from without. There'd be nothing to *endure* here—not even the heat.

Noah nudged me out of my reverie. "I learned this shit in college," he said. "C'mon. Before the FSU kids come in here to fuck."

"Yeah," I said distractedly, once more thumbing a button that flooded a diorama Everglades.

FADE IN

EXT. U.S. ROUTE 27—AFTERNOON

GLENN

What we should've done is alert every local newspaper and tell them that three strapping lads were redoing Lawton. Then people would've come out of the woodwork. We could've gotten our characters that way.

NOAH

They would've all been seventy-five years old.

KENT

That, or insane.

NOAH

Yeah, I don't know how I'd feel about people being able to track us. Knowing the area where we're camping at night.

KENT
(to Glenn)

God, Jim was boring. Maybe next you want to fall in with some mall walkers?

GLENN
(carefully)

Trying to collaborate with you is like trying to collaborate with the little girl from *The Exorcist*. Everything gets the bile.

KENT

It's constructive criticism.

GLENN

I need to call my wife and tell her that being around you guys only makes me love her more.

FADE OUT

MILE 312 — PERRY

WEATHER THE STORM YOU CAN'T AVOID, AND AVOID THE STORM YOU CAN'T WEATHER

Three days straight we walked the sinuous hills surrounding Tallahassee. After lunching at one convenience store, we were offered some advice by the attendant on duty: "Avoid small towns . . . and also big cities. Just, avoid everywhere, if you can manage it. The rednecks are gonna wanna play with you." From him we purchased a fritzy Bluetooth speaker so we could listen to the news. We received so many election updates that the catchwords of freedom, corruption, and middle class abstracted into a fine mist. Later, the radio briefed us on the Mean Season: a hurricane watch had been issued for the northeast coast of Florida. Hooking like an uppercut toward us was Matthew, a storm that had killed a hundred people in Haiti and was expected to intensify into a Category 4 before making landfall somewhere between Cape Canaveral and Jacksonville.

"Cross Jacksonville off the list, then," Glenn said.

"Christ Jesus hallelujah," Noah rejoined.

The sky bore no trace of the coming blow; it was the threadbare blue of cotton work clothes scrubbed too often. That evening, we were turned away from a horse breeder's gate via video intercom. ("Mr. Glenn. *Mr. Glenn.* There have been a series of horse butcheries lately, and I would like you to move on.") Following that failure, we resorted to SOP when in desperate need of a place to rest our heads: We checked Google Maps for nearby churches. We called one located deep in the woods off the highway. They said fine.

A thing you should know about Google Maps, friend, is that for whatever reason, when you're out in the bumblefuck boonies, Google Maps will occasionally toss up digital mirages. A hair salon actually located in Pensacola will appear in the dark heart of the scrubland. A down-home restaurant established generations ago in Panacea will pop up along a stretch of weeds hundreds of miles away. Or, in this case, a "primitive Baptist" church will appear to be *here,* when in fact it is quite far away in the opposite direction.

Which matters a lot when you are walking! When you are walking beside the highway! Long after the sun had set, we slipped into our reflector vests and pressed on, eventually turning off the main drag onto a network of winding dirt paths. We searched for the phantom church.

I don't know that I can communicate to you the totality of the blackness. Among the trees, it was as if a fire blanket had been thrown over us. Now and then, we passed under a gap in the branches, and there we glimpsed faraway stars glistening like larvae in pitch. We kindled our cell phone flashlights. Shallowly, they punctured the dark.

"White guys!" Glenn said. "We have no natural predators. So, go climb a mountain. Walk a thousand miles through inimical infrastructure. Fly blind into some thirsty vigilante's electrified fence."

"Ah, jeez," I muttered. My beam had alighted on a ghostly Confederate flag staked in a circle of worm-eaten driftwood.

Headlights appeared a few dozen feet behind us. "I think we should prepare to get played with," Noah whispered. We drew together until our shoulders abutted. Even so, we touched fingers to one another's elbows, for the small reassurance.

A Crown Vic with illegally tinted windows pulled up. It idled. It dusted us with grit as it accelerated down the path.

"I know we keep making *Heart of Darkness* jokes," Glenn said hurriedly in a low voice, "but I'd much rather be traveling up the Congo River right now."

At our approach, all sounds flattened like wrinkles under an iron. The loudest thing going was the squeak of my pram's springs, which pinged our location as regularly as sonar. We came to the spot on our phones where the church was purported to be. We walked past it, then back. Then past it, then back. We leaned against a low fence. We squinted into the nullity. A square of light appeared. Out of it poured many hounds, barking wetly as they raced for us.

So we ran. We reeled off-road, we crashed through the brush. The pines seemed to part and leer, like a crowd making way. "Oh, Christ," Glenn hissed. "Oh, Jesus, Jesus, Jesus." Our phones' beams stirred the dark.

That's when a thick shaft of high candlepower lit us up. Hackneyed as it sounds, we froze like deer. Panting, we tried to shield our eyes. "Ah, hello?" Glenn called out. "Sorry, hello?"

No response but for the sound of twigs snapping nearer. Without lifting his own feet, Noah shimmied into a ready position. He patted himself for the retractable baton, couldn't find it, and so held his fists loosely in a low boxer's guard. Glenn, flooded with fearlessness or the profoundest ignorance, took a few steps toward the light.

Below it, a nickel-plated revolver was thrust.

This time, I made no mention of brotherly love. I raised my hands with Glenn and Noah.

Whoever it was at the other end of the gun—we were on *his* property. And in Florida, that meant he was well within his rights to shoot us dead. He could Stand His Ground. We were about to get Stand Your Grounded.

I shrieked "No!" Perhaps because adrenaline was swamping my brain? Perhaps because my lizard self had ticked the "fight" box? "Nono!" I repeated. I lowered my hands. "Hey!" I said. "No!"

I advanced a few paces with my pram. Perhaps because I was being courageous? If only. Courage is acting rightly in the face of fear. It is understanding and *fearing* the threat of death even as you disdain it. If you do not feel fear, however—are you being courageous? Are you not being, in fact, a dumbshit? An insouciant who, were there any justice in this life, was about to be thrust into the truth of the Panhandle? If not the truth of this world as it is experienced by anyone other than a white male dumbshit?

"We're just looking for a goddamned church!" I cried, as if affronted. "Come on!" I implored, as though appealing to our right to go where we pleased.

The spotlight and firearm were lowered. We saw the stranger for what he was: a wizened old man, his posture curling him into a question mark. Behind his Coke-bottle lenses, his pupils were obscured by a gauzy pallor, as if spiders had spun webs across his eyes. "You thought my house was the church?" he asked in a wavering voice. "Y'all just walkin'?"

"Yes!" I roared, bug-eyed and heaving.

"Y'all thought it said on your machines this was the church?"

"*Yes!*" again.

"Oh, that explains it." The old man tucked his pistol into his waistband. "C'mon, this ain't the church." He brought us to the front of his property, where a large pickup truck was parked in the driveway of a decrepit house.

"You can just throw your barrow in back there," the man said. "Y'all hiking the Florida Trail?"

". . . Yes," I said, hollowed by the comedown. Noah helped me secure our gear in the tool-crowded truck bed.

"Happens all the time. People hiking that trail, they look on their phones when they're in between sections, they think this here's a spot to camp. You know, I 'bout shot y'all for prowlers," the man said.

"We know," Noah said.

Noah hunkered in the bed of the truck. Glenn and I squeezed into the cab. "My name's A.C.," the man said. "Russell. A. C. Russell." He proffered his right hand while simultaneously turning over the ignition with his left.

"Hey," I replied. "I'm a Russell too."

"The Lord—He works in mysterious ways," A.C. said. He pulled onto the unlighted dirt road. "I don't know but that you might be kin to me. Y'all are kin to me regardless. Now, I just got done driving back from Arcadia, where I was working a job. But this church y'all's looking for is only four miles the other way."

"Well, we just wanted to say, for one, thank you for not defending your property," Glenn said. "And, number two, for taking us to the church. We were on our last legs back there."

"Hey, y'all are kin to me. I was born, raised, and I lived my life within five miles of the church we're going to. My grandson got baptized there not too long ago. Church was formed by my ancestors in

1850, before the war. Why I 'bout shot you back there is we had a lot of break-ins in this area recently. Kind of a situation we never had before. Caught a couple of 'em a few weeks back—young fellas stealing guns and prescription pills out of trailers. On drugs, I figure."

"Yeesh," Glenn said, modulating himself. "I wouldn't have blamed you."

"I could give you a ride into Perry tomorrow, if you wanted. I like picking up the hitchhikers sometimes. One of 'em, kid from Miami, he says to me, 'You know, you gotta be more careful.' I says to him, 'Oh really?' Then I showed him this—"

With a flick of his wrist, A.C. snapped open a straight razor. "I said, 'Son, the *Lord* is with *me*. I'll be all right!'"

A.C. steered us onto the misty lawn of a wooden church bookended by a couple dozen tombstones. He cranked the parking brake, turned with seriousness to Glenn and me. He slid open the cab's rear window so Noah could hear. He asked the three of us: "Now, y'all love the Lord, don't you?"

"Yessir," we said.

"And you know where you're going when you die?"

"Yessir," we said.

"God bless you boys," A.C. said. "If I had a half a mind, I'd go with you."

A.C. then demanded that we take down his home phone number and his mailing address. He made us promise that we'd contact him should we ever find ourselves in a jam. Whatever we needed, he'd get it to us. "It's important that y'all keep doing what y'all are doing," A.C. said.

He didn't belabor the point. But he didn't need to. We've received similar sentiments from others along the way. They'll pull over to take selfies with us, or they'll want simply to shake our hands. They'll tell us they're happy that *somebody* is fool enough to do this. Or they'll tell us what A.C. told us—that this is their dream. They want desperately to walk out the front door and just keep going. To abdicate all responsibilities and sacrifice their privilege in the most extravagantly useless manner possible, like a libation poured out to placate a god.

We disembarked. We waved. A light rain began to fall, a harbinger of Hurricane Matthew. Sullen wafts of mist rolled our way over the graves. Glenn and I worked quickly to pop our tent. Noah did likewise. That is when a *different* pickup skidded onto the church-yard, chewing up turf.

"What y'all doing here?" a camo-hatted young man asked through the driver's-side window. His left arm was hanging out of the cab; his right was hurriedly doing some unseen thing.

"Camping," Glenn said vacantly. "We talked to Pastor Williams . . . are just . . . camping."

"Pastor Williams," I agreed.

"Oh! Pastor Williams," the man said. "Well, y'all are OK then. Just wanted to check you out. Because some tweakers'd stolen the sound system out of this church the other week."

"Tweakers," Noah said. "Of course."

"I'll tell Pastor Williams y'all are OK," the man said, revving his engine.

"Pastor Williams," I said.

And with that, the playing ceased. The next day would be our last in the old man-killing parishes of the Panhandle, where we'd come to feel lost, unhappy, and at home.

By midmorning, a hurricane warning had been put into effect from northern Miami-Dade County to the Altamaha Sound between Jacksonville and Savannah. Governor Rick Scott told the east coast of Florida to prepare for a "catastrophic" strike. "You need to leave," he said. "Evacuate, evacuate, evacuate." Our phones sang with alerts from news outlets estimating that two million evacuees were now headed west, fleeing the first major hurricane to make landfall in Florida since 2005.

"This storm will kill you," the governor added. "Time is running out."

The sky above turned cloudy and unfocused-seeming as we marched inland. The westbound lanes of highway became clotted with wide-load trucks towing double-wide trailers; with meeping family sedans; with so many recreational vehicles.

"You know," Glenn said amid the honking horns, "I always hated walking."

"You're just realizing this now?" Noah asked.

"Somehow. In Toronto, I always try to bike everywhere. Even the coffee shop two blocks away. Walking always seemed like a monumental waste of time."

"We could buy bikes at the next Walmart," I pointed out. "Attach one of those children's trailer-buggies to the back. Tow our gear."

"I've *been* voting for this," Noah said.

"I still don't know if I'm there yet," Glenn said. "But, I mean, if a bike just gets me away from some of *this*." He spun once with his arms outstretched. "All of this Rebel flag, meth lab, *Breaking-Bad*-slave-compound militia business. Like, 'I got a God-given right to defend my crappy, ignorant life! You wanna make my existence better? You wanna send my kids to school? You wanna give me healthcare? Fuck *you*!'"

On the empty, opposite side of the highway, a couple of phone trucks sped east toward the fray.

"I apologize for that," Glenn said. "The road scrapes away your personal and political mythologies."

Come late afternoon, a cold wind was gusting into our faces. The sky had gone corrugated with low slate clouds. Under such auspices, we entered the depressed city of Perry. Like a lot of formerly bustling midsized communities in north-central Florida, Perry is where all hope for modest mastery over practical lives has been obliterated by larger market forces. Vocations, economic identities, solvent businesses that *aren't* dollar stores or chain pharmacies—these things are gone, and they aren't coming back.

The place was unsettling in part because it had been unsettled. Most of those who *could* leave, *had*. Those who'd stayed behind did so because they wished to live by the old ways; they found meaning in their order. But the narrative which had assured these people they'd be all right if they remained loyal to what had been given—this narrative no longer obtained. Industry needn't be loyal to anyone beyond the boardroom. Industry pushed the plunger whenever it pleased, exploding mills and factories. In due course, the human remainder thumbed their own plungers.

"Man am I glad to be entering through the black part of town," Noah said.

"Absolutely," I agreed.

"I will take chuckling derision over flint-eyed enmity every day of the week," Glenn said, waving to a group of laughing older women standing on a porch.

We walked miles of cracked, sloping sidewalks. At one intersection, a grease-streaked younger woman wearing a flapper's feathered headdress approached. She had a rather large pinecone tucked under her right arm. Something about her seemed spring-loaded. I expected at least one trash can neurosis.

"You boys homeless?" she asked.

"Are *you*?" Noah responded.

"You going to the Gandy then?" she wondered. "To the hurricane party?"

I shrugged. "Lead the way, ma'am."

The flapper walked us past the vestiges of economic optimism: shuttered bookstores, auto shops, internet cafés, family diners. She said, "People been pulling up all day."

We arrived at the Gandy Motor Lodge. It was a formerly trim, now derelict fifties motel spread out under oaks stoled with moss. These trees thrashed in dumb assent with the wind, working their forked limbs as if spellbinding the dozens of trucks and RVs packed into the parking lot. All very foreboding, yet clusters of people were milling about drinking from red Solo cups, maybe dancing a little, crossing in and out of open rooms. Our flapper said see ya and went to join them.

We booked the last vacant suite. While Noah and Glenn readied our gear for the hurricane party, I spent some time in the bathroom washing and scrutinizing a face that no longer resembled my own. The skin was as tan and burnished as a well-oiled Rawlings mitt. In contrast, the scleras were startlingly white, fried-egg white. Cheekbones and a jawline had resurfaced, I saw. The mullet had gone blond and feathery from exposure. This visage was not *radiant,* or *sun-kissed,* except insofar as a man marooned on a desert island could be said to be *radiant* or *sun-kissed.*

I did not want to film with strangers. I wanted a reprieve from dynamism.

"Let's go, funboy," Noah said, knocking at the door.

"Yeah, yeah," I muttered. I reached down to my left big toe, pinching its nail between thumb and forefinger. I pulled it up and out like the gull-wing door on a DeLorean.

I tossed the nail in the toilet. I took a last look in the mirror. I hoped that what was hard to endure in the present moment would be, one day, sweet to recall.

Dispersed about the parking lot were grill stations manned by drumstick-shaped dads in shorts. They were jabbing at and flipping the meatstuffs they'd brought from home, which would have spoiled in a power outage. Strangers handed them mixed drinks, a tacit barter for the barbeque. Many of the drinks were (*bluck*) White Russians made with milk brought along for the same reason as the meat. A litter of children was chugging this whole milk straight from the carton in between bouts of winging footballs around the parking lot at groin level.

"Hooo baby," Noah said, grimacing as he calibrated our shotgun mike. "In lotso foot pain, brother. Gonna drink it far away."

Glenn had me interview a few of the older women ringing the pool, which was drained and somewhat suggestive of an open sarcophagus. They weren't worried, they said. They were from Ormond Beach, Flagler Beach, Daytona. A couple of them seemed to be of Eastern European extraction, for they gave off a turnipy warmth. "He can blow *me,* this Matthew," said one. She followed a grunted laugh with a long slug of her drink.

Their disregard—it reminded me of the hurricane parties I attended in my youth. Let me preface this by saying that at my Miami Catholic school, we didn't have snow days, naturally. We had hurricane days. A lot of them. Tropical storm days, too, and flash-flood days. Days in which the cancellation of class meant less "where shall we sled" and more "will we have a place to sleep after this?"

Which is not to say that these days were gloomy. Oh, no. As you can see, a strange glee arises throughout the peninsula on these worst days of the Mean Season. A kind of swaggering, both-hands-beckoning, devil-may-care attitude. This filtered down to kids like me. I came to understand that, every year, Mother Nature would try to tee me up, knock me out—and there was honor in not flinching.

I knew little of hurricanes' actuality. For example, I did not know that the Spaniards had appropriated the word *huracán* from the native Taínos of the Caribbean. They did so because *el huracán* was a force the Spaniards had never before reckoned with. The phenomenon was so much more powerful than Mediterranean storms, so seemingly *purposeful* and *directed*. Each one acted as if it were an agent carrying out orders from on high, settling debts and relaying messages like a mob enforcer, or the accuser who toyed with Job.

The colonists learned to identify the signs of its approach: aching bones, severe headaches, premature births, ants climbing up the walls, saw grass blooming like crazy. Such were the results of plunging barometric pressure. I wonder now: Maybe that's where our giddy bluster came from? The hydrostatic mass rushes out to sea, and everything in nature runs, hides—but not us. Even when the mandatory evacuation siren sounded—not us. We hunkered down, painted phrases on our plywood as if *el huracán* could read. We jutted our chins and pointed at them.

And we threw parties in honor of our audacity. Outside: a monster whirlwind born from a vacuum. Inside: Life! Rollicking hubris! The candles as well as the booze got brought out as soon as the bathtub and washing machine were filled with water. The best part, for a kid like me, was when the eye passed over us. An eerie jaundiced truce in the middle of the tempest. If the adults were shithoused enough to go with us (or shithoused enough not to care), we kids would tour the damage. We weren't property holders! It was fun! It was like seeing Santa's list made manifest: who's been naughty, and who's been nice.

I got a lot of muddled theology at my Catholic school. Some of the nuns held peculiar heterodoxies regarding Limbo and the presence of aborted babies therein. As to the question of theodicy, or why God allows bad things to happen to good people—it was rarely if ever broached. So, imperfect in my understanding, I'd race around the storms' destruction in order to see for myself the divine hand of providence. Our neighbor, Arnold the barber, was spared! That made sense. The mean *abuela* who pretended like she wasn't home every Halloween? A tree fell on her car! The world added up. *El huracán* shook down wrongdoers for things owed, penances gone unsaid.

It was apocalyptic, this understanding of mine. Apocalyptic in the true sense of the word: *apokalypsis,* from *apo,* meaning "un-," and *kalyptein,* meaning "to cover." I thought hurricanes uncovered what had been lying beneath all along. My brashness in the face of such storms flowed from this belief, too, I think. Me and my family were fine people. What did we have to worry about?

Now, prior to the latter half of the twentieth century, this connection between hurricanes and those affected by them had remained private. Acts of God came and went. You suffered through them or were spared. You held out little hope that human vulnerability to "natural disaster" could ever be eliminated. You simply weathered each storm in turn, hanging on to the understanding that human beings and forces of nature stand in a relation of complementarity and interdependence and, consequently, must be granted equal respect.

Technological innovation, bureaucratic growth, and evolving public consciousness post–World War II changed that. Hurricanes were transformed from private catastrophes into public events of the first order. Florida-based research facilities, tracking and warning systems, emergency management teams, and the Weather Channel's Jim Cantore all worked to promote a sense of administrative control that stood in sharp contrast to the acknowledged unpredictability of earlier eras. More than ever before, it seemed, people and property were protected from cyclonic fury.

Then came Hurricane Andrew in 1992. Peak winds: 175 miles per hour. Storm surge: 17 feet. Death toll: 51. Homes destroyed: 80,000. Total damages: $30 billion. My neighbor Arnold—wiped out. The rectory across the street from my grandfather—a shambles. The farming folk of Homestead, as well as the Air Force base there—sayonara. Homes built by a subsidiary of the Walt Disney Company—as good and pure an enterprise to my young eyes as Holy Mother Church— these homes folded so fast under Andrew's strain that the builders were class-action sued for fraud. My own house was halved in the storm.

Before I could process this, I was bundled off to live with some relatives out of state. My parents repaired. When I returned to Miami, my Catholic school placed me in a kind of group therapy for kids who'd lost everything. Here, they finally taught us about theodicy, albeit in a roundabout way. Through talk therapy, we were made to understand that we were *not* bad people, or even half-bad. Nor, though, was this imbecile chance. The counselors did not want us to think of Andrew as accident. God was here, they told us. His hand was in this. But we can't know how till Judgment Day, since we are but humans.

Thus did a crack appear on the surface of my childish faith. This crack widened into a fissure and finally a break when I was teenaged. I refused to read into Hurricane Andrew's wreckage. I would not divine it as if it were tea leaves. Find the small voice of God in the storm? No. What happened to us was an accident within the economy of dumb matter. Nothing less, and certainly nothing more.

And, don't worry, I won't delve into how I came to reexamine theodicy, and make my peace with it, and forgive my younger self for being so obtuse. (Once my Ivan Karamazov moment had passed, I realized: By complaining about injustice and evil of this world, I was tacitly admitting that this world is not as it was intended to *be;* I was affirming the existence of a good Creator via the intensity of my complaint.) I will merely make clear that I *still* refuse to believe that the pitiless circle of nature becomes intelligible, endurable, and even morally beautiful because of some belief in a general happiness arising out of individual miseries. I *still* refuse to assent to the idea that every up and down along the sine wave of the Universe is solely the effect of a single will, sans any deeper mystery of created freedom. Suffice it to say I now understand that the Good Book does not ascribe any meaning or purpose to suffering and death. Suffering and death are privations of the good—they mean literally nothing in and of themselves—and this fact is perhaps the most liberating and joyous and *good* aspect of the Good Book. There can be no moral justification of the "natural" evil inherent to the present cosmic order. Evil's here and will continue to be till kingdom come. To say so doesn't deny evil's horror; it denies the possibility that we can abolish it.

Well and good. Yet I must confess that I felt the ol' end-times titillation circling my nipples when I saw Matthew draw nearer on an RV television. I was once again anticipating revelation. Not in the moralistic sense, though. This time, I had faith *el huracán* might reveal something different.

I was hoping that, for all the "natural" evil wrought—the blasted homes, lost lives, swamped hopes and dreams—*el huracán* might clear out some overgrowth and uncover a bedrock truth: We cannot estrange ourselves from this world, no matter how hard we try. We are and always will be dependent, contingent, interknit creatures. To delude ourselves about this is destructive in the extreme. Believing ourselves exempted from nature is the kind of misperception that leads to a ruthlessly utilitarian vision of the earth. Seen through this lens, Mother Nature appears distinct from us. More than that, she looks like she was made to serve. From her we take raw material and shape it into whatever we wish. We can, say, uproot mangrove swamps, fill them in, build luxury condominiums along the ersatz shoreline, pressure-cook the atmosphere by flying to those condominiums every winter—and then we can act surprised when a naturally occurring phenomenon emerges out of that warmed water to knock it all down. We can *rebuild in the exact same spot,* just as willfully, just as unsustainably, certain in our delusion that the storm won't be back, at least no time soon, and anyway there's honor in the chin jutting.

El huracán is a destructive force, but it can also spur growth. It overwhelms and inverts, like a wildfire. It shakes stuff up, à la earthquakes. Wipes the slate clean, flood-like. Behold, it makes things new.

"We cannot welcome disaster," Rebecca Solnit wrote, "but we can value the responses." This is, I believe, the true meaning behind "natural" evil. It is not the facile response—that *these things happen for a reason.* Suffering and death are not morally intelligible. Christ, they would be far more terrible if they *were.* No, suffering and death come and go on the wind. But what we choose to do in the aftermath? That means the world.

~~~~~~

Glenn, Noah, and I had nothing to contribute to the hurricane party, materially speaking. But we learned, canvassing the scene, that that didn't matter. Drinks were passed to us like relay batons. RV burgers were on the house. People were grateful that we were recording this, regardless of whether they'd see the footage someday. They acted as if they had to live up to it, this posterity. They were doubly inflated—by the booze as well as the camera.

Laurent over there was leaving behind two classic cars in his garage in Coquina Key. Darryl told us that he lacked flood insurance but wasn't scared. There was much *woo!*ing and razzing. A lot of flipping Matthew the bird. These partygoers described how they had acquired property, had raised children, had had decent unsaintly lives grow up around them until, now, they rattled around inside of those lives like they rattle around in their RVs. Like marbles rattle around in spray-paint cans. It was clear that some of them *wanted* to be emancipated from those lives.

Noah took frequent breaks to rummage through Igloo coolers. He invented a signature cocktail for the occasion: pouches of Capri Sun squeezed into clear plastic cups half-transluced with cold, cold grappa. Contrapuntal streams of music blared through open motel-room doors, the Scorpions' "Rock You Like a Hurricane" doing battle with Led Zeppelin's "When the Levee Breaks." Women wearing coral lipstick handed us paper plates piled high with Ruffles. We were given Gatorades to go with our hybrid aperitifs.

The evacuees recognized that we were weirdo dirtbags, and they loved us for it. We were bohemians! The closest thing to bohemians they'd seen in north-central Florida! We held some allure. And Noah leaned into this. Hard. Deep into his cups, he fronted like he was some undiscovered hilljack Errol Morris. He started flirting with one free-spirited woman who'd outfitted herself with as many leather tassels as possible. "A creative person doesn't stop at *any*thing," I heard this woman say, pushing a fingertip to Noah's chest. "And you're a creative person, aren't you?" The dark ecstasy of eclipse was creeping across Noah's face. "I am a true admirer of life," he answered.

Witnessing this, Glenn said: "Eeeee."

Nearby, the tasseled woman's . . . fella? old man? . . . lugged propane tanks, handles of rum—anything with a handle, mostly. He laughed, shook his head. He himself had struck up a rapport with the flapper, still carrying her pinecone like a running back with a football. Glenn was impressed that she remained upright. I shared with him some words of wisdom: Do not underestimate the stamina of the psychologically unwell. They will exhaust you long before they exhaust themselves.

Glenn and I pulled Noah away from his fringed ladylove. Together, we drank heinous milk-based cocktails, we investigated the open rooms. In one, elderly were playing pinochle. In another, preteen boys had set up their Xbox. "Hey, my guys," Noah said. "You know what I call my old girlfriend?" The children blinked at him. "The ex-box!" he cried.

"All right, man," I said, patty-caking Noah back out the door.

No rain was falling. We didn't know it yet, but no rain *would* fall here. Matthew was churning alongside the central coast of Florida, his eyewall brushing St. Augustine—but the hurricane would come no farther inland.

We wandered into a room in which bikers or biker cosplayers were engaged in a game of Twister, denim scouring denim. Their costume suggested that these men and women were looking to retain youth, or perhaps youth's rebelliousness. But youth's pliable rebellion had turned brittle, from the sun maybe, and inelastic rebellion appeared to be something they could no longer stretch beyond without breaking, as with a dried-out rubber band. Noah accepted a strange concoction from one such man on the sideline of the game. Noah eyeballed it, swirled it, sniffed it. Then he threw it back, as dispassionate as an engineer performing an integrity test. The same man then offered Glenn and me a few bumps of cocaine, which we took. When the game of Twister threatened to devolve into a more ignominious entertainment, we got out of there.

We retreated to our room to swap out batteries for the film gear. There, Noah collapsed the way an imploded building collapses, sliding toward the center of the earth with no loss of upright bearing. Glenn and I threw a duvet over him, returned to the movable feast. We plopped onto lawn chairs at the lip of the empty pool, Miller Lites bulging our pockets. Glenn rolled film.

GLENN (O.S.)

How would you describe the people at this party?

KENT

Like they're ten minutes from horking.

GLENN (O.S.)

Take two.

KENT

They are grown-up adults behaving as . . . as basically everybody in Florida is presently behaving, on the macro level.

GLENN (O.S.)

Better. I like it.

KENT

They're telling themselves, *The wagon has not yet reached the guillotine. Until then, we are immortal.*

GLENN (O.S.)

Print it!

Glenn powered down the camera, laid it on his lap. "Zero part of me believes this movie is going to be my big thing," he said, a little giddy from the coke. "But that just means I'm more committed! More committed, and less confident!"

"Fuck your confidence," I said, my knee joggling at three hundred beats per minute. "You're in an empire, bro! And when empires act, they create their own reality. We are history's actors."

"You are Rome, I'll give you that!" Glenn agreed, pinching the bridge of his nose while rocking in his chair.

"So let's start acting like it!" I said. "For the doc's sake."

"Art is not truth," Glenn said, recalling our writing classes. "Art is a lie that enables us to recognize truth."

I gestured expansively with my beer can ringed between two fingers. Around us, motel doors started shutting. "It's all in the art," I said. My skin prickled to gooseflesh. I was certain that the first girthy raindrop was about to hit. "We're gonna get no credit just for living the thing."

"To us," Glenn said, offering his can in a toast. "Nobody's heroes. Everyone's fools."

"For Florida," I countered.

THE TRUMPET SOUNDS, AND THE SLEEPERS WAKE

We rasped drawn-out, fetid moans the next morning, our throats like sepulchers opening. To steady ourselves, we took analeptic swigs of flat beer from the cans scattered about our motel room. We stepped into a dry but unceasingly windy morning. Torn clouds flew overhead like the last shavings of a buzz saw nicking through wood. The greater St. Augustine area had seen some damage, but on the whole, the state was spared. Again. For now.

We walked off our hangovers in the space of a few hours. My newly bare toenail bed was raw, pink, puckered. Staring at it poking out of my sandal, I was put in mind of schizophrenics who self-enucleate. We camped behind a fenced-in power station. We woke up and walked some more.

Glenn has developed open sores on his hips and shoulders from bag-related chafing. Still he maintains that he positively *cannot* push a buggy against traffic. It's a psychological thing, he says. He likes to be that many extra feet away from the oncoming lane, in case he needs to dodge an out-of-control car.

Wasn't much to see alongside the shimmering ribbon of asphalt: uncrushed beer cans; snakeskins; the agonized death masks of squashed varmints; teak-colored dip spit trapped in water bottles. The pine barrens had given way to farmland and open pasture. We were drawing nearer to the plains of Alachua County. If I knew anything about breeds of cattle, friend, I'd be more specific than *black, white, brown, and tan cows munched on grass whilst little birds pecked at their backs.* I admired the scene. More, I gave thanks to God that we'd made it through the long canyons of whispering trunks. At last! We were on ruminants' ground.

I frog-walked Rock-a-bye Thunder the wrong way down landing-strip-length right-turn-only lanes, Glenn and Noah flanking me. We passed big-box stores whose approach ways and parking lots were themselves a quarter of a mile long. We passed prefab homes under construction. Ads for accident and personal-injury attorneys. Churches whose signs trucked in automotive metaphors. "God accepts trade-ins," read one. "A bad attitude is like a flat tire," read another. "You ain't going anywhere 'til you fix it."

I wore a sloppy, ecstatic smile. To the west, the sore orb of sun was suffusing the prairie with golden-hour light. *This light is the color of thin dreams and conquistador obsession,* I thought. Then I laughed and thought, *That thought is ridiculous!* So, too, was the one that followed. But, hey, I had it. *In this moment,* I thought, *with my body worked to exhaustion, I feel as if I am leaping into the infinite with every step. And, every step after that, I feel as if I am falling surely back to the finite.*

I was beginning to attend to the road—to the world around me—in a new way. I don't know if it was the lifting of the heat, the retreating of the pines, the shitcanning of the walking shoes in favor of flip-flops. Whatever it was, I found myself able to disport centrally in mute calm, even as cars sped past and sprayed me with grit. Deep down and deep inland I bathed in a mildness that was something like joy. I was freed from the mental demons and smart-phone-enabled gremlins that would have otherwise tugged at me like fiends did Saint Anthony, layering the moment and keeping me earthbound. Achieving this state at my desk in my "home office" would have required superhuman self-restraint. Here, though—pulled out of time, road placid—I was able to direct my attention fully. I could scrutinize the integrity of each hour as though beholding it through a jeweler's loupe. Here, I had *no choice* but to master the habit of attention, which is the substance of prayer.

"Something in our soul has a far more violent repugnance for true attention than the flesh has for bodily fatigue," the great mystic Simone Weil wrote. "This something is much more closely connected with evil than is the flesh. That is why every time that we really concentrate our attention, we destroy the evil in ourselves."

Then there's also W. H. Auden, who said: "To pray is to pay attention to something or someone other than oneself. Whenever a man so concentrates his attention—be it on a landscape or a poem or a geometrical problem or an idol, or the True God—that he completely forgets his own ego and desires . . . he is praying."

I had slipped the surly confines of the cell between my temples. I'd achieved a state of perfect receptivity, of exuberant compassion toward all around me. In these few moments, I was intimately conscious of my condition on this earth—that of a pilgrim. I became deeply aware of the fact that I have here no lasting city; that my stability and security consist in being rooted to something deeper. This ecstasy was what all the walking narrators of the past several centuries have been writing around, I realized then. This and not confession or self-discovery was the point of a long walk: to explore the sacredness of the world around me, and to find my self-expression in expressing exactly that. The wonder of loving and living beloved.

While appreciating this, I happened to glance downward. I saw that midges had breaded my bleeding feet like a couple of veal parmigianas. I stopped, screamed, and kicked. My detachment arrested, I overheard Noah talking.

"Three of us, and we need a room tonight," he said, holding his speakerphoned phone flat on his palm.

"Like a husband and a wife and a child?" an ancient-sounding man drawled.

"No. Like friends."

"Man-friends?" the proprietor asked. "I can't be having no three man-friends having a time tonight."

"I don't think we'll be having ourselves a time." Noah sighed.

"Call me back later. I got a married couple in one of my rooms. Turned out they was having some kind of spree in there. With strangers. I gotta run them off. Call me back later. You can have that room."

"An orgy, huh?" Noah said, pocketing his phone. "On the banks of the Suwannee River. At the one-star Dive Inn."

"The end of every day feels like the bus scene at the end of *The Graduate*," Glenn said.

ANOTHER LOUSY DAY IN PARADISE

Outside Gainesville, we entered a long gully of fast-food franchises and home-furnishing superstores, the kind of miracle mile spoking into every medium-sized city throughout America. These strips are ugly and exhausting to drive through—to say nothing of walking through—because they assault with a dissonance of messaging. They're the visual equivalent of several dozen radio ads blaring at once.

"I think I finally understand the obsession some people have with finding *the real America*," Glenn said as we passed a Captain D's Seafood Kitchen. "This is it. If you're trying to look deeper than this, you're missing the point. And that's probably unacceptable for some."

Heavier flows of traffic zoomed by as rush hour neared. Peering into these windshields, we saw countless examples of the blank forgetfulness that an ever-moving perspective affords. That is: One-half of the driver's brain was occupied by the immediate and *almost* automatic decision making of driving; the other half was in a peculiarly distracted and suggestible state, sort of like a channel surfer's. When any of them noticed—suddenly, although it was sudden only for them—the trio of drifters staggering eighteen inches from their lane line—they spasmed behind the wheel, reacting as though they'd seen some ghosts.

After a while, the commercial strip petered. We followed the highway as it cut through pastureland that was in the process of becoming suburban developments. Here the shoulder narrowed considerably, leaving me no room for error as I piloted Rock-a-bye Thunder against the flash-flood current of rush hour. Glenn and Noah walked with a foot in the dry drainage ditch to our left.

Double-barreled waves of tightly packed cars pulsed at us from the other side of a low hill. Whenever their surge was sluiced by a red light, we jogged for a few seconds, trying to gain ground. We hoped to obtain the relative safety of a sidewalk before the sun dipped lower.

Very often I had to slalom off the shoulder onto the lip of the drainage ditch in order to avoid Rorschach blots of roadkill. Glenn gloated: "*This* is why I said no to that buggy." "Smells like a literal killing field," Noah said, covering his nose while running.

Though I am neither a veteran of foreign wars nor a doctor without borders, I know what death smells like. Thanks to the many, many pulped critters encountered along this journey, I can pronounce with authority that death smells musty, and that mustiness has depth as well as presence. Within it, hot like a filament, is a hint of latex. Redolent of, say, gloves that have been used to locate and remove an abscess, gloves which were then locked in the trunk of a car abandoned in the rainforest. "Sickly sweet" will do in a pinch.

Noah stopped short when he noticed an amphibian in his path. "Tiny frog," he said, still with his hand over his nose and mouth, "how did you get here?" I paused alongside him. "Tiny frog," I said, "did you just sit down to die?"

Glenn walked over, said, "Tiny frog, get out of here before you get run over by a mobile movie theater!"

We amused ourselves with this frog for, oh, ten seconds while traffic streaked by. As we did so, a sense of dereliction of duty crept over me. I glanced up. I noticed a champagne-colored GMC truck screaming downhill toward us. Its right-side tires were riding the line on the shoulder. Then, as if noticing my noticing, the truck drifted back to the center of its lane.

"Heads up," I alerted. "Got an erratic one here. Gold truck."

Noah and Glenn paid heed. Instinctively, they leaned forward on the balls of their feet. The three of us attempted to Care Bear Stare the truck into remaining in its lane.

The truck's windshield was darkly tinted, however. We couldn't make pleading and/or disapproving eye contact with the driver. We couldn't see if there even *was* a driver. The *Duel*-ish quality of this standoff froze us with dread for the three Mississippis it took the gargantuan truck to close the distance. When it was about thirty feet away, the truck jerked suddenly to the right. It now straddled the shoulder and the lip of the ditch. It accelerated.

"O why did we fear him," the poet Robinson Jeffers wrote, "for Death / Is a beautiful youth and his eyes are sleepy." A nice sentiment, Robinson, to be sure—but for us Death manifested as a five-thousand-pound crew cab intent on touching grille to brow and transmuting our consciousnesses into rose Jell-O. Yet like the bard, the three of us were entranced. Fixed in place. I even tilted my head forward a bit, as if to catch a whisper.

"Holyshitjump!" Noah screamed, freeing us from our enchantment. I shoved Thunder into the roadside ditch. The three of us followed after it, leaping like stags. The truck missed us by inches, sounding its horn as it passed. The wake of displaced air seemed to propel us that much farther. We rolled to a stop in the dry bed amid spilled gear. Glenn scrambled to check for breakage. Noah clambered to the shoulder in order to take down the license plate number of the truck, which had glided smoothly back to the center of its lane. He couldn't see the leftmost characters.

The questions came tumbling out of us at once: *Why? What the fuck? What was he doing? What did he think we were doing? Mad-dogging him? Wishing a motherfucker would? Who's that funny to? How had we shaken this fragile man? Surely he was a man? What did we represent to him? Did he think we were making some kind of political statement? Did he see our powerlessness and say to himself, "Now I will teach them a lesson about the world's relationship to powerlessness"?*

We walked on, humiliated and seething. We were officially twice shy. I forgot to check if the tiny frog was OK.

Glenn ducks into our tent nimbly, whereas I hurl my body through its threshold like a fish passed between mongers. I make my bed against the far wall; Glenn rests by the zippered, semicircular entrance. Our tent is long enough that we can store some valuables at either end and still be comfortable.

It doesn't matter to me where we camp, since I have an inflatable mattress pad. Glenn brought along no such thing and so demands that we bed down on only the mossiest of grasses. He bitches nightly about my pad. Not because he is covetous of it, but because it has been grimed black by my feet. It looks like an expressionist charcoal drawing drafted by a primate, except, again, it was my unsandaled feet. There are also a few calligraphic strokes of blood and pus, from my wounds.

In the tent, sleep comes fast and bereft of dreams. My own stink—the arch smell of lactic acid stripping the finish from my brain—no longer wakes me in the night. It wakes Glenn, though. He likens the sourness rippling from me to a ribbon tied to an oscillating fan. For his part, a piercing fetor opens around him like a popped umbrella whenever he removes his shirt.

Exhalations and personal vapors get trapped in our tent, causing it to warm considerably throughout the night. Were it made of clear plastic, it would fog like the windows of a car parked at a lovers' lane. Glenn and I fart with abandon, is what I mean to say. We are as at ease around each other as a crabby old couple. And, like an old couple, what we do together is less important than the fact that we do it together.

The evening of our brush with the GMC truck, Glenn set up the gear inside our tent to film a little unbosoming.

<hr />

FADE IN

INT. TENT UNDER A BRIDGE—DUSK

Glenn is lit harshly in a spotlight's glare.

> KENT (O.S.)

Looking like you're in *The Blair Witch Project*.

> GLENN
> (exasperated)

Right. Feeling like it, too, under this bridge.

> KENT (O.S.)

Nobody's gonna see us. If you'd just ducked under the gate that I spotted on Google Maps—

> GLENN

That's private property!

> KENT (O.S.)

It's an empty lot behind a strand of trees along an unlit highway! You're not going to get deported, man.

> GLENN

It's not the deportation I'm worried about! I'm worried about all these nutjobs running around with all kinds of guns, or attempting to run us over for points like it's a video game.

A couple of cars pass over the bridge. One of them drifts onto the rumble strip that fronts the guardrail, producing a sound like a romance-language tongue roll.

> GLENN

See?

KENT (O.S.)

It's an adventure. You can't have a paper asshole on an adventure, man.

GLENN

I'm definitely down for adventure. But my days of adventure no matter the consequences have come to an end, dude. I'd feel like such a dick if something happened to me on this trip, and my wife found out it was because I'm camping under a bridge like a sex criminal.

NOAH (O.S.)
(shouting from other tent)

You jabronis should've gone to law school.

KENT (O.S.)

You got stuff to lose. I don't. I get it. Still, man. You gotta be open to the story. Do it for the doc. Everything—in service to the doc.

GLENN

Damn the repercussions? We're going to live forever on celluloid?

KENT (O.S.)

That's right. The Florida Glory that eluded so many.

GLENN

I guarantee you you'd feel differently if anyone was willing to have a child with you. You, though—you operate so as to not owe any emotional or social credit to anyone. Self-sabotage as a means of self-protection. Won't let anyone help you. As soon as relief is proffered, the firewall comes down. Thinking you can achieve something like emotional self-reliance. Very immature.

KENT (O.S.)

I would argue it's very *American*.

GLENN

Maybe this *will* be my big break. Maybe I've got a tragic case study on my hands. You thinking that this Florida project is going to work wonders; the audience knowing that the real wonder is in watching your delusion unfurl. My own *Burden of Dreams*.

KENT (O.S.)
(quietly)

Whatever.

The men fall silent. Katydids begin to chirr like lighters failing to catch.

FADE TO BLACK

WHERE RUDER FORMS SURVIVE

Unbeknownst to me, Noah and Glenn had conspired to take this weekend off. A few weeks ago, I guess, they invited their significant others to Gainesville, a college town oasis where there are decent restaurants and fancy coffee shops. They'd booked separate twee B and Bs.

"I mean, I just assumed we'd all stay in the hostel downtown," I said, trying to hide my hurt.

"I need to refill my heart with my wife," Glenn said. "I need to replenish my red blood cells. As you are a joy vampire."

"It's this," Noah said, shrugging apologetically, "or we take road wives."

We reached the Gainesville City Limits sign. Glenn wanted Noah and me to stand in front of it and expound upon the time we spent here, the friendship we developed. I did not want to do this. We were *so close* to finishing off the day. You simply do not stop a walker who is this close. *Glenn should know that by now,* I thought.

"Where are we, Kent?" he asked. His tone was as condescending as a child psychologist's. "Can you tell us where we are? Can you tell us where we are, and what it means to you?"

"What the fuck are you talking about?" I said. "Look behind me. The sign. The sign is telling you where we are. Kind of question is that?"

"Fuck you, you pedantic shit," Glenn shot back. "Don't tell me my questions are dumb."

"Don't treat me like I'm some asshole off the street!" I countered. "Don't give me the regular interview shit. Just tell me what you want, and I'll give it to you."

"That's not how journalism works, man."

"Guys," Noah tried to interject. "Let's just get this done."

"What is wrong with you?" Glenn asked rhetorically. "Sometimes I wonder: Did I really spend this much time, money, and energy to be patronized by a dickhole for *months*? I know you think your ruinous inner and exterior life is some expression of, like, unique and devastating honesty. But it is emphatically *not*."

You fucking . . . passive-aggressive nurser of hurts, I thought. *You work so hard at keeping your small mean feelings hidden. Only in the rare argument do they appear. Hiding them even from yourself. Not willing to be seen taking your small mean everyday revenge on me, which, granted, I have sometimes earned.*

But what I said was: "I'm sorry that your questions are stupid."

"I *definitely* don't want an apology," Glenn said. "I want less commentary. Less demeaning bullshit. It isn't just the shit talking of three guys hanging out! It's this Chinese water torture of criticalness. You don't offer any helpful suggestions. You just shit on what I'm doing. And then act like you're this guy who's so aloof he can't take all of this to be quite real."

Glenn looked me up and down. Then he continued: "I have no idea what's pretense and what's dedication with you."

Though this bothered me—I *do* want to pull my weight, I *do* want this documentary to succeed, I *do* care about Glenn—I let none of these bubbles rise to the surface.

"I *am* helping you," I said, half-believing it. "To be not this way. To get you to stop being so sensitive."

Indignation raised his eyebrow. "Just so I get this straight," Glenn said, "you're doing *me* a favor by relentlessly playing me for a fool? You're teaching *me* emotional maturity?"

"That's right," I said. "Teaching you to be Zen. Stoic. These are like koans."

"These are like koans," Glenn repeated.

Noah whistled.

"Yeah, so, like—when I say you are a human golden retriever, so boundlessly prepared to be happy, and so ready for everyone else to be happy along with you—that's a compliment, by the way, you're a friendly guy—but when I say that, it's meant to, like—you're supposed to think it over, while you walk. *Is it true that I'm this way? Why or why not?*"

"That hardly seems like something to make fun of me for."

I went on telling Glenn that he was morally and imaginatively naïve, a serene simpleton. I informed him that my efforts at finding something deeper in him had been an all-around failure; that interacting with him was like tapping my fingernail against a bright porcelain glaze: High pure notes ring out, but not one scratch is left on the surface.

"Look, it's OK!" I said. "You are Canadian. You're the son of a distant queen. It'd be weird if you *weren't* an obsequious mediocrity."

"In fact," Glenn said, "it all feels rather indiscriminate."

"I get it. I get why it has to be so pedestrian with you."

Now, I did not *really* want to be saying this. In the heat of the moment I did, maybe, sure. I wanted less to win an argument than to cripple. I wanted to see Glenn's face buckle like the body of a man whose Achilles tendons have been cut. Looking back on it, though, writing it out—I recognize that it was not my finest hour.

It is well to explain to you here that an inner diabolism haunts my underconsciousness. I don't particularly care for it. I'm not proud of it. I wince inwardly whenever this reflexive antagonism flares up. Yet there it is, the fact of the matter: A snickering imp lives within me. A seditious and inebriating familiar spirit. If another exalts himself, this spirit humbles him. If another humbles himself, this spirit lifts him up. I go on confusing and contradicting the other party until the other party, through word or deed, proves that he, too, is a monster that surpasses all understanding.

"Trolling," I believe the kids call it. Acting like a provocateur and a trickster, and then gaslighting those who took the provocation seriously. Unparseable layers of irony, earnestness, persona, and performance drifting and overlapping until it becomes impossible for the other party to determine whether the devil horns are on or off.

Not that the genuineness of my actions matters in the end. I exploit the other party's kindnesses and weaknesses; I wind them up; I watch as they are transformed into unwitting performers. Often I do this for fun. More often, I do it for profit.

"Cuntishness as buffer," Glenn pronounced. "It's *me* who gets it. Sure, I know only what you let me know about you. But because of what I know, I know empathy is a real struggle for you. Totally.

"Your soul's like your dumbass buggy," he continued, giving Thunder a nudge. "It's the perfect vehicle for you. You've both been left alone too long. You're both rusting from the inside out. You're both too weak to do the real work you're here to do."

"All right, guys," Noah said, repacking his portion of the gear. "The light's gone, so we can just do it somewhere else tomo—"

"The castle of your . . . your entire life . . . was built on sand, homie," Glenn said, reaching for the lapel mike pinned to my collar. Clumsily or purposefully, he thumbed the point of its pin into my flesh. "It's all coming crumbling down."

It wasn't the pain but the principle of the thing. I shoved Glenn. He came back at me and, God love him, he twisted my nipple. Glenn gave me a purple nurple, friend. What was left for me to do but put shoulder to thigh, wrap up, and drive? That's just good tackling form.

So we had ourselves a dustup. Boys will be boys and all that, even when two of the boys' wives are en route. Understand, I'm stronger in the upper body but taper to a fine point below. Glenn used this to his advantage after I'd gone to ground with him. He wrapped his slimming but still trunkish thighs around my midsection, used them to prize me off of him. We rolled about the gravel and roadside garbage as if our shirts were afire.

Noah did not rush to intervene. Something in him—something like in a dry drunk with a beer placed before him—recognized that if he even *touched* this, tragedies would ensue. Instead, he circled us with a hypertensive flush to his face. He looked as though he dearly wished to make himself understood; he also looked as though he'd be able to make himself understood only by way of strangulation.

Glenn and I completed one last revolution before releasing each other from the clench. We lay panting together, supine and slightly baffled, like postcoital lovers. Then Glenn pushed himself up from the dirt with his left elbow. He leaned over and gaveled a fist against my solar plexus. "You make it so it's either spar with you or feel bad all the time," he said, wiping his nose with the back of his hand.

He refused to make eye contact once we'd regained our footing. To the back of his head, I said, "Those whom He loves He chastens, Glenn." I regretted it immediately.

"What you two idiots should be thankful for," Noah said, slapping the filth from our backs, "is it wasn't necessary for me to call upon my murder technique. Anyway, we could use a break."

Once we reached downtown Gainesville, Glenn and Noah went their separate way. I noticed not only that they were relieved to be rid of my company—but that I myself shared their relief.

THIS LONGING FOR COMPLETENESS IS CALLED "EDUCATION"

You know what they say: Each successive generation is, in effect, a conquering army of wee Huns who must be civilized before it's too late. I decided to do my part in that civilizing mission. I offered my services to the current dean of the journalism school at the University of Florida. Who, turns out, is my old thesis adviser, a genial diet book author. The man used to smile everywhere below his eyeballs while going over my avant-garde, thirty-thousand-word-story drafts with me. He did so once again—smiled a smile that was pure exercise of will—when he saw me stride into the patisserie for our lunch meeting.

I filled him in on my professional arc, making it sound more ascensional than the top-of-the-coaster drop it had become. To account for my appearance as well as the sickly sweet aroma emanating from the area of my feet, I filled him in on the doc, too. That's what did it. The dean invited me to talk to his magazine-writing capstone course. Long ago, I had taken that course. I had loved that course. I had been inspired to live my present life thanks to that course. Here, now, I could pay it forward.

More essentially, I could array our GoPros and film a scene for Glenn. Present him with a funny little make-up gift when we see each other next, like.

The following day, I went to pay my respects to the Ritz, the apartment complex where Noah and I had our meet-cute. What I found in its place was Cyclone fencing and hip-high weeds. The squat, off-white, two-story building had been razed some time ago, apparently to make way for luxury condos catering to well-heeled parents and alumni. Its demolition had left a gap in the row of student housing like that of a pulled tooth. And as is the case with a pulled tooth, all I wanted to do was prod the painful absence.

But I had children to inspire. So, somewhat somber-hearted, I crossed UF's campus to meet with the dean in the new "integrated newsroom" that football boosters' money had paid for. "Here's where we teach drones," the dean said, "and there's where we do 360-degree video." All was glass and steel, a fine architectural metaphor for a vocation purported to trade in transparency and the effacement of mystery. It was also the utter opposite of the shabby and avocado-carpeted college I'd loved so well, with its wood-paneled dark rooms, printing presses, and permeating aura of obsolescence. This "integrated newsroom" was a lame reproduction of the very thing that had destroyed journalism: Silicon Valley, right on down to the napping stations, dearth of walls, and young people sitting in headphoned silence before computers, tablets, and phones.

The dean must have misinterpreted my gasface, for he then added, "Oh, no, don't worry—we have extracurricular seminars on social media management."

He ushered me into a conference room and said he'd be back in an hour. I set up my cameras, took my place at the head of the class, sized up the dozen students peppering the few rows of tables. They looked . . . exactly as students looked when I went here. I would say that their big sneakers and graphic tees revealed in each an angry baby howling to be dressed . . . but I was dressed similarly.

I knew them: They had arrived on campus with the preconceived notion of an educated person being someone possessed not of a particular body of knowledge, but of an approved suite of skills and opinions. They were here to acquire the expertise necessary to acquire a job that might cancel out the debt they were presently acquiring. Their first two years of study had been given over to remedying their eighth-grade reading and writing levels. This was handled by graduate teaching assistants (and adjuncts!) who toss off A's because they know they won't sniff a faculty job without good student evaluations. The students know this, too, so the customer-is-always-right attitude is rampant. These children spend perhaps four hours a week on coursework; then they drink themselves unconscious Thursday through Sunday, networking for the future.

Their heavy-lidded eyes stared out at me from atop their folded arms. I contrived to begin. I could not begin. Their heads burrowed into their folded arms.

I'd led enough workshops and seminars at Columbia to know that I would need a Contigo full of hundred-proof to get through this. I pulled long and hard from the one I'd brought with me. I rocked on my heels, which had grown bristly with concentric circles of callus. I began.

I introduced myself, detailed my transcript history, swore that I was Just Like Them. I euphemized the documentary project. I rattled off the names of some magazines I'd written for. Kvetched about escalating rents in gentrifying Brooklyn. "Who here has seen *The Devil Wears Prada?*" I asked. No response. "All right, well—who here subscribes to *The New Yorker?*" Crickets.

I sucked at my thermos full of sunshine with renewed urgency. "OK, fuckers," I said. "Who here in this *magazine-writing class* thinks they want to be a writer?"

The children glanced around the room. "Sounds cool, I guess . . ." one young man said.

I rubbed my face with both hands, let them fall to my sides. "Look," I said. "I'm gonna tell you what I wish someone had told me at your age."

I slugged two-thirds of the Contigo in one go. "At least one of you wants to do this," I said. "I know it. One in twelve. I was the one in twelve. The one of you . . . I sympathize. Having been divested of any hope for love, or being seen by those who mattered most, you turned to writing. Whoever you are—listen up."

As a contemporary American writer, I said, you will have more freedom than virtually any other writer does, or did. How will you choose to put this freedom to work? What impossible goal will you attempt to effect while flexing your finite abilities in an imperfect medium? Will you oppose the neoliberal order? Cis-hetero patriarchy? The endless cycle of consumption and waste?

"Me," I said, "I like to lodge my opposition to the market by writing long, reader-unfriendly works."

I also try to honestly portray the humanity I see struggling in a fallen world, I told them. I try to reconcile a longing for grace and redemption with a deep sense of human imperfection and sin. Evil exists, that much is certain—but the physical world I see and describe is not evil in and of itself. We make it so.

More than anything, I said, I try to take the long view. Try to keep one eye fixed on history while keeping the other trained toward eternity.

I polished off the Contigo. I grimaced, *ahhh*ed. "Look, you're free, sure. But, brass tacks—if you're going to be a magazine writer, you're going to have to deal with magazine editors."

Bumbling on, I said: "You will prepare for these editors a free-range, pan-roasted squab of a story, OK, and they will take it, and they will rip it apart, and they will pluck nuance and complexity like so many fine bones." Then they will run the meat of your story through the grinder with some inorganic binding agents added. They'll extrude the pink slime of this new "story" into a nugget shape. Drop it into the fryolator. Crisp it into something that is easy to swallow and shares well. "And all this while *proper* writing becomes this *niche* commodity that gets consumed *only* by people who seek it *out!*" I said, scanning my audience in search of an *Amen!* Receiving none, I said: "Ah, hell. It's gone. It's over. It's something else now. It's just visions of a Netflix deal dancing through every writer's head.

"But no," I said, contradicting myself, walking back my despair for the sake of the hypothetical student who cared. "No, really. You shouldn't beef with these editors. Most of them are kind, patient. They're professionals who could have been *lawyers*. You know? *Ad execs*. But they chose *words*. They went with vinyl when they could have jumped to any streaming platform." I looked to the ceiling, bit my lip, shook my head as if in grateful wonder. Even so, I continued, you will need to familiarize yourself with the politics and cosmology of this editorial class. You will need to learn how to deliver on their expectations. "This is the secret," I said, lowering my voice after propping myself against the edge of the table in front of me. "This is the secret to all publishing, from magazines, to books, to I don't care what. If you *really* want to get published, what you do is ape the stuff that's already succeeded. You go after the consensus. You tell a story to these editors about the things they already believe to be true. You hand them a mirror they can see themselves in. Or see themselves as they wish they were.

"Now, if that sounds less like writing than flattery, well . . ." For a couple of beats, I considered how best to conclude this thought. "Not everybody is cut out for this business. I'm not even sure I am, now that I think about it."

I was sweating boisterously at this point. And if at this point it occurs to you, dear friend, that I was making an ass out of myself—it didn't to me.

"Nonetheless!" I shouted. I scrutinized the students. They were listening, all right. Uncomfortable as they were, they treated me with the politeness they might show a man discussing his own private religion. And I was so full of boozy *joie* that I loved them for it.

"Just . . . just ask yourself this," I remember myself saying. "What do you give highest value to? Figure out what that is—what you bow before—and you will come a little closer to understanding yourself, and what you want out of this. Ask yourself: What are my forces? What am I aligned with?"

I placed a hand to my chest like a doyenne with the vapors. I had a chunky burp to hold in, yes—but also I was moved. For their part, the students looked at me as though my skeleton was incandescing.

"Make yourself a servant of that thing. Writing is serving. *Living* is serving. Choose what you're gonna serve. If it's success—get derivative. If it's yourself? OK then. You want to write about your odyssey toward self-liberation? Hey, that's basic as all hell, but you do you. Point is, you gotta serve *some*thing."

My own face flushed as I took in theirs, pimples and foaming beards and all. They had a helpless vital pathos about them, like dogs with their first red erections. I'd made it thirty minutes into the allotted hour. I started for the door before I broke down.

"I don't know, man," I said over my shoulder. "We're gonna have to come up with something going forward."

A FRIEND IS, AS IT WERE, A SECOND SELF

With what remained of my shore leave, I wheeled Rock-a-bye Thunder to a bike shop. The affectless hipster I paid ten dollars to tune her up told me all was for naught. Rock-a-bye's rivets were rusted out, her spokes were loose, her cracked tires belonged to a gauge he'd never seen on this continent. The stroller was knocking on heaven's door, he said. Prognosis: two weeks.

Lugging my pack was a nonstarter, as you know. So I got to thinking. What could replace a pram? A wheelbarrow? A Radio Flyer wagon? One Craigslist search and thirty dollars later, I had my answer: a jogging stroller! Jog-a-bye Thunder is a regal purple, and she comes equipped with bicycle tires, shocks, a handbrake, and a seating area deep enough for multiple packs. She's got a *cup holder,* friend.

When it came time to depart Gainesville, I met Noah and Glenn southeast of downtown. They walked up grinning and grab-assing. They were actually *beholding* one another without my intermediary position refracting the light. They'd spent the long weekend going on double dates and, having just seen their wives into a cab bound for the regional airport, they radiated post-conjugal-visit contentedness. The both of them glowed as if heavily moisturized.

"Check her out," I said, pushing down on the jogging stroller's handlebar and popping a modest wheelie.

"Hell yes," Noah said. He bent down, strapped in his pack next to mine. Then, straightening, he pulled me into him by my elbows, gave me a lingering hug. I hugged back.

"There's a storage area underneath, if you'll notice," I said to Glenn.

He sauntered nearer. He slid on his sunglasses as if to protect against the shit-eating grin shining out of his face. "I missed you, fucker," he said, giving the pressure point in my shoulder a too-hard pinch.

"I missed you, too," I said, scowling, backing out of his grasp.

"Stockholm syndrome," Glenn said. "It's a beautiful thing."

"I've learned to love the little things about you guys," Noah added, "since all the big things, no one could possibly love. It'd be wrong to."

Everything was forgiven, everything was the same. In the space of one long weekend, our gall had turned gilt.

Redoubling our good mood was our discovery of a *wooded bicycle path* running parallel to the eastbound highway. It was wooded enough that, for the first time, we neither saw nor heard traffic. We were not blown about by autos, and we were shielded from the murdering sun ball! What a difference it made. We could pick shapes out of the fenland clouds. We could listen for the thrum of deep, generative energies.

Mostly, we walked side by side in a coterminous solitude, as happy as could be.

Sooner or later, the day began to relax its strain. The sky rouged. The mosquitoes rose. I noted in my pad, *Friendship is like metaphor: So long as it is still living, friendship—like metaphor—is inexhaustible and not fully explicable.*

Shadows solidified. The horizon split evenly between SweeTart pink below and artificial raspberry blue above. As we had encountered no one else along this path, we decided to pitch camp in the leaf litter adjacent to it.

Noah propped a spotlight, and Glenn set the camera on its tripod. A light breeze beat up the sound of palm fronds collating. Leisurely, we erected our tents.

A large brown anole scampered onto Glenn's and mine. The lizard fanned its dewlap once, twice. "What is that," Glenn asked flatly. "I am assuming it is about to jet me with black goo from a sac."

"They don't bite," I assured. I looked to Noah, who winked at me. "You can just grab it by the tail and fling it into the trees." Glenn reached for the anole's tail carefully, with thumb and forefinger, as if selecting a canapé from a tray. The moment it was pinched, the lizard's thick tail was jettisoned—its signature defensive maneuver. While Glenn took a couple seconds to scream, the anole scurried into the underbrush.

"What did you *do?*" Noah kidded.

"What you told me to do!" Glenn cried.

"It's still *moving!*" I said. At this, Glenn lifted the detached tail to eye level and saw that it was writhing like an unattended fire hose. He blurted the rudiments of a swear before attempting to fling the tail into the underbrush while simultaneously hopping away from it. In the process, he tripped over a tent spike and went down in a heap. Noah sprang to his feet in a state of great concern. He rushed toward Glenn, hopped over him, and checked to see if the camera got all of that.

Once I'd swallowed the last of my laughs, I said, "It's an invasive species," as if this would console Glenn. "That's why it's got that *Jurassic Park* escapability."

"Silver lining," Glenn said, dusting himself off, "is I'm starting to think there's no such thing as being out of place here."

"That one didn't go into the can," Noah said, looking with vexation at the camera's digital panel. "Wasn't recording."

"How long do you think it's going to take you to go through this footage?" I asked Glenn.

"The rest of my life," he said.

"You could hire an assistant," I suggested. "Someone to catalog, transcribe."

"I would have to make them sign a nondisclosure agreement. Lest they see how we are the most unsympathetic characters in the history of story and alert the Twitter mobs. It's problematic, to say the least, when the resolution of every scene is either 'This sucks dick' or 'We're some bitches.'"

"It's transgressive," Noah said.

"Clearly, it doesn't bother *me*," Glenn said. "But in terms of the no-sympathy stakes? I think we're sweeping them."

"Disconcerted Glenn is funnier than regular Glenn," I said.

"Disconcerted Glenn is just Glenn." He got up and replaced Noah behind the camera. He rolled film.

GLENN

(disconcertedly)

We're not spending most days in interesting places, or particularly beautiful places. I guess if where we were walking was truly beautiful . . . I probably wouldn't worry as much about the footage.

KENT

A mountain range, however sublime, can never produce a plate of riblets.

GLENN

Seriously, though. I'm afraid we aren't getting the *real* Florida. Right now we are just drifting through towns barely scratching the surface.

NOAH

But really getting to know gas stations and maniacs.

GLENN

I'm failing as a journalist and filmmaker.

NOAH

Of *course* we're not getting the real Florida. I couldn't tell you what that *is*—but I *do* know you don't get to it by being, like, rigorous professionals.

KENT

He's right. You wanna *get* Florida? OK, well—you *get* Florida by inventing an interpretation of it. Preferably a for-profit interpretation. Think of, like . . . Seaside. Seaside *got* Florida by substituting its own simulation "Florida" *in the place of Florida*.

NOAH

We've talked about the bikes, but lately I've been straight-up fantasizing about buying a used car. Just some beater. Then we drive it around, and we actually have time to find weird stuff, hang around, stage things, film. And nobody'd know we're not walking.

KENT

I'm down.

GLENN

Right. So you're saying that actually doing this straight is the *least* Florida thing we could be doing.

MILE 475 —— ST. AUGUSTINE

DISASTER TOURISTS

Lining our approach into St. Augustine were more and more Hefty bags filled with waterlogged trash. Mattresses, strips of insulation, large appliances, and pestiferous living room sets had also been curbed in Hurricane Matthew's wake. I was forced to slalom Jog-a-bye around this detritus as well as heaps of branches and brown fronds that had been massed chest-high on the sidewalks.

We entered North America's oldest city in the brassy glare of late afternoon. Glenn got many nice magic-hour shots of the Castillo de San Marcos, a masonry fortress shaped like the starry compass in a map's legend. Although the Castillo has presided over the St. Augustine Inlet for more than four centuries, it can do little to protect the city from the Atlantic floodwaters that have been encroaching with alarming frequency. Governor Rick Scott has put aside the task of combating sea level rise because he's skeptical of man-made climate change; he has forbidden bureaucrats from even *printing* the term "climate change" in official documents. Planning efforts at all levels of government have been thwarted. Florida's environmental agencies under Governor Scott have been downsized and retooled, even as waters rise across coastal Florida at rates faster than previously measured. In addition to more flooding at high tide, these heightening sea levels mean massive surges during tropical storms and hurricanes.

The tourist core of St. Augustine had been drained and tidied by the time we showed up. Visitors were mobbing the Castillo as well as the olde tyme simulacrum of Spanish Florida that abutted it, no waders necessary. Though by the look of things, frozen drinks in plastic whale bones were categorically necessary. We endeavored to join these visitors. But first—a motel, and showers.

It seems like a cop-out, I know, yet the fact of the matter is: The more developed an area, the more difficult it is to camp there surreptitiously. Simpler to take turns shelling out the hundred or so bucks for a Red Roof Inn. And I don't even mind the cost, since it'd take something like twenty nights of hotel stays per month to match my Brooklyn rent.

No, all is roses when we enter the exquisite sameness of a motel room. The air is unscented. The bed corners are hospital tight. The TV remote waits on the end table like a suicide pistol. Part of me wants to weep then, weep like someone who has suddenly found solace and can hardly conceive of the darkness to which he'd been confined.

We plopped onto the beds, we checked our phones, we performed the Dutch drudgery of bailing out the day's flood of news, notifications, and #content. We sniffed out every single electrical outlet, plugged in our gear. We backed up our footage, we planned our route. We decided that we deserved an evening on the town.

I less "woke up" than got ejected, gasping, into the morning's bladed light. Was there a dusty thudding inside my head? There was. Did my mouth taste like a desert sin? It did. Was I *positive* that I just saw—for one lucid second—leering over me—against the whirling backdrop of the motel room walls—a demon? We're all adults here, friend. We know from the physical chastisements of a hangover.

Brittlely, I pushed myself upright. I tottered to the bathroom. My torso ached deeply and all over, as though I had undergone an operation to remove a vestigial organ. I felt lighter but also hollower. I'd ditched some ballast.

For reasons unclear to me, Glenn and Noah were supine on the carpet, as motionless as limestone kings carved atop tombs. "Guys," I croaked. "Guys, what'd we end up doing?"

I dug through Glenn's bag, looking for the camera. I found *it* but not the memory cards, the external drives, the remote mikes. Below my heart, panic lit a stove flame.

"Get up!" I shouted. "Glenn, Noah—up! Our shit's missing!"

We ransacked the room but found nothing. Well, nothing aside from a greasy bag of cocaine. "Easily three eight balls left," Glenn adjudged. Noah had a slightly firmer grasp upon the previous night's events. "Let's talk to the Tall Teller," he suggested. "He'll know what happened."

That suggestion made no sense to me. I went along with it anyway. Glenn bought a memory card at a nearby CVS and began recording as we dipped into the stream of foot traffic on St. George Street, the ancient main drag that was now bracketed by faux-Spanish villas, wooden barracks, crystal shoppes, and "authentic" tapas bars.

Down the chintz chute we went, shouldering past honeymooning couples and families sporting plastic conquistador helmets. These throngs were here for the history. And there *is* history here, to be sure, but it is obscured by the Pirate Soul Museum and the Fountain of Youth Spa & Laser Center. St. Augustine's history has been refurbished in much the same way that a prized game animal is refurbished by a trophy hunter. That is to say: It has been neutralized, stuffed, and mounted. St. Augustine today is a taxidermied approximation of its former self (with flattering if absurd flourishes embroidered here and there, for presentation's sake).

Accuracy? Accuracy's got nothing to do with it. History qua history matters only to the extent that it can be monetized. That it can be disarticulated into a series of attractions—a competitive advantage. Loads of other coastal towns have white-sand beaches and umbrella cocktails, but where else in Florida can you visit a building that is more than seventy years old? This is what the tourism industry boils down to: *difference.* Tourists aren't necessarily searching after historical purity, or luxe pampering, or simple R & R; they want *difference.* They want something they can't get elsewhere. Something that might change them. Ultimately, ideally, tourists are looking to experience something so different and so transformative that they just might return home improved versions of the persons they were when they left.

Is that going to happen for many tourists in St. Augustine? Almost certainly not, no. At least not if they're Floridians like me and Noah. We came of age within touristic infrastructure; more of the same will not be granting us opportunities for personal renewal. If they're tourists from Latvia, on the other hand? Sure, why not. The haunted Huguenot cemeteries and faithfully reconstructed galleons might do something for them.

The lure and blur of the real. That's what St. Augustine's had to work with. That's why the city developed into a historical fiction like Colonial Williamsburg, except with even fewer fucks to give re: verisimilitude. Does that make St. Augustine a less-than-authentic attraction? Lord, no. St. Augustine is as real as the taffy pullers along St. George Street. St. Augustine is a real place run by actual citizens who work the tourist core but live far outside it, who pay authentic taxes and support genuine schools and hospitals, and who day after day conjure the fantasy of *difference* which tourists come to experience. This-all is as real as the stakes involved. Because if St. Augustine ever fails to convince people to visit? That's it. Once outsiders stop buying into the illusion, St. Augustine ceases to exist.

If that sounds like the dictionary definition of a Ponzi scheme—well, it is. No one here disputes this. St. Augustine in particular and Florida in general exist only so long as ever more people show up, buy land, build homes, pay sales tax—or at least drop a few thousand bucks during their stay. If the fiction ever dies—the reality dies with it.

"I don't know how much longer I can take the smell of caramel," Glenn said as we pushed upstream against the tourists. "How much further is this guy?"

"Don't either of you remember?" Noah asked. "Last night?"

I consulted my memory. I recalled: coquina walls covered in lime wash. Cypress columns rooted in flagstones and sawdust. Lagers in incongruous steins. Balconies, grilles, shutters. Solid surfaces and delicate screens; wide bright courtyards and deep shadows. A guy named Duane who sold us coke. After that, things grow darker and more fluid. The echo, the splash, the boom, and the roar of fast currents sink this memory under the rush of liquid.

"Nope," I said. "Got nothing."

Glenn demanded that we stop for espressos before venturing any farther. We sat for several minutes on sticky patio furniture outside of a gelato parlor, blowing on paper thimbles. A single fritzing nerve caused my left eyelid to flutter as I watched members of a bachelor party guffaw their way to a distillery tour. Snatches of the previous evening flickered to life in my mind's eye. The shame I felt then rhymed with the shame I felt the night before.

"Google says the Teller's up there, just past the Florida Cracker Café," Glenn said, yawning. "I guess we should hurry this up. My body is really committed to not being awake."

We approached a cedar stall, no bigger than a tollbooth, and found the Teller in the window: top hat, pencil mustache, black suspenders, black string bow tie like Colonel Sanders's worn over a mint green dress shirt straining against a muscular torso. The Teller smiled when he saw us, his eyes sinking into his crow's-feet like change lost to an old leather couch. "Lookit these three assholes!" he called out. His smoke-cured Carolina accent was of the type in which "pen" is whittled into "pin."

"You boys decided to take me up on my offer?" he asked, leaning out of the booth. "Make me the next big reality star?"

Last night's flickering frames sped up. They resolved into memory: The so-called "American Tall Teller" arrived at the bar to much fanfare following his last ghost tour of the evening. He glommed on to the same bachelor party we had glommed on to. I don't remember much about these celebrants other than that they were replacement-level dudes. They fell back on movie quotes in lieu of actual dialogue. They originated nothing, could keep the routine going—that's all.

And they took to the Tall Teller like pigs to slop. For them he recounted stories that unfolded as easily as deep-creased maps. He rehashed his days living in the woods and bathing in a creek while doing street magic in Virginia. Then it was on to the decade spent as a backup dancer. "Wait a minute," Noah interrupted, squinting. "Aren't you Wildcat Jerry?"

"Correct you are," the Teller said, a tequila in his left hand while his right was positioned as if to sprinkle a secret ingredient. "I trained under Wahoo McDaniel and Swede Hanson. Wrestled in the WCW."

"They debuted the crossover Japanese wrestlers against you," Noah said, nodding harder. "They kicked your ass."

"The craft, I conquered," the Teller lamented. "The craft's politics, I could not conquer."

That image is then replaced in my mind's eye by a technical difficulties test pattern. When the picture returns, we're at a crappy duplex, presumably the Teller's. The bachelor party had come with us, unfortunately. A dough-faced broheim wearing a lacquered shako, of the Prussian style, ralphed off the balcony. *That* I recall. Also: the Teller passing around a framed picture of himself in which he's shaking hands with Jimmie "J.J." Walker.

While the bachelor party waited for the Teller's drug dealer to arrive, the man himself put on a VHS copy of *Cutthroat Island,* in which he had a small role. Noah, Glenn, and I were ushered into a spare bedroom full of Bob Marley posters. "Look, boys," the Teller said, "I'm a big fish in a small pond here." He lowered his voice. "Anybody can tell some assholes a story, but it takes a special person to entertain. What I'm proposing to you is a *reality* show. A reality show where the Tall Teller searches America to find out what the best ghost story, tall tale, or legend is." He noticed our eyes icing over. His hand gestures became more emphatic. "I'm talking genuine historic tales, tales that have been with us for hundreds of years. We'll examine these stories, spin 'em, and determine if it's a true tale or a conjure-up. What do you say?" He cracked open a laptop, played us some poorly edited test footage. "It's History 101—if somebody don't tell these stories, you don't keep the ghosts alive."

I snapped to in front of his booth. "You really don't remember, huh?" the Teller asked me. "Well, I know who got your stuff. I'll take you. I'll even only charge you half price, since you told me you used to hustle tourists, too." He played my ribs like a xylophone with his elbow.

Evenings, the Teller plied his trade as a ghost tour guide. But during the day, he worked as a hansom-cab driver. We climbed into the Teller's open carriage, and he hee-yawed us through the tourist district. We rolled past the 540-room Ponce de León hotel, which now is home to Flagler College. "Named of course for Henry Flagler," the Teller relayed. He told us that this hotel was the very first to be poured entirely out of concrete and wired for electricity. "Same New York architecture firm that did the big library in Manhattan?" he said. "They did this hotel first. And Tiffany's—she did all the stained-glass windows."

Opened in 1888, the Ponce de León was a monumental success, drawing the likes of President Teddy Roosevelt, Mark Twain, and Babe Ruth. It was so successful, in fact, that Henry Flagler built the Hotel Alcazar directly across the street in order to house the guests who couldn't get a room at the Ponce. This gangbusters business convinced Flagler that he needed to develop the Atlantic coast of Florida into something like an American Riviera.

It was to be his second act. Henry Flagler had already conquered the business world, rising from relative Connecticut obscurity to amass a mind-bending fortune as one of John D. Rockefeller's partners in the Standard Oil Company. Reasonable people expected Flagler to retire to a life of leisure. Flagler, however, was something less than reasonable. Instead of playing out his string yachting or whatever, he relocated to Florida's sandbox in the late 1800s. And he brought his checkbook with him.

After building the Ponce and opening the less pretentious Alcazar, Flagler purchased nearby short-line railroads. He rebuilt them to accommodate heavier and more frequent traffic. He conglomerated the whole thing into the Florida East Coast Railway, and he extended it from St. Augustine down the hitherto unvisited shoreline. By the time Flagler died in 1913, it was possible for a socialite in New York City to hop on a train and head straight for Key West.

Flagler did to Florida what other millionaires and developers had already done to the West: He tamed it in reverse. He built infrastructure in advance of, not in response to, the people and the cities that infrastructure would serve. Before any demand existed, Flagler imposed his transportation system, his ideal landscape, his totalizing vision. *If I build it, the people will come,* he figured. (He was right.) And because Flagler was sole owner and architect of his designs, he was also the sole beneficiary of their revenue, since Florida collected no income tax. (It still doesn't.) The state never saw a penny from Flagler.

"You boys really ought to jump out and get some shots of me explaining this," the Teller said over his shoulder.

"We would, Wildcat, if we knew our shit was safe," Noah said.

"Duane's got your shit!" he responded. "C'mon, the shot's perfect."

The Teller framed himself between the Ponce de León's twin 165-foot towers. "Tourists weren't called 'tourists' until Flagler got here," he told the camera. At first, they were called "strangers." As in "Yankee Strangers," since most came from the Northeast. To class up Flagler's undertaking, the term "tourist" was imported from Europe. "Noblemen touring around the great cities, that kind of thinking," the Teller said.

But there were as yet no great Florida cities to tour. The first strangers came on the recommendation of their physicians, who for some reason thought the fartgas atmosphere would do consumptives good. These tuberculars—as well as those with jaundice, dysentery, diarrhea, gout, syphilis, and ringworm—were ordered to take the waters in Central Florida's natural springs. "Consumptives are said to flourish in this climate," poet Sidney Lanier reported. As you should by now suspect, he wasn't being completely honest. Lanier had been hired by a railroad company to write a guidebook in which he rhapsodized about Florida's recuperative powers, describing "cadaverous persons coming here and turning out successful huntsmen and fishermen, of ruddy face and portentous appetite, after a few weeks."

Regardless of actual medical outcomes, this idea of Florida as site of renewal and rejuvenation persisted as a powerful metaphor. The state began to attract healthier Yankee Strangers who arrived via Flagler's railroad in search of agreeable weather as well as geographic novelty. These Yankee Strangers especially enjoyed the exotic flora and fauna. They liked to buy rides on paddle-wheel steamers, so they could chug up pristine rivers and shoot whatever stirred on the banks. A few were self-styled entrepreneurs who made for the Everglades, where they hunted alligators for their hides and wading birds for their fashionable plumes (some of which were worth their weight in gold, thirty-two dollars per ounce, back in New York City). Colorful tree snails they harvested to extinction.

In the course of a few decades, Florida—the wonderland lauded for its *difference* from the rest of the nation—became less diverse, less natural, less original. In order to keep people coming, the state pivoted from the living aesthetic that had been so central to its selling of itself. Florida turned to the artificial. It began to look and feel like what businessmen *thought* such a place should look and feel like. From there, it was only a matter of time before every two-bit developer was trying to pull a Flagler and transform some stretch of Florida into their imagined paradise.

On Valencia Street, a flock of Spanish tourists, here to see what they were vaguely responsible for, I guess, stopped to photograph us. We prodded the Teller back to his driver's seat.

"You boys want me to swing you around the Fountain of Youth Park?"

"No," we said in unison.

We rolled to a combination tourist tram station / mini golf course. There, a short man dressed as a jaunty pirate was singing sea chanteys for a queue of indifferent elderly.

The Teller whoaed his horse. He called out to the pirate: "Dee! Fellas wanna have a word."

Noah hopped from the carriage. He strode briskly at this pirate. "Where's our shit, bro? What happened to our shit?"

"Hey, hey, easy," the pirate said while stealing a glance at the elderly.

This is where it gets embarrassing, friend. *More* embarrassing, I should say. It was I who purchased the cocaine from Duane at the Teller's. That much became clear. However, what also became clear was that in purchasing this half ounce—stocking up as we left, you see—I came to realize I did not have any cash. "Was *y'all* that proposed it," Duane said, pointing at me. "Y'all said you'd hock your gear. Good thing you came back, too, because I was gonna sell this shit soon as I was done here."

"What the fuck, Kent?" Glenn said. "You told us you paid for it!"

Duane rooted around in his weathered shoulder satchel. He produced our drives, our mikes. "That'll be three hundred fifty, y'all."

My friends decided not to join me at the Hilton, where I withdrew $350 for Duane and $100 for them from the lobby ATM. After that, we said goodbye to the Teller, giving him a few last minutes of camera time and making reality-show promises we had no intention of honoring. On our way back to our motel, I tried to laugh the matter off. But Glenn and Noah weren't having it.

"I was about to kick that man's balls off," Noah disclosed.

I told them I did not remember the transaction, which was true. Furthermore, I told them, I was sure I mentioned my intent. They were probably just as far gone themselves. Anyway, let's hook up the camera to the TV. The tape will out.

INT. SMOKY, DREARY, CARPETED APARTMENT— EARLY MORNING

The AMERICAN TALL TELLER crouches next to his bulky, convex television. From this position, he telestrates his old magic shows for the bachelor party–goers.

TELLER

I started incorporating dancing into the magic, you see.

The frames fast-forward. Now the Teller has put on his old wrestling videos.

TELLER

I remember that guy well. He really taters you.

The Teller can hardly be heard over the raucous hum of male confabulation. The shot drifts through the room, settling momentarily upon a man in the corner who appears to have gone cataleptic. The corpse-rigid legs extending before him are all that keep him in his chair. The camera then locates Kent and Noah, who are quite obviously in the bag. Noah is watching the wrestling, as rapt as a drunk man can be. Kent's face, however, reflects a dimming light.

TELLER (O.S.)

Yeah, my turn now. You want some? I'll give you some!

Kent looks for the camera, finds it, moves for it. His body accompanies him in lagging sections.

KENT

(spreading arms)

I got this text from my super, telling me the mailman keeps looking for me. Sign a registered letter. That's from Uncle Sam, Glennzo. Thirty-*eight* grand now. At *least*.

Noah lurches off the wall, moves from background to foreground. Kent's eyes are blank. Consciousness's stylus is no longer etching wax.

KENT

We need to get real, man. Shift gears.

Offscreen, there is a burst of shouting, jocularity. The camera pivots, zooms in on DUANE THE PIRATE as he enters. If they could, the bachelors would lay down a path of palm fronds for him.

FADE OUT

FADE IN:

INT. SMOKY, DREARY, CARPETED APARTMENT— HOURS LATER

Filling the frame is Kent's face. A thin band of iris rings each of his dilated pupils like the stone lip of a deep well. You can practically hear the blood hissing through his veins—a sparked fuse.

KENT

Harken unto me, you dipshits! The footsteps were accidental yet the destiny could be no other. We're not gonna soften now. Oh, no. We're gonna intensify what we are! This is the one and only ticket— intensify.

Sequins flash in his eyes.

KENT (CONT'D)

Art is not documentation but *transformation*.

He moves to a nearby end table and beaks deeply of the bachelor party cocaine.

KENT (CONT'D)

Said it before and I'll say it again: Florida was founded by artists! The people who came here—artists! They added artifice so that suckers'd think there was *less* artifice. Dredge a canal half a mile inland, boom, that's waterfront property. No one can argue it's not. And if history's taught us anything, which it hasn't, it's that fantasy, advertising . . . fucking . . . *salutary fraud* have shaped this place far more than truth ever could.

Behind closed lips, Kent's tongue moves over his teeth.

KENT (CONT'D)

If we don't stumble across what we need—fuck it, we'll mock it up. Because that's what the place was founded upon. Faking it till you've made it. Convincing people it's real—people who *want* to be duped, mind you, who *want* to believe—

NOAH (O.S.)
(screaming at television, everyone)

PINFALL, CACTUS JACK!

Kent's eyes widen. His train of thought crashes off a cliff.

FADE OUT

MILE 510 ⸺ STATE ROAD A1A

HAVERING TO YOU

To celebrate our crossing of the five-hundred-mile mark, we played The Proclaimers' "I'm Gonna Be (500 Miles)" on our Bluetooth speaker and said not one word to each other.

⸻

CATCHING THE SPIRIT

After Daytona Beach (the less said, the better), we turned toward the interior of the peninsula once again, moving southwesterly into first-generation suburbia: brick-and-mortar homes, modest and reasonable, shaded by oaks. We were headed for the Cassadaga Spiritualist Camp, the largest such community in the South and the only year-round Spiritualist camp in these United States. Cassadaga is made up of fifty-five homes on approximately fifty-seven acres of land. Those who reside in it have chosen "to share in a community of like-minded people where they can live, worship and work in harmony with their beliefs," as Cassadaga's promotional literature puts it.

These Spiritualists have faith in a higher power. Call it what you wish: "Great Spirit," "Universal Energy." Like Protestants, they believe that no man or institution can mediate an individual's experience of the Higher Power. Unlike Protestants, they recognize no particular savior. Spiritualists believe that all of the major prophets have been inspired by the Higher Power throughout the course of history. According to them, these prophets bore the same message: the Golden Rule. "Do unto others as you would have done unto you." Problem is, the followers of these individual prophets organized themselves into corporate structures, into religions. These rival religions then overlaid dogma and tradition upon the Golden Rule, eclipsing its simplicity and obviousness. Petty dissensions led to war, war to general human misery, et cetera and so on.

Nothing too controversial, right? It jibes with the syncretic, humanistic theology embraced now by about a quarter of this country, a belief system that sociologists in the mid-aughts classified as "Moralistic Therapeutic Deism." A few core tenets were identified:

- A Higher Power exists who created and ordered the world and watches over human life on earth.
- This Power wants people to be good, nice, and fair to each other, as taught in the Bible and by most world religions.
- The central goal of life is to be happy and to feel good about oneself.
- The Higher Power does not need to be particularly involved in one's life except when it is needed to resolve a problem.

Where Cassadaga's Spiritualists split from followers of Moralistic Therapeutic Deism (as well as most orthodox faiths) is in their belief that a person's soul hangs around after he or she dies. And this loitering soul—it's just *dying* to talk to a trained medium. "Mediumship, when done in the true sense, will produce a real understanding of this existence and level of interaction to and from the spirit realm," Cassadaga's literature says.

You need not be a medium or "healer" to be a Spiritualist. Even so, the faithful number only 500,000 in the United States. This number represents a significant decline from the heyday of Spiritualism in the mid- and late 1800s. Back then, Spiritualism's two founding sisters, from Hydesville, New York, were touring the country, conducting these new rituals called séances, talking to ghosts on behalf of people like Mary Todd Lincoln and Horace Greeley. Spirits were also communicating with regular folks in any number of ways—table tippings, communicative creakings, messages received by automatic writers, Ouija pronouncements. (Never mind that a lot of these regular folks had just lost loved ones in the Civil War and were willing to believe just about anything if it eased their pain.) Spiritualism seemed to represent a new frontier in metaphysics.

In the midst of this fervor, a young man named George Colby was told during a séance that he would found a Spiritualist community in the South. His spirit guide—a Native American specter named Seneca—led him to a spot where, ahem, underground rock alignments generated magnetics and harmonics and created a spiritual vortex. Around the same time, wealthy New Yorkers from the Lily Dale Spiritualist Community of Lake Cassadaga approached Colby about creating a wintertime retreat in Florida. Before too long, a forty-room hotel and some stately Victorian homes had sprouted above the spiritual vortex. Cassadaga got its own railroad station, too, so well-heeled Spiritualists could make like their tourist contemporaries and ride the rails from New York, Maine, or Iowa straight there.

Spiritualism's founding sisters would go on to confess their fraud before dying penniless, insane, and addicted to drink. No matter. Those dissatisfied with conventional Christianity as well as those attracted to alternative belief systems found themselves drawn to Cassadaga's vortex. The community of Yankee Strangers built itself up. The Spiritualists weathered early fights with their Baptist neighbors; they experienced something of a renaissance during the New Age movement; they still manage to pull in about 150 people for their Sunday services. Including us.

"Who knows what today will bring?" I joked as we neared the camp.

"They do," Noah said. "The mediums."

"I'm trying to go into this with an open mind," Glenn said. "But I have a feeling it's going to be locked shut, combination spun, by the end."

Cassadaga embraces tourism, but at its core it is a residential community of about fifty practicing mediums and healers. Its "downtown" is a small post office and a couple of psychics on one side of the road, and then the forty-room hotel and camp-owned bookstore on the other. This is the line of demarcation. Everything behind the hotel is part of the camp (even though the hotel no longer is). Everything on the post office side of the street is non-camp-sanctioned. "Leeches," the camp members call these outsiders who arrived in the eighties.

Many luxury sedans were pulling up to the allegedly haunted hotel just as we were. Most of them were from Orlando and its constitutive suburbs, which are a forty-five-minute drive away. All of them were here for Halloween weekend.

Older men in khakis and floral-patterned shirts were milling about the hotel's lobby, a section of which had been transformed via bedsheets, plywood, and protuberant nails into a fun house called Clown Town. That, or they were drinking the bar dry while their wives, daughters, and significant others browsed the public corkboards and Trapper Keepers for suitable mediums.

"I'm not trying to sound sexist," Noah said as we powered up our film gear.

"Here we go," Glenn said.

"But I expect three-fourths to four-fifths of the clerics or whatever to be middle-aged women. And for the few men to be the high priests. Slash sexual-predator-type grifters."

Walking the camp's oak-lined and moss-hung streets took less than half an hour. Amid the peeling Victorian homes were traces of rural eclectic: a yard edged with miniature American flags; a Buddha wearing Mardi Gras beads and sunglasses; a Saint Francis statue overlooking golden sphinxes; a second-story door with no stairs leading to it. We admired the Eloise Page Meditation Garden, a shady lot filled with statuary, benches, and memorials to noted Spiritualists. We reflected upon Spirit Pond, which is where the ashes of dead mediums are sometimes dumped. Around us, visitors moved with purpose. We flagged down a few, interviewed them. They said they came here because they sought closure with a deceased loved one. They said they came here because they wanted to talk to God. One woman said she didn't mind paying $120 an hour to "know for sure there's another side." Inwardly, I said a word of thanks for our not encountering a parent who'd lost a child.

A couple of visitors told us that they also attended classes for mediumship "accreditation" that were offered here. Everyone, it seems, has one of the nine gifts of the Spirit. And everyone can have that gift "unfolded" for a nominal fee. "Get accredited at Cassadaga," one Wilford Brimley–looking guy told us, "and it's accepted everywhere, no question."

As the 10:30 a.m. Spiritualist service approached, we made our way to Colby Memorial Temple, a Mediterranean Revival–style hall erected in 1923. No crucifixes, crescents, or Stars of David to be found—instead, a troubling number of sunflowers had been planted around the building. We asked one besuited middle-manager type what gives; he recited: "As the sunflower turns its face to the light of the sun, so Spiritualism turns the face of humanity to the light of the truth."

"Rad," Noah said.

"I sense you need some healing," the man said. "Come. Come to the healing gazebo."

He held the door for us as we crowded into the small, circular structure adjacent to the temple. Sunlight filtered through gauzy white curtains; multiple window-unit ACs whirred our sweaty skin into braille. We took the last three seats along the room's perimeter and waited our turn to be "healed." I was called up first by our middle-manager friend. I sat in the center of the gazebo next to a large man in an *Are We There Yet?* tee who had his own healer. Our middle-manager friend washed his hands in a small dish. He asked me, "What is in your mind right now?"

"My feet hurt, and I miss my toenails," I said.

"Hmmm," he said. He turned my palms up and placed them in my lap. He stepped behind me. Then he wiped his wet hands over his closed eyes. He gripped me by my shoulders. "Think of something that needs healing," he directed. "So, my feet?" I said. Gently, he touched my temples, my arms, my legs. I perceived no energy flowing to or from me. Which is not to say that this was an unpleasant experience. It felt *nice*. Nice the way someone at Supercuts massaging your scalp as they shampoo you is nice.

"How do you feel now?" he asked after three minutes of soft nudging.

"Fine?" I said.

"Well, improvement usually takes more than one session," he admitted. Passed my way was a donation plate gone leafy with twenty-dollar bills. "May the healing power of healing spirit be with you each moment of each day," our new friend whispered in my ear. I dropped a fin into the dish. "Much obliged," I said.

"Thanks, but no thanks," Noah said, exiting the gazebo with me. We waited a few minutes for Glenn to get healed. He emerged saying he *did* feel a third hand on his shoulder after the dude had moved on to his head. "But mainly the thing I thought of was how bad my shoulders hurt."

We entered the temple as its bell began to toll. It was a large, airy, downward-sloping hall with particleboard ceilings from which dangled six black orbs on chains. About a hundred people—most of them older women in pastels—sat in central pews and rows of chairs radiating from a stage containing something akin to a public-access talk show set: comfortable chairs, ferns, a piano, pink drapery, air-brushed paintings of the stars and planets as well as one single sun-flower. Soft flute music wafted out of unseen speakers. "No kneelers," I pointed out.

The reverend was a short, middle-aged man with a full head of brown ringlets. He started things off by lighting three candles, explaining that this one symbolized body, this one mind, and this one spirit. Then came hymns, invocations. So far, so harmless—even if my own convictions prevented me from saying "amen" to any of this stuff. Certainly I was not going to recite their Declaration of Principles, which included claims like:

5. We affirm that communication with the so-called dead is a fact, scientifically proven by the phenomena of Spiritualism.

9. We affirm that the precepts of Prophecy and Healing are divine attributes proven through Mediumship.

The congregation was invited to line up along the walls for their spiritual healing. Those who'd already been healed were led in guided meditation by the reverend: "You begin to feel your mind relaxing . . . You forget the past, and your imagined failure . . . Now is the time when you say, 'I want to focus on my own well-being' . . . I see the light being absorbed into the body, and becoming light energy . . . This is happening because I love myself, and I want to experience love and happiness . . ."

As chairs scraped and some guy tickled the ivories, I began to think of the great psychologist-philosopher William James. He'd described nineteenth-century phenomena like Spiritualism in his landmark study, *The Varieties of Religious Experience.* In it, James categorized these "anti-religionists" as individuals who very much like the glowing, white-hot charisma of certain creeds and their geniuses. What they *don't* like are the politics and the lust for dogmatic rule that are apt to snake in and contaminate the originally innocent prophet or concept. To these anti-religionists, history makes it clear: When followers codify their encounters with the Higher Power, bad things happen. Encounters with the divine come to mean "religion," and "religion" comes to mean "church," and "church" comes to mean hypocrisy, tyranny, meanness, exclusion. The Spiritualists, the "anti-religionists"—they are *pro* spontaneity, *pro* authenticity. They are *anti* orthodoxy, *anti* intellection. They are, in fact, damn near Romantic in their *pro* inspiration, *anti* tradition tack. *Pro* individualism, *anti* conformity.

Inspired myself, I flipped open my notebook and wrote: *To these individuals—be they Spiritualist, Moralistic Therapeutic Deist, whatever—the overcoming of an inherited religion is seen as an achievement of maturity. Finally throwing off [Catholicism, Judaism, Jainism] like a clip-on tie after church is considered a liberating act. You are finally free to begin the process of* becoming. *Of determining who you* really *are, digging your Authentic Self out from under religiously imposed hypocrisies and psychological impedimenta.*

I continued: *They believe the Higher Power wants me to find My Truth. I am to do this by custom-designing My Truth as if at a Build-a-Bear Workshop, taking whatever works from wherever I can find it: East, West, Global South, it's all good. Having found My Truth, I must beware of anyone who attempts to impose theirs. All proselytizing is a mask of righteousness worn over a will to power. There is but one authority, and it is moi.*

Amen I say to you, the Golden Rule can be updated to read, *You do you, so long as I remain free to do me.*

The guided meditation droned on. "Follow your soul, not your mind." That kind of thing. Stop listening to your head, because it leads you astray, and start listening with your center. Breathe in the life-giving Universal Spirit, which fans your Divine Spark; trust not your craven ego; turn away from the allure of your pain-body; relinquish future and past so that you may live no longer in anxiety and regret; blah blah. Things got very Krishnamurti-Gnostic up there.

"It's time to stop stopping to think," the reverend said. "Here, now, you live *your* truth."

Noah leaned over and said, "All this 'golden streaming light' talk is making me have to piss. I'll find you guys outside."

A Spiritualist matriarch come all the way from Connecticut preached the homily, entitled "This Wonderful Journey of Self-Discovery." After that, the congregation beseeched the Infinite Spirit a few more times. While stifling a yawn I stretched and gazed about—and noticed that Glenn was actually doing it. He had closed his eyes and was holding his upturned palms in front of him as though he were a mendicant. He was repeating after the reverend: "This happens because . . . I love myself . . ."

I nudged Glenn when the reverend announced there'd be a new members' gathering after the final blessing. An instrumental version of "All You Need Is Love" ushered us out of the building.

We followed the congregants into the temple's parking lot. And what did we find there, adorning the chariots of these spiritual spirits, these freethinkers who choose seeking over submitting, believing over belonging? Why, a ton of *Hillary for Prison 2016* bumper stickers. That's what.

Like a deep-sea anglerfish waggling its bioluminescent lure, we pretended to futz with the boom mike. Almost instantly, congregants approached. "The spirits are wise," said one mom-mulleted woman who declined to give a name (yet was a dead ringer for the Realtor whose billboards we'd been passing on the highway). "They want to guide and uplift us. Wouldn't it be egotistical *not* to hear what they have to say?"

A burly guy in a motorcycle club jacket told us, "I actually *want* to come here." Fanned behind him, his motorcycle clubmates nodded. "When I thought about going to church before, it was *hell* this and *shame* that. Here, it's positivity."

We thanked them for their time, and we went and joined the new members' gathering in progress in the century-old Andrew Jackson Davis Building. Here, neophyte mediums were pacing the creaky salon, practicing their gifts on a few dozen volunteers who pecked at complimentary donuts.

One smoky-eyed woman introduced herself as a confident person who knew she was intuitive since childhood. In Puerto Rico, she said, she always had that sense of just "knowing." She received spirit visits from many of her friends and family members at or after the times of their passing.

"Let me touch with you over here if I may," she began. One raised hand had a question about a departed father. The medium answered, "When he was on the earth plane . . ." This segued into "Don't let things get you down . . . he's behind you, pushing you up . . ." before ending with "Strong vibrations . . . just keep going."

Another medium, with long, floss-colored hair, took the floor. Hers was a strong connection to the Spirit Realm *and* the Earth Mother, she said. Although her grandmothers had made their transitions to the Spirit Realm, they came often to visit her at the old family home, especially now that it was in disrepair and in danger of foreclosure. Their spirits turn on lights and open cabinet doors. They also highlight water damage and locate palmetto bug nests.

This medium walked along the walls studying the blurry enlargements of old lithograph postcards that lined them. Abruptly she spun around, slapped both hands to a sunflower-tableclothed table, and peered across at an elderly invalid who was breathing through an oxygen machine.

"You've got some energy inside of you," the medium said. "I see you're hooked up to some oxygen, but there's a little ball of energy inside of you . . ."

The collection plate was passed onto the invalid's lap. She glanced down at it, then back to the medium. Behind the oxygen mask, her sunken face wore the startled, ring-mouthed expression of a mummy, or a baby removed from the breast.

"I'm getting the word . . . 'feisty,'" the medium said, fanning the air as if to bring a smell nearer. The invalid's eyes widened; her nods were barely perceptible. The medium began nodding, too, and smiling.

"I don't know how *feisty* you were," she said, ". . . but it's still there! It was there before, and it's there now! You know, you're not giving in . . . You don't want to give in! You've got time to come! You really do!"

The medium took one of the invalid's hands, saying, "You're going to keep going, kid! That's what they're telling me from the other side. 'She's got it! She's got it!'"

Hearing this, the invalid smiled like someone so happy to be disabused of a particular, lingering fear: that we live and die as we dream—alone. Her nurse reached into her purse for her.

~~~~~~

Glenn did as instructed. He let his hand drift over the board of psychics until he was guided by the Universe to one picture: Darcy. Darcy was a bright, quippy blonde in her early fifties. Originally from Kentucky. Originally a midlevel executive for Hilton in Orlando. Darcy was starting the new, more evolved phase of her life.

"Once you come here, you just keep coming. You get sucked in," she told us with a laugh as she walked us to her . . . I guess you'd call it her studio? Her atelier?

"*You* might even get sucked in," she said to the three of us in mock warning. "We never proselytize; people just stop on the side of the road because they're pulled here. How do you think *you* got here?"

We arrayed our film gear around Darcy's suite, which was full of crystal pyramids, crystal dolphins, bookshelves lined with self-affirmational tomes (and one Make America Great Again cap). She sat Indian-style and barefoot in a wingback chair and motioned for Glenn to have a seat in the one opposite hers. Out of frame, Noah monitored the camera, and I watched the battery levels on the mikes.

First, Darcy explained how she was not a fortune-teller. "Mediums don't glimpse the future," she said. They deploy a sixth sense that captures vibrations. These vibrations convey information. A *good* medium is like a tuning fork reverberating in perfect harmony with the resonance of the Universe.

"What I'm going to do is step into our vibration and pick up the people who are a part of our vibration," Darcy said. "Then we'll talk to these people in the vibration. I hear them in my left ear. For a lot of mediums, it's the left ear. A couple other people hear it in their mind's eye."

Darcy closed her eyes, jutted her chin, gripped the arms of her chair. "I am getting a fenced backyard . . ." she began. "I am getting a woman. I am getting a little thickness around her head. I don't know if she had dementia or anything . . ."

"I am getting . . . a caring person, but a person who might not have communicated as well as she wanted to . . ." Here Darcy cracked an eye and looked at Glenn, who was looking back at her sidewise.

"Wait, no," she tried again. "Now I am getting . . . that you are getting a lot of your strength from your male side of your family. I am getting . . . that you are a lot like your dad. Does that make sense?"

I turned to Glenn. His eyes were waiting for mine.

"Is this anything you recognize?" Darcy asked, her lids still closed.

"Within a broad realm," Glenn answered, still staring at me.

"Now I'm moving to the heart chakra . . . I am getting . . . Oh, OK. I just had a man come in here, so I'm checking in with him as well . . . Strong-minded man, not thin, a strong-willed man . . . Do you have a man from your family who's in spirit?"

A stone punched through the frozen surface of Glenn's demeanor. His icy outer layer cracked, webbed, dissolved. "Yeah," he said. "Yes. My father's dead." He straightened up in his chair.

"He spent a lot of time in his head?" Darcy said. "He was one who did work that used his head. He had a lot of creativity. He might've been a manager or a leader? Someone who drove things, led people . . ."

"Yes!" Glenn's enthusiasm startled Darcy. She kept her eyes closed, though a grin began to nibble at the ends of her smile lines.

"As I'm working with his vibration, I'm sensing that you might have a lot of his characteristics. He's telling me . . . he's telling me that he went to the school of hard knocks? Or maybe you did?"

"Mmmmmaybe," Glenn said. "You'd really have to stretch that metaphor to include us."

"I think that's what he means?" Darcy chuckled. "He's telling me that you're both men who're able to overcome?"

"Sure, I think that's fair," Glenn said.

For the next twenty minutes, Darcy offered Glenn one nebulous characteristic after another. Glenn considered each, saying nay or yea with certain reservations. Together, they outfitted more or less ideal versions of Glenn's dad, Glenn, and the relationship they shared. Watching this, I thought: *Reminds me of how Noah and his buds create a communal fiction while playing Dungeons & Dragons.* But more than that, I thought: *It's like two people working on a police sketch.* "*I'm sensing that the man had . . . a defining physical characteristic?*"

Indeed, Darcy disclosed her reading in a manner that was very familiar to me, a part-time instructor of young people. Almost every one of her statements curled upward at the end—"upspeak," as it is known. ("I feel that . . . he wants you to settle *down?*") Practically everything Darcy proposed was appended with a question mark, as though she sensed that a flat-out declaration would open her up to argument.

And Glenn—sweet Glenn, son of the attenuated North— Glenn did not wish to quibble. He seemed too embarrassed to do so. *I* was certainly too embarrassed to do so. Embarrassed for him, embarrassed for Darcy. Embarrassed for all of us. Every time Glenn affirmed her, I was secretly relieved. This, I came to understand, was what greased the whole works.

You, the customer, *want* to preserve good relations at all times. You want to be in harmony with the spirits. You don't want to be the one who *disputes,* who says *maybe this* but *definitely not that.* Doing so would amount to drawing distinction. And you don't want to do such a thing, not after that affirmational church service. You want to go along to get along. Go with the flow. Encourage, and you will be encouraged in turn. To sigh *"Nah"* is to close yourself off to the Universe and its vibrations, is it not? What's more, it is discourteous. After all, *you* are the one who came in here asking for advice or guidance. Asking for advice or guidance is in nine cases out of ten touting for flattery. And now that you've got it, you're going to *reject* it?

"Around you," Darcy said, opening her eyes, "and you, too"—she looked at Noah—"and you as well"—she turned to me—"I'm picking up a lot of men? A lot of male energy? Men kind of standing alone? Kind of, you know, finding themselves on that path? Men seeking, men searching?"

While keeping his attention locked on the camera's flip screen, Noah let out a short, mirthless sound. A pause inflated—then popped like a soap bubble.

"What I'm hearing is that this is taking you closer to your heart? And how you approach life in general? The spirit took me into the heart chakra, that's why. It's connecting the head and the heart for you? That's part of your life journey?

"And as you transition back to the life before this journey, it feels as though there's change coming with that? More depth?"

"Like, deeper pockets?" I asked.

"What I'm saying is that I'm picking up children? Children. There's children with this situation?"

"OK!" Glenn clapped his hands together. He circled his finger at me and Noah, the universal wrap-it-up gesture. "I think that will do. Thank you very much. I guess that'll be . . . ?"

"Sixty dollars is our suggested donation," Darcy said, licking the tip of a ballpoint pen in order to write out a receipt.

INT. CLUTTERED HOME OFFICE—LATE AFTERNOON

Kent sits uneasily on a sunflower-print couch next to JULIAN, the plump, horseshoe-bald, Platonic ideal of a BUFFALO SNOWBIRD. Shelved around them are books and cassette tapes pertaining to the 150 precepts of Spiritualist natural law. Silhouetted in the sunshine along the window ledge behind them are plaster statues of religious figures as well as vases full of peacock feathers. Julian holds his hands together above his lap, but his fingers are not quite steepled. He is rubbing his middle digits together, smiling at the camera.

GLENN (O.S.)

So, Julian, if you could introduce yourself.

JULIAN

Well, let's see. I was a real estate broker up in New York. Had a hundred agents, three offices. I was a New York mortgage banker. Had a hundred fifty employees and clients like Kodak. But I was very out of balance in life. I worked twenty-five years, seven days a week. I basically ruined two marriages, focusing on all my empires. Heh, you could say I was like a mini Donald Trump.

JULIAN (CONT'D)

Are you guys familiar with what an "aha moment" is? When answers come to us, but not in our conscious minds? Well, a year to the day from my last divorce, all four of my corporations went into insolvency. There was nothing I could do about it. It was like sand going through my fingers. It was a multimillion-dollar bankruptcy.

GLENN (O.S.)

Maybe *not* so mini, eh?

JULIAN

I was a member of seventeen community organizations back home. I left those behind, too, to come here. Arrived in 1997. Became a Reiki master. Do you know Reiki? Went from being a multimillionaire to here. Do you know any other spiritual counselors with an MBA?

KENT

I mean—money can't buy you unity with the Great Spirit, right?

JULIAN
(wistfully)

When I was younger, I'd get a burr under my saddle—and *peew!* I was out of here. Now, I meditate. Meditation is *listening* to the Spirit. Prayer is asking. I ask, and I ask. And I don't see that door! So maybe this is where I'm supposed to be, in the end? This is where the Universe wants me to end my life on this plane?

Glenn, Noah, and Kent exchange glances while Julian continues to smile at the lens.

KENT

Stability! You know? If the Universe is everywhere, then you don't need to seek Him—It?—elsewhere. Right? Wouldn't that be the logic? It isn't the Spirit who's absent from us but we who are absent from . . . It.

JULIAN

Let me tell you something. You like this house? I own it. This and the one next door. You know the woman who gave you guys your reading earlier? She's my wife. Well, not technically my wife. She's been divorced twice before, too. We know the runaround. She wanted me to get my real estate license four years ago. *OK!* I said. Twenty percent of what I do—it's real estate.

NOAH (O.S.)

A fine house. What abou—

JULIAN (CONT'D)

One of John D. Rockefeller's accountants built a house here. I can sell it to you, should you guys ever want a house. You have to be a member of the camp association, though, to buy it. You have to be a Spiritualist. But here's the thing—you can own these homes, right? Own your own castle, the American Dream—but the camp association owns all the land *beneath the homes.*

Julian shifts his head from cocked-to-the-right to cocked-to-the-left. All while maintaining eye contact with the lens, stroking his fingers.

JULIAN (CONT'D)

We've got 175 association members, but only 44 homeowners. If you lose your membership, you lose your house. If you die, your next of kin has to sell your house to another Spiritualist. No banks will loan here. You have to find a cash buyer or be willing to take on a mortgage in return. So, to answer your question: My name is Julian, and I've got a couple of properties I bought right at the height of the housing bubble that I sure would like to sell.

GLENN (O.S.)

I say hang on to them, Julian.

KENT

Yeah, you never know. You're pretty high and dry here, right? Once the coasts start flooding, and the property values plunge, you could have a couple of primo pieces on your hands. I'm sure people'll be willing to believe whatever shi—

JULIAN

Oh, you're not one of those who seriously believes global warming, are you? You don't *actually* believe that we could seriously impact Gaia?

KENT

. . . shit.

JULIAN

We like to think we're so powerful, don't we? We like to think that it's *us* who controls the Universe. And not the other way around.

NOAH (O.S.)

Julian, goddamn it.

JULIAN

We cannot rend the garment of the living God. You understand that, though. I'm receiving a very understanding vibration from you. Are you sure you don't want to move to Cassadaga?

Julian leans back, laughs. His hands uncouple and float to their corresponding knees as lightly as a fresh sheet thrown over a mattress.

JULIAN

Now, Kent, do you have an active prayer life? Is there a spiritual tradition that you follow?

KENT

I'm a Catholic, yeah.

JULIAN

Do you believe you're a perfect child of God?

KENT

I'm a Catholic—no.

JULIAN

In the eyes of the Universe, you are a perfect child of God. It's just, do you choose openness or do you choose fear?

KENT

Oh, I choose openness, Julian.

JULIAN

One of the things we do in spiritual healing is help you erase those negative perceptions. We help you remember *who you are*.

KENT

I want to do that, Julian, believe me. I want to remember who I am. But first, let me tell you *my* truth. Then maybe you can help me get the Universe to actualize it.

FADE OUT

The human need to believe—to embrace explanations—is as pervasive as it is strong. Given the right cues, we are willing to go along with just about anything. We'll put our confidence in just about anyone. This—all I disclosed to Julian as if he couldn't possibly have heard it before.

"Good divination is the art of a good story," he agreed. Julian was very astute, I must say.

Our minds are hardwired for narratives. We *crave* them. And when ready ones aren't available, we contrive them. Stories about our origins. Our purpose. We contrive stories that supply the reasons *why*. "Human beings don't like to exist in a state of uncertainty,

Julian" was what I said. "When something doesn't make sense, we want to supply the missing link."

This is what the confidence artist is, of course: that link. Someone who's only too happy to provide you with *exactly* what you need to hear *exactly* when you need to hear it. The confidence artist exists because everyone, now and then, whether they want to admit it or not, desires a little . . . *magic,* let's say, for lack of a better term. The too good to be true. (It's never too good to be true if it's you—*you,* not those other schmucks and marks—to whom it rings true.) And since this desire has always been with us, that means the confidence artist has always been with us. But when he *thrives* is during times of upheaval. When the old ways of doing things, of looking at the world, no longer suffice. Droughts, plagues, revolutions. Gold rushes, territorial expansions, demographic declines. Whenever transition is afoot, so, too, is the confidence artist.

He's a linguistic alchemist. He takes anxiety and disquiet and with his silver tongue he turns them into gold. In this he is similar to the writer—he *is* an artist, after all—seeing as how the both of them have a gift for dissembling. The both of them can create characters who convey sincerity, dependability, vulnerability as needed. They can present as credible, and that's huge, since the credibility of the teller is very often the test of the truth of a proposition. "Reliable" narrators through and through, the both of them know how to work an audience, how to get disbelief suspended. They do more than pull strings; their cogged circles fit into the various gearwheels, and all revolve.

Confidence must come first. Confidence is a voice, it is a gesture, it is a pretense, it is a ruse. To establish confidence in the worlds of storytelling or swindling, one simply . . . acts confidently. Which is to say, one does what one can to come across as well established. (Harder than it sounds; much practice is needed to come off as unpracticed.) That achieved, one makes sure to meet the expectations of the genre being worked. In the writer's case, that can be anything from tell-all memoir (extreme suffering leads to self-deliverance) to rollicking travelogue (numberless perils return the writer to where he started, wiser and more content). The scammer's categories are no less well worn: there's the money-box scheme, the Spanish Prisoner, the pig in a poke, the jam auction, the pigeon drop.

One takes care to select and present only the most pitch-perfect details. One anticipates the audience's questions, concerns, and objections, and one moves to manipulate them before they even register. Most of the concerns, anyway. You don't want your okeydoke to seem *completely* scripted. You have to act natural. You have to provide your mark with enough leeway to play the part required of him. Remember, friend: Believability hinges on the person being asked to believe. The principle at work is the same whether you're spinning a yarn, grifting a mark, or baiting a mousetrap. You load your trap with cheese, yes, but just as important, you leave room for the mouse.

The first Spiritualists were excellent storytellers, excellent confidence artists. They responded to and profited from the grievous bewilderment of those who had lost loved ones to total war. "We affirm that the existence and personal identity of the individual continue after the change called death," the Spiritualists assured these mourners. (And continue to assure them, as it is their Principle Number 4.) Then they told the mourners what they were hearing from the other side. Which, what do you know, coincided almost exactly with whatever it was the mourners needed to hear.

None of *that* did I mention to Julian. Instead, I asked him if he wouldn't like to coauthor a little something with me. "You ever seen *Nanook of the North,* Julian?" I asked. "What about *F for Fake?*" When he didn't answer, I said: "Doesn't matter. Let us introduce the wonderful mysteries of Cassadaga to the widest possible audience, hey?"

INT. CLUTTERED HOME OFFICE—EARLY EVENING

Kent sits smiling on a sunflower-print couch next to JULIAN, the plump, horseshoe-bald, Platonic ideal of a BUFFALO SNOWBIRD. Julian holds his hands together above some sheets of paper in his lap. He, too, smiles at the camera.

JULIAN

Kent, I want to thank you for having a reading with me. Even though, according to your own faith tradition—

Julian glances at the sheets in his lap.

JULIAN (CONT'D)

—consulting horoscopes, astrology, palm reading, interpretation of omens and lots, the phenomena of clairvoyance, and recourse to mediums all conceal a desire for power over time, history, and, in the last analysis, other human beings. They contradict the honor, respect, and loving fear that we owe to God alone.

KENT

(closes eyes, nods)

JULIAN

Nevertheless, you are embracing your openness at Cassadaga. I honor you for that. The Great Spirit honors you for that. You are embracing your loving openness to the unlimited power of Spirit. Whom we now invoke.

Julian takes Kent's hand. Both bow heads.

JULIAN

Mother-Father God, Infinite Intelligence—as we come to you today with Kent, seeking guidance in his life, help us to discern the meaning of these words. Help us to put a layer of white light around him, to only allow the highest and the best through . . .

JULIAN (CONT'D)

As I step into your vibrations, Kent, I sense that you are approaching very fast the end of a seven-year cycle in your life. I'm sensing that . . . as you move nearer to 2017 . . . you're going to start effecting some changes. In your life. In the world.

KENT

Interesting!

JULIAN

"Seeking" means discovering how we fit into the puzzle. Why our piece is here, and how we can connect it. I'm sensing for you . . . the spirits are telling me . . . Love. They're telling me that your next cycle will begin with tremendous love.

KENT

Am I finally going to find the love of my life, Julian?

JULIAN

The spirits are telling me it's deeper than that. Deeper than a person. Now, Kent, the Universe—are you familiar with the anthropic principle?

KENT

Enlighten me, Julian.

JULIAN

The anthropic principle says that the observer is as essential to the creation of the Universe as the Universe is to the creation of the observer. Does that make sense to you? We are here observing the Universe, and it just so happens that the Universe we're observing is perfectly compatible with us, the people who observe it.

KENT

You're saying we're here because we are *meant* to be here.

JULIAN

That's right! The science backs us Spiritualists on this. Things are as we find them—*just so*—because we are both the causes *and* the effects of the Universe.

Julian re-steeples his hands. He steals a peek at the papers in his lap.

JULIAN

The Universe is not only *like* us—it exists *because of* us. We follow the Universe, but we can lead it, too. You've heard of the power of positive thinking? Well, it's one of our natural laws in Spiritualism. Things can be exactly as we *want* them to be. Because we are both the causes and the effects.

KENT

(nodding)

So you're saying that . . . the subject *is* the object. The question *is* the answer.

JULIAN

(smiling like Cheshire cat)

That's right. That's right. Love is what led you here. Love led you here so you could see that love is what moves you. Do you understand? That's what the spirits want you to know. It is not you who has chosen them, but they who have chosen you. The line between them and us is only temporary, you know. They want you to remember that. They want you to make your life a gift for your beloved.

KENT

And our documentary, Julian—what do they say about that? Are we going to redeem Florida? Are we going to die trying?

JULIAN

Now, remember, everything I'm telling you is potentials and possibilities. You don't have to listen to anything I tell you. But I'm sensing about you, and about your energy, which Glenn and Noah share, is, ah, the spirits, they are saying—

Julian fumbles with the papers in his lap. Kent's glare ratchets toward him like the head of a socket wrench.

JULIAN (CONT'D)
(relievedly)

That what you're making will be more than a documentary. *Anybody* could have made a documentary about Florida. Given a by-the-numbers account. But the vibrations all of you are giving off—

KENT

Yes?

JULIAN

What you're doing will bring about a change in *consciousness*. A change in the way people perceive this place. A change in how they *act* toward it. The Universe wants you to understand that this is a holy task. You have been chosen by love for the sake of bearing love.

KENT

So according to the Universe, the only way forward is for someone to love Florida?

JULIAN

This is what the spirits are telling me.

KENT

That when people see someone loves Florida—even if it's an arbitrary love, like family love, or country love—people will see Florida is *worth saving*?

JULIAN

Love is never blind, Kent. If you take anything away from this reading, I hope it's this. The last thing love is, is blind. Love is bound. But the moment you bind your heart in love? That's when you realize your hands are truly free.

KENT

Wow. I think I speak for the three of us when I say that that was more than expected, Julian. Quite the *treat* on Halloween, heh. I wish we could stay longer and bask in the, you know, vortex of energy here.

JULIAN

Well, our doors are always open in Cassadaga. All perfect children of God are welcome to join our association. And should any perfect children of God wish to know more—about Spirit or anything else— they can reach me anytime at WE ARE ONE REALTY. That's WE ARE ONE REALTY, all one word, at Hotmail dot com.

FADE OUT

IT'S UNCLE WALT'S WORLD;
WE'RE JUST LIVING IN IT

We knew we were nearing Orlando when the diversity of trash along the roadside broadened considerably. Streets and state roads broadened, too. Traffic: greatly accelerated. We also encountered many pedestrians, which was rather surprising since year after year Orlando is rated at or near the top of the list of deadliest American cities for walkers. In 2016, Orlando regained its crown, barely edging out the runners-up: Tampa, Jacksonville, and Miami.

The company of other walkers, we assumed, would be a boon. Strength in numbers; can't run us all over; that kind of thing. However, since these were *Orlando* pedestrians, their presence ended up being less than heartening. Vapors poured from their eyes like effluvium rising off of asphalt in a rain. Many had lips so lined and suncracked that they appeared to be sewn shut. Or it's possible that they weren't returning our howdies because they took us for narcs.

At least we were blessed with stretches of virgin sidewalk fronting subdivision after subdivision. The old cliché is that Central Florida's subdivisions were named after the things wiped out to make way for their construction: Cypress Pointe, Clear Lake, Panther Run, et cetera. This cliché is, like most clichés, ten thousand percent true.

Local tax revenue was high enough to furnish big public parks with batting cages we could camp behind. Doing so felt as wishful-thinking ridiculous as putting a lampshade on one's head in order to hide. Still, nobody called the cops on us even after we awoke to the pinging clatter of batting practice. This way, we were able to park-hop across the Greater Orlando metropolitan area, that sprawling conglomeration which lacks for any clearly identifiable boundaries or civic identity—and which so perfectly stands in as a synecdoche for Central Florida.

"Yikes," I said, breaking the relative quiet as we skirted another Mediterranean-styled shopping plaza. "I've actually eaten in that Ruth's Chris Steak House."

Not too long ago, these Orlando 'burbs were orange groves. And not too long ago, there was nothing more quintessentially *Florida* than orange groves, oranges, orange juice. (That the fruit is non-native is both beside the point and entirely the point.) In the 1950s, Americans purchased more oranges than all other fresh fruit combined. Hamlins, Temples, Parson Browns, Lue Gim Gongs, Sanford Bloods—they were like edible advertising. The vision of Florida as a garden of earthly delights was seeded into millions by way of these healthful, noon-bright treats. (Many of which had been exposed to ethylene gas, shocked with cold, covered in wax, scrubbed with detergent, or simply dyed orange in order to achieve their radiant color.)

The fecundity of grove towns like Clermont, Leesburg, Citra, Dunedin, Winter Haven, Frostproof, and dozens more turned Central Florida into the world's leading producer of oranges. Even when demand for the fresh stuff flagged, frozen concentrate was invented to reenergize the market. Unlike California's navel orange, Florida's most popular type, the Valencia, was perfect for juicing. Three-quarters of the 1960 crop traveled to consumers in tank cars, not crates; by 1980, that proportion had risen to 90 percent. Then, when things were sunniest, a series of devastating freezes halved the state's production. Brazil stepped up their citrus game in response. For them, oranges were a cash crop; 99 percent of their production was for export. Florida couldn't compete at that scale.

Enter: the developers. Hundreds of thousands of acres of prime grove land were transformed into trailer parks and cul-de-sacs within the last few decades. Juice plants, packinghouses, and the unique sand-hill environment have given way to strip malls and single-family homes. Lake and Orange counties (over which Greater Orlando straddles) once accounted for one-quarter of Florida's citrus. Today, the counties constitute less than 2 percent. The workforce that used to pluck fruit? They now cater to the 66 million tourists who flock to Orlando year in and out, cementing its position as the most popular tourist destination on Planet goddamned Earth.

No other place in America has been so quickly and thoroughly (re)shaped by tourism. Consider: In 1950, about 186,000 people lived in the Greater Orlando area. On the eve of Walt Disney World's opening in 1971, the metropolitan population had ballooned to 522,575. It surpassed 1.6 million in 2000. It swelled to 2.13 million within the last two decades. As the former mayor Carl T. Langford put it: "I spent thirty years of my life trying to get people to move down there [to Orlando], and then they all did." He offered this quote from North Carolina, where he lived out his last years after claiming that Orlando had become too congested for him.

Orlando and its economy have expanded at one of the fastest rates in the nation, but the value of that expansion has not kept pace on the individual level. Growth in annual earnings per worker has been very slow and well below national averages. Real wages in Orlando have been stagnating for decades. In some areas, they've fallen. Such is the Faustian bargain at the heart of Orlando's (re)shaping: shitty pay and iffy quality of life alongside exponential growth.

"What is clear is this," concluded the *Orlando Sentinel,* "the nation's 27th-largest metropolitan area excels at little beyond being one of the world's top tourist destinations, and it lags behind most comparably sized U.S. cities in virtually every category." Indeed, when compared with those cities, Orlando ranks near the bottom in things like home ownership, per capita income, and school spending. On the other hand, if you were to look at who's leading whom in service jobs, overcrowded schools, crime rates, commuting times, and pedestrian fatalities, you'd see that Orlando *dominates.*

Its story reflects the state's. The number of service workers in Florida increased *twentyfold* from 1950 to 2000. Contrast that with the state's number of farmhands (stayed the same); construction workers (increased threefold); manufacturing workers (doubled); and government employees (increased fivefold). The macrocosm (Florida) and the microcosm (Orlando) both run on low-skill, minimum-wage service jobs because that's what touristic infrastructure is built around. There are lawyers, doctors, cops, teachers, and accountants in Orlando—but practically everyone else is a laundress, fry cook, trash hauler, deliveryperson, baggage handler. Not to mention desk agent, customer-service representative, Uber driver, long- and short-haul trucker. Waiter. *Bartender,* by God. Not so many sommeliers or concierges, but a goodly number of ice sculptors. Cartoon character suit wearers. Pretty much anybody you don't have to give health insurance to.

"Welp." Glenn gestured at the pipe-cleaner palms, at the eight lanes of roaring traffic, at the zombified pedestrian limping our way.

"Let's play a game," Noah suggested. He selected a business at random—a nearby tobacconist—and Googled it. "Yup," he said. "Part of synthetic drug sting, according to the *Sentinel.*"

All theme-park-adjacent lodging was booked. It took many minutes of app thumbing for us to locate a room in a welfare hotel on a dark side street in the downtown business district. House policy required that guests pay in advance, in cash, which I did. Noah helped me carry Jog-a-bye up the narrow staircase. Glenn killed the AC, hit the lights. We three jumped into the queen-sized bed, happy if only to have a roof over our heads once more.

After a few quiet moments, Glenn said, "Guys?"

The three of us were lined up Kilroyishly under the covers, our eyes fixed on the blotchy stucco above.

"Guys."

The walls blinked red then blue as a police car passed.

"Tell me if I'm crazy. But does this mattress feel damp to you?"

"There's a more important question to be asked here," Noah said to the ceiling. "Is forty dollars too steep a price to pay to sleep in someone else's urine in downtown Orlando? Or is it exactly the right price?"

Glenn had made some inroads with a guy whose Facebook page said he "played" Jesus Christ at the Holy Land Experience theme park. So Glenn spent the next day trying to Skype with him, to assure him we were legit. Noah volunteered to do all of our laundry. "You could fold our drawers into paper airplanes" was how he put it. "I would also like to be alone."

Meaning I had the day to myself. Not knowing what else to do, I made for the Orlando Welcome Center, where I purchased a five-dollar all-day pass for the International Drive Trolley.

If you've ever been to Orlando, friend, you've been to International Drive. It is the 14.5-mile strip of hotels, restaurants, hotels, time-shares, souvenir shops, lesser theme parks, laser tag emporiums, curio museums, outlet stores, and hotels that's "as well-known in Boston, England, as it is in Boston, Mass.," as the line goes. And this is an important point to make. For so very many of the millions of tourists who come to Orlando, *this*—Disney, Universal Studios, I-Drive, all of it—stands in for America itself. "No matter where you travel in the world, you run into a startling number of people for whom Orlando is America," John Jeremiah Sullivan has written. "If you could draw one of those *New Yorker* cartoon maps in your head, of the way the world sees North America, the turrets of the Magic Kingdom would be a full order of scale bigger than anything else."

International Drive is not Orlando's main thoroughfare—that'd be Interstate 4, which runs parallel to I-Drive—but as International Drive comprises five-hundred-plus businesses selling everything from digital cameras to golf clubs, weeklong stays to Argentinian steaks, it is far and away the most vital artery when it comes to Orlando's economic health. This despite the fact that until very recently, I-Drive was nothing but sand, pines, and palmettos. What happened was an attorney turned developer named Finley Hamilton, who went looking for ways to profit from Walt Disney's 1965 announcement that he would build a huge new theme park southwest of downtown. On April Fools' Day 1968, Hamilton paid $90,000 for ten acres of scrubland. This patch of nothing was accessible only by dirt road—but Hamilton figured that Disney-bound tourists would spot his new Hilton Inn from the interstate, take the nearest exit, and drive north on the paved road he would build.

He bought and flipped more acreage along his road in the months preceding Disney World's opening. "I came up with International Drive," he later recalled, "because it sounded big and important." Within a few years, I-Drive included a dozen hotels, two dozen restaurants, and four gas stations, most of which were clustered at the road's two major intersections. Then the nation's first water park, Wet 'n Wild, opened in 1977. Just like that, I-Drive went from a place to sleep and eat to a destination in its own right. Arriving not long after were your Ripley's Believe It or Not!s, your Skull Kingdoms, and the like.

In short, International Drive has developed into a tacky gauntlet whereby families are stripped of armloads of cash on their way to and from Disney parks. It, like Greater Orlando, is premised upon one thing: Uncle Walt's sloppy seconds.

I hopped on the International Drive Trolley at its southern terminus, so very excited to be aboard a motor vehicle. This being Florida, where fixed meanings are prohibited by the spirit if not the letter of the law—the Trolley I boarded was not a *trolley* trolley. It was a bus. A bus done up fancy-like in trolley drag, but a bus nonetheless, with slatted wood benches, interior lights sculpted to resemble gas lamps, and a whole honking gaggle of Europeans. Europeans slung with water-bladderesque purses on the thinnest of straps; Europeans smoking unfiltered cigarettes; Europeans wearing capris hemmed at inspired lengths. Together we rode from South I-Drive to SeaWorld, where the Continental children *oooo*ed at the expanse of parked cars glinting in the sun. We passed an empty municipal bus, which led me to speculate: *I bet this is the most used public transit route in the state*.

We gathered more passengers outside an outlet mall. Their wrists were braceleted with the woven cardboard handles of upscale shopping bags; their smiles communicated the bliss of completion. We accelerated past the noodly, Lovecraftian slidescape of Wet 'n Wild. Someone dinged the ding for WonderWorks.

In terms of gross economic power, the tourism industry is in the uppermost tier along with energy, finance, and agriculture. Worldwide, it generates $3 billion in business every single *day*. If frequent-flyer miles were a currency, it'd be one of the most valuable on the planet. Why *shouldn't* tourism have its own city the way oil has Abu Dhabi and film has Los Angeles?

Orlando is tourism's pantomime capital. But that's not all due to Disney. Contrary to Uncle Walt's founding myth, roadside attractions and theme parks had been dotting city and state long before his arrival. It's just that their theme was, well, "Florida." Sunken Gardens and Jungle Gardens dazzled Depression-weary Americans with imported grugru palms, Madagascar screw pines, and the greatest concentration of orchids in North America. Silver Springs, Cypress Gardens, and Weeki Wachee Springs took a similar tack—"Come marvel at Florida's splendor!"—while adding canny advertising and gimmicks like alligator wrestling to the mix. These "natural" attractions were equal parts organic phenomena and human cultivation. Their grounds had been processed and "improved," just like the canned and sprayable foodstuffs then appearing on supermarket shelves.

This was midcentury, when a Florida vacation was seen as a marker of middle-class status. What's more, a Florida vacation underscored one's support of and participation in the American way of life. You drove your new car to new national wonders like Marineland, where intrepid scientists had trained bottlenose dolphins to perform tricks, and in exchange for your hard-earned money you got the sense that you were combatting global Communism.

Around the same time, the superhighways were snaking their way into the peninsula. The interstate program—the most expensive and elaborate public works program of all time, mind—was at once a Keynesian economic driver and a geographic equalizer. The impeccable government roads stretched down the Gulf Coast, along the Atlantic coast, and across the gaps in between, buttressing Florida's sky-high growth like a trellis around a sprout. Tourists no longer had to rely on railroads, bus schedules, or dicey Southern byways while traveling to the Sunshine State. Now, millions of them could pick up and go whenever the mood struck. They could chauffeur their families to *difference* within a matter of hours, riding the interstates the way aristocrats had ridden Flagler's trains a generation prior.

This democratization of travel was precisely what Walt Disney observed on November 22, 1963, when he flew over Orlando in a private plane, assessing the area's potential for his Disney World project. He looked down and saw Interstate 4 intersecting with Florida's Turnpike, both roads teeming with fast-moving traffic. Not far away from this hub, he eyed a vast stretch of virgin swamp. "This is it!" Disney exclaimed over the roar of engines.

With such a combination of highways and undeveloped land, Disney could build his dreamed-of tourist mecca—America's "total destination resort," as his planners referred to it. He bought up 27,000 acres, anonymously and piecemeal, from Central Florida farmers, ranchers, and rural landholders. For two hundred dollars per acre, owners were more than happy to sell to one of the five dummy corporations orchestrating Disney's clandestine "Project X." In time, the locals noticed that the ground was shifting beneath their feet. Rumors ran rampant as to who or what was purchasing southwest Orlando. In October 1965, one headline in the *Sentinel* read: "We Say 'Mystery' Industry Is Disney." A year later, Uncle Walt officially announced his plans for a "bigger and better" version of Disneyland in Florida. The Associated Press crowned him "the most celebrated visitor since Ponce de Leon."

While the Disney saga unfolded, many of Florida's established attractions were being bled dry by the new interstates, which bypassed their locations along the old roads. Rainbow Springs, Sanlando Springs, Dog Land, Everglades Tropical Gardens, Florida Reptile Land, the Waite's Bird Farm—they died off. Frog City, Sunshine Springs and Gardens, Atomic Tunnel, Shark World, Bongoland, and—alas—Midget City, too, went under. Times were tough in the early '6os. Perhaps this explains why Disney's announcement sounded like a godsend to these beleaguered mom-and-pop enterprises. "Anyone who is going to spend $100 million nearby is good, and a good thing," the owner of Cypress Gardens was quoted as saying.

And he was terrifically wrong. About his own prospects, but also about the size of the investment. Disney promised more than $600 million. He was going to build a Magic Kingdom five times larger than the one he'd created in California. He also vowed to construct a rapid transit system as well as a thousand-acre industrial park and a jetport. "But the most exciting and by far the most important part of our Florida project—in fact, the heart of everything we'll be doing in Disney World," Disney said in a promotional film, "will be our Experimental Prototype Community of Tomorrow. We'll call it Epcot."

Disney claimed that this model city would "take its cue from the new ideas and new technologies that are now emerging from the creative centers of American industry. It will be a community of tomorrow that will never be completed, but will always be introducing and testing and demonstrating new materials and systems. And Epcot will always be a showcase to the world for the ingenuity and imagination of American free enterprise."

Sound familiar? Like the Spaniards and Flagler before him, Disney was taking his second chance in Florida. *His* grand design—the reason why *he* was clearing forests, draining wetlands, remaking the place in his image—was to fashion *his* idea of utopia. "I don't believe there's a challenge anywhere in the world that's more important to people everywhere than finding solutions to the problems of our cities," he said. "But where do we begin—how do we start answering this great challenge? Well, we're convinced we must start with the public need. And the need is not just for curing the old ills of old cities. We think the need is for starting from scratch on virgin land and building a special kind of new community."

The way Disney sold it, Epcot would be a working community of twenty thousand. "It will never cease to be a living blueprint of the future, where people actually live a life they can't find anywhere else in the world," he said. "Everything in Epcot will be dedicated to the happiness of the people who will live, work, and play here." The idea was to build high-density apartments surrounding a business center; beyond that would be a greenbelt and recreation area; the outermost rings would be low-density residential streets. There'd be "playgrounds, churches and schools . . . distinctive neighborhoods . . . and footpaths for children going to school" in Disney's proposed utopia. A multimodal transportation system incorporating surface trains, a monorail, and a "webway people mover" would render automobiles unnecessary, à la Seaside.

Then came the rub: "To accomplish our goals for Disney World, we must retain control and develop all the land ourselves." Disney demanded municipal bonding authority, three highway interchanges, and the creation of two municipalities together with an autonomous political district controlled by the company. In effect, Disney wanted his own corporate-controlled state within the state. "A sort of Vatican with mouse ears," the historian Richard Foglesong termed it. In return, Florida would receive a perpetual stream of visitors, more sales- and gasoline-tax revenue, a long boom in construction and service jobs. "You people here in Florida have one of the key roles to play in making Epcot come to life," Disney inveigled, like a true confidence artist. "In fact, it's really up to you whether this project gets off the ground at all."

And the people of Florida bit.

Though Disney wouldn't live to see it, he was granted his Reedy

Creek Improvement District, which is still "governed" by a supervisory board "elected" by the landowners—i.e., the Walt Disney Company. As described by a former head executive, Reedy Creek "gave us all the powers of the two counties in which we sit to the exclusion of their exercising any powers, and of course it let us issue bonds. We could do anything the city or county could do. The only powers that still reside on us from outside are the taxing power of Orange County, the sales tax of the state, and the inspection of elevators."

Reedy Creek handles its own planning and zoning. It lays out roads and sewer lines, licenses the sale of alcoholic beverages. Building codes? Psh, Reedy Creek *employs the building inspectors*. It employs its own fire department. Contracts its own eight-hundred-member security force. Technically, it is within Disney's rights to build an airport and a nuclear power plant within the Improvement District, if Disney so desired.

But that whole utopian city thing? The enticement that ultimately sealed the deal for the people of Florida? It was all a ruse. The Experimental Prototype Community of Tomorrow was just another theme park. And though more than 55,000 people work in the Reedy Creek Improvement District by day; and though more than 100,000 patronize its stand-alone restaurants, clubs, and theaters every night—Reedy Creek retains a permanent population of about fifty. Most of whom are company executives or their family members.

Walt Disney demanded and received the powers of a democratically elected government, and his corporation ducked the botheration of, you know, constituents. Constituents who might challenge Disney's top-down plans or even vote them out of power. The constitutionality of this arrangement has never been challenged. I suppose this proves no one minds the arrangement all that much. But I tend to think otherwise. I think it proves that the people of Florida are no different from patsies across time and space: too ashamed to admit when we've been had.

"By turning the state of Florida and its statutes into their enablers," T. D. Allman writes, "Disney and his successors pioneered a business model based on public subsidy of private profit coupled with corporate immunity from the laws, regulations, and taxes imposed on people that now increasingly characterizes the economy of the United States."

So, huh. I guess Disney *did* get his "showcase for free enterprise" and his utopia both, in the end.

....

Along the north end of International Drive, things got a little scooter-trash. More frequent were the all-you-can-eat buffets, mini golf courses, and mirrored emporiums selling watches in bundles of threes. So, too, the Sunshine State–themed motor courts out of which lived the recently homeless or the soon-to-be. A few of the trolley's children grew restless when we passed a museum that went by the name of "SKELETONS." *That's new,* I thought.

I was put in mind of my own childhood trips to Orlando. (Hey—we are no more immune to the inveigle than the rest of you.) My parents would pile my sisters and me into our van predawn. We'd drive up, hit the parks, drive back in the gloaming. Grade school and high school graduations also included trips here. Likewise my college commencement. It's a Special Place for us, too. Weird to think about, I know. Like seeing one of the cooks come round from the back of the house to dine at the counter.

I stretched out as the Euros exited the trolley. To the driver they trilled thank-yous, their English scented with accents that sounded the way flavored waters taste. The driver looked at me in the rear-view mirror. I twirled my up-pointed index finger. I rode until the sun went down.

....

While I was out cruising, Glenn was being a professional, locking down our day with Jesus. The guy was surprisingly amenable, Glenn said. "Though I guess he's supposed to be? I don't know, you tell me." Jesus agreed to meet us at Epcot the next day.

We *could've* met him at the Holy Land Experience, where Jesus plies his trade, but Glenn wanted the juxtaposition. Christ and Mickey Mouse, et cetera and blah blah, a ham-fisted visual metaphor the Germans will probably love.

The Holy Land Experience would've made for striking foot-age, though. The park was opened in 2001 by a Messianic Jew who believed his ministerial calling involved the conversion of his tribes-people to Christianity. Needless to say, the man's attraction struggled to find its audience. In 2007, he sold it to the world's largest religious TV conglomerate, the Trinity Broadcasting Network, for $37 million. Trinity decided to revamp the whole operation. "A faith-based version of Universal Studios" was what they envisioned.

First off, the austere and historically accurate stage shows had to go. In their place: a dozen razz-dazz song-and-dance numbers performed at regular intervals throughout each hot Orlando afternoon. The tunes are originals and the actors blow-dried pros who perform with the verve of true believers. Their big crescendo is the bloody reenactment of the crucifixion occurring every afternoon at 5:00 p.m., when some fifteen hundred guests crowd around a loin-clothed Jesus as he belts out his solo while being nailed to a cross. Six minutes after his body is delivered to the tomb, a shout—"I am alive!" A beaming, gold-spangled Jesus emerges from a cloud of smoke to announce that the sick shall be healed, the last shall be first, and the exit is through the gift shop.

The Holy Land Experience attracts a quarter million visitors every year (and is exempted from its share of taxes thanks to a religion-related loophole), yet Trinity Broadcasting has claimed that their park is a money loser. Recently, Trinity auctioned off hundreds of ornate thrones, statues, and a winged Harley-Davidson in order to defray park costs. (Kept off the block: the network founders' multimillion-dollar homes in Orlando, Texas, and Tennessee.) Trinity ran appeals for donations on crawlers below their programming. Programming in which—let me be clear here—these hydra-headed flimflammers preach a heresy that goes something like this: God has no use for the puny achievements of men (true) → yet the only way to know one's standing in the eyes of God is to take stock of one's worldly achievements (false) → and the only way to *increase* one's worldly achievements and thus one's standing in the eyes of God is to faithfully give what little one has to the Pharisees onscreen (false, God, false) → after which time, like a slot machine that always pays out, God's favor and grace will redound at a rate of seventy times seven (Jesus, no).

Trinity's is an impressively diabolical shakedown. (Though to be fair, their shakedown is not exactly contrary to the Calvinist theology imported by the Puritans.) It capitalizes, quite literally, on an antique struggle within the wider church. For millennia, certain Christians have really, *really* wanted someone to tell them that the New Testament affirms *who they already are,* rather than—as is actually the case—affirming the kind of person they are not, and probably would not wish to be. They will pay good money to the confident charismatic who declares their version of the Good News: that by dying on a cross, Christ saved them from the burden of having to act like Him.

These thoughts and others I was free to pursue while our Uber sped past acres of undeveloped and illegal-to-walk-through greenery surrounding Epcot. Walt Disney had chosen Central Florida for this negative space as much as anything else. No seediness, no disorder would be allowed to abut his realm, as had happened at Disneyland in Anaheim. Here in Orlando, a nimbus of pristine nothing rings his Magic Kingdom.

It was not hard to spot Jesus at the gate, for he came robed in an off-white, shawly vestment. His hair was as you'd imagine, long and brown with chestnut strands that caught the sunlight. His beard, however, was . . . uncharacteristic. It blotted his pitted cheeks like lichen on a rock. Furthermore, the man was shorter than the inspirational posters had led me to expect. Swarthier, too. Kinda had a down-and-out Pete Sampras vibe about him. *Which is probably closer to the historical Jesus,* I rationalized as we approached.

Glenn hailed him, shook hands, introduced us. "Rodrigo," Jesus asked us to call him. "Though my friends can call me Roddy." We paid for Roddy's ticket, we had our thumbprints scanned. We spun the turnstiles. A wave of relief overwhelmed us as we plunged into Disney.

Relief because little can possibly go wrong here. Relief because little can possibly *happen* here—at least insofar as "happening" involves "happenstance," which requires some measure of chance or uncertainty.

"How many of these people do you think secretly work for Disney?" Glenn asked as we made for the nearest Starbucks. "My guess is thirty percent."

We got our coffees, we directed Roddy to a relatively untrafficked section of the park's lagoon to conduct a background interview. People rubbernecked, but not as many as you might think, since Roddy had donned a fitted baseball cap. Nor did our hobbles draw attention. It's not like anybody else in Orlando was striding upright with the dignity of destination about them.

Receiving permission to film on Disney grounds is famously difficult—nigh on impossible. We solved this problem by ignoring it completely. Glenn mounted his camera; Noah quickly miked Jesus up; I took a seat on the bench next to him.

EXT. EPCOT CENTER—EARLY AFTERNOON

RODDY'S black, logoless cap is so large that its flat brim juts from the spot where his eyebrows should be. His RESTLESS HANDS reclasp over his lap as if he is intricately and continuously high-fiving himself.

GLENN (O.S.)

Roddy, OK. Could you tell us when you started acting?

RODDY

Man, yeah, I'm a natural actor.

KENT

How about: What came first for you, religion or drama?

RODDY

Oh, drama, baby. That drama came first.

KENT

(blinks)

RODDY (CONT'D)

So like I first used drugs around this time. The high school time. Using took away the sense of alienation. I smoked weed and abused my prescriptions to cope with an alcoholic family. Not having friends at school, I felt like it was always "them" and "me," you know? Like I was the fucked-up one.

KENT

Ahhhh . . .

RODDY

I ran away from home at twelve. I fell into a cycle of living on the streets. The first time I overdosed, I was fourteen. Then, you know, I robbed a convenience store at gunpoint for a book of matches. What the fuck, right? I knew I was crazy. But the drugs made it OK. Sleeping in dumpsters, freezing in garages, constant starvation. I was haunted by this feeling, you know. That I was different from other people. That I was an alien walking among the earthlings.

KENT

Why don't you tell us what it's like for you in the Holy Land Experience?

RODDY

Right, OK, so. Each day, five days a week, you know, Jesus gets there, he's wearing his blue jeans, running shoes. Gold cross on the chain, all that. Change in the cast lounge, pray, put on microphones like this one. Then, showtime. Jesus's got two shows in the marketplace, then two passion plays. Those last fifteen, twenty minutes. It's a lot! You gotta rely on the Holy Spirit to do that!

KENT

Does it help to refer to Jesus in third person? Help it seem not sacrilegious or something?

RODDY

No so I finally hooked up with a girl I met at a concert. Using my homelessness as, you know, an excuse to move in with her family. I ripped off her parents. And we took off for the streets. By that time, I was overdosing every few weeks. One of those times I was hospitalized, and she left. I tried to kill myself in a bunch of different ways. Finally, I almost did. Overdose. At the hospital, they didn't know who I was. I didn't have no ID. They found me lying in an alley somewhere. The doctors told me afterwards that no one had visited me. No one cared. Full force, I felt the total emptiness in the heart.

KENT

But you *are* Jesus, right?

GLENN (O.S.)

(speaking quickly, holding out phone)

On your Facebook page, it says, look, here, it says: "I am Jesus." Location: Orlando. "I am Jesus at the Holy Land Experience."

RODDY

Yeah, bro. It's like, I *become him* when I go there. You know? I'm just so full of the Holy Spirit when I'm there. Love, bro. I can cast out demons when I'm there, you know? When Jesus is up there performing miracles of healing, I'm like, *I can do that too,* you know? After the show, I go up to people, and they tell me they have liver problems, they have COPD. I put my hands on them, I feel the love of God go through me, and I say, "I cast you out!"

KENT

You ever been to Cassadaga?

RODDY

It's like, I've cast a demon out once already, with the help of my Higher Power, right? I am a grateful disciple of God and a recovering addict who just celebrated eight years clean through NA and the grace of God. I live with the mental illnesses of severe depression and schizophrenia. And yes, I've been blessed with a very fulfilling life.

NOAH (O.S.)

Seriously, guys?

FADE OUT

Technically, Roddy wasn't lying. *Technically,* he *does* play Jesus at the Holy Land Experience. Just . . . in an unofficial capacity. If there's anyone to blame here, it's Glenn and his shoddy research. But then again, what can you expect from some internet searches conducted after fifteen hours in the sun?

We turned the gear back on, we interviewed Roddy in what *I* felt was a very considerate, respectful manner. He told us he's from Delray Beach but works part-time in food service here. Before that, he lived in Port Arthur, Texas. Before *that,* Chicago. "I'm from everywhere, man," Roddy said. "I been everywhere." He could afford his frequent trips to the Holy Land Experience on account of cast members who slipped him complimentary passes, he explained. He told our cameras that going there gave him the strength and courage to live by the principles when recovery didn't make sense. "The depression didn't go away. Instead, it got worse. I heard voices and saw people who weren't there. And this was me *not* using drugs, but I was still hallucinating. I was feeling alienated, hopeless, useless, worthless. But then I saw some preachers on TV. It was like a sign from God, you know? I realized I don't have to walk this walk alone. God had a plan for me."

He went on in this fashion for some time, detailing among other things the time rival gang members stuffed him in the trunk of a car. ". . . And he puts that gun to the side of my head and I heard a pop, felt that heat," Roddy regaled the cameras. He wasn't kidding when he said he had seen and done some *stuff.*

Roddy winding up where he's wound up makes perfect sense, though. For Roddy is representative of that most unfairly maligned sociological phenomenon, the "Florida Man." As you might recall, "Florida Man" was a meme that went viral in 2013 and endures to this day. The idea behind it was simple enough: Aggregate news headlines in which the principal actor is identified as "Florida Man." "Florida Man Does X." "Florida Man Arrested for Y." "Florida Man Found

Guilty of X and Y While Under the Influence of Z." The joke was that Florida Man is the superhero America never asked for but nevertheless deserves. And that joke blitzed across the pop cultural landscape. National Public Radio, *The New York Times*—a lot of major news outlets picked up on it.

Florida Man, it would seem, captures something essential about how the rest of the country conceives of my home. The meme gives shape to a sentiment that had long gone unarticulated, at least at the national level. According to it, the archetypal Florida Man can be pared down to three basic qualities. The first is intemperance. Florida Man is almost always drunk, high, or tilting toward some as-yet-unnamed state of chemically altered consciousness. "Florida Man Arrested While Wearing T-Shirt That Says 'I Have Drugs,'" reads one entry in the series. "Florida Man Pocket-Dials 911 While Cooking Meth with Mom," reads another. "Hallucinating Florida Man Seeing Imaginary Aliens Walks into Store with Large Knives and Asks Not to Be Eaten." "Florida Man Walks into Bar, Downs $80 Worth of Shots, Sets Fire to Trash Can, Punches Everyone in the Face."

The second aspect of Florida Man's character might have been guessed at already. That is, Florida Man's truest and only recourse when faced with life's challenges is: violence. Absurd, hyperbolic violence, the kind rarely given expression outside of cartoons. "Florida Man Says He Had No Idea Beating an Alligator to Death Was Illegal." "Florida Man Gets into Brick-Throwing Fight with Identical Twin Brother." "Florida Man Mistakes Girlfriend for Hog, Shoots Her." "Florida Man Arrested for Hitting Drag Queen with Tiki Torch While Dressed as Member of KKK Now Running for Mayor."

One might say that these first and second characteristics flow from and feed into one another. This would be correct. It is also correct of the third and final aspect of Florida Man's triune character— namely, that he is something of a confidence artist–cum–Quixote. Florida Man dreams big, impossible dreams and, goshdarnit, he cannot help but strive after them. For instance: "Florida Man Accused of Memorizing Stolen Credit Card Numbers in Order to Live at Luxury Disney Hotel, Again." "Florida Man Arrested for Allegedly Fixing Cars with Play-Doh." "Florida Man Shows Up to Bank Robbery Drunk, in Taxi." "Florida Man's Church Loses Tax-Exempt Status Because It's Reportedly Just a Nightclub."

Florida Man is from somewhere else, Cleveland or Cedar Rapids or Pascagoula, but he drove south down the map into tract homes and accessible beaches. He drove all night and then through the dawn so that he could arrive, take off his shoes, fall asleep on the sand, and wake up to perfectly spaced stars. On the Gulf Coast, the Atlantic coast, in Central Florida, South Florida—Florida Man has woken up all over the state.

Or else he was born here. Florida Man needn't be a Yankee Stranger. Florida Man, like the ideal American, is defined not by place or past but by process. Florida Man is forever "becoming," is always on the make. As such, a person *metamorphoses* into Florida Man. He arrives here or was born here, he finds out it's all an okeydoke, and rather than give up or move on, he doubles down. Slowly but surely, he gets filtered through the state's socioeconomic (and judicial) layers the way a drop of rain hits ground and seeps toward rock bottom.

You can find Florida Man anywhere along that downwardly mobile trajectory. There he is—clocked out of his job but dawdling in a Caribbean-themed bar, comparing his mortgage contract alongside an Amway brochure. There he is—underemployed, resting against a boardwalk's piling, wondering if he should commit mail fraud in order to get his car repaired. There he is—self-medicating as Jesus in a Jesus-themed park.

Some guys learn from their mistakes; all Florida Man knows is to raise the stakes. He's an American hero, well and truly—a hero who cannot recognize the villain he has become.

So it was in the spirit of apprentice Florida Men that the three of us tried our damnedest to make this situation work. Ex-junkie as Redeemer of the Experimental Prototype Community of Tomorrow. "We can fix the intro in postproduction," Glenn assured. Noah justified it: "Wouldn't the *real* Jesus show up as the guy they kick out of the Holy Land Experience, anyway?"

I agreed. "To the extent that you did it to the least of my 'cast members,' you did it to me."

⁕

I could describe Epcot to you, but why? Every year, more people come to Disney's asphalt-and-fiberglass play places than visit the

Eiffel Tower, Taj Mahal, Tower of London, and Pyramids *combined*. There's a good chance you're one of those who've been here, done that. And even on the off chance you aren't—Epcot contains not one referent you haven't seen or experienced one trillion times already, every day of your life, in the outdoor malls, airports, top-shelf arenas, cruise ships, fast-casual chains, and "revitalized" downtowns of the late-capitalist West. (It is here we should remember that the word "utopia" was derived from a Greek pun for "nowhere.") If anything, Epcot's age and relative staidness appear touchingly quaint when compared to the latter-day pleasurescapes it inspired. Much of the fun to be had here is not unlike the fun to be had in a living-history museum: Whoa, check it out, one of the very first "managed experiences"! Lookit how they did it way back when. Get a load of the crude methods they used to cover up every trace of noncommodified, nonregulated, unsimulated, un"real" reality.

Does anyone *really* want to know about "Ellen's (as in DeGeneres) Energy Adventure"? "Mission: Space," "Imagination!," or "The Seas"? "Innoventions"—I had to take a break from walking in order to squint at that word on our map. Was it an actual English noun that I knew, or was I suffering through another bout of heat-induced aphasia? Twenty seconds later, I had convinced myself that "innoventions," like "imagineer," is not yet a real word, and I moved on to "Living with the Land."

"What're we supposed to be learning here?" Glenn asked loudly during a cartoon screening in which the animals of *The Lion King* work together to make a jungle resort marginally more eco-friendly. "That if we keep doing what we're doing, environmental destruction may happen in the future? But since it's already happening, it's OK, since we're also making tiny strides to make it better?"

Roddy, rapt, shushed him. Unlike Glenn but like most of the other guests, he had merrily and instantaneously adapted to this psychic environment. Roddy was happy to be free from freedom for a little while.

Back in the sunshine, we walked about and wondered what to do next. Glenn, as always, followed the principle *When in doubt, shoot B-roll*. He stalked Roddy as he strolled by gray-faced Mouseketeer apparatchiks and rail-thin New Englanders. Past soft little screeching boys and girls so early accustomed to mother love. Betwixt the regardful eyeing traded by brown-skinned families and those wearing Make America Great Again hats. Through the *yearning*. More than amusement, there is yearning for amusement at Disney. The overheated, despondently mute families trudging along—they appeared to resent the fact that they were not having fun. Not having fun at Disney? Surely this indicates some sort of moral failing on their part?

In this uncanny valley, I noted in my notebook, *it is the disheartened, the ambivalent, and the human that begin to seem unreal.*

"Yo, J.C.," Noah said, lowering his GoPro camera. "You allowed to drink?"

"Hell yeah I can drink," Roddy said. "I can outdrink you, and *you, and you*. Just don't gimme no junk, you know?"

"Around the World with Jesus Christ?" I suggested.

"Around the World," Noah agreed.

"Why not," Glenn said. "Futurism is dead. Everybody! Just . . . travel and consume."

We entered the World Showcase, a series of elaborate national pavilions set up to exhibit the cultural splendor of human civilization. Really, though, it is a lap of seventies-era themed bars, restaurants, and gift shops encircling a man-made lake. It is intended for those who cannot afford to (or do not wish to) visit the real countries represented therein.

A dense column of slow-moving tourists threaded the Showcase. I spotted far fewer children here than anyplace else in Orlando. The visitors were mostly young adults. Many were wearing Mickey Mouse Club sweaters or Minnie ears. They were gleefully snapping selfies of themselves eating Dole Whip. They had an air of ironical self-awareness about them.

"Wait, are all of these countries from the Northern Hemisphere?" Glenn asked, surveying the list of Canada, the United Kingdom, France, Morocco, Japan, America, Italy, Germany, China, Norway, and Mexico. "That's *great*," he said with a laugh on his lips.

He meant *great* in that many would find it *not* great; they would consider it racist and supremacist and yadda yadda. The First World–centricity reflected an indifference to present-day standards of cultural sensitivity. Yet it was this *indifference* that was "great" to post-tourists like Glenn and the young wisenheimers around us.

Before we can unpack this, we have to understand something else. The great floodgates of the wonder world have swung open. In 2012, the United Nations celebrated the milestone of one billion international trips taken in a single year. This was a milestone, but one that was in line with the 25 million international trips taken in 1960, and the 250 million taken in 1970, and the 536 million taken in 1995. So many people travel now, and the business of travel has become so intertwined with national (and local) economies, that a country like Thailand can be the world's biggest exporter of rice while still relying on tourism to be its biggest earner.

Mass travel has converted the entire earth into capital and her peoples into a consumer base. Everyone everywhere now hankers after *difference*. Why? Existential modernity, maybe? That is, a modern person travels because he or she (consciously or not) feels rootless or spiritually homeless and believes *real* reality and genuine living are to be found elsewhere. In the past, or in other, more "primitive" cultures, or purer, more "authentic" lifestyles. Anywhere, really, but where the modern person happens to find herself most days.

Problem is, as ever more people seek out and consume difference, difference becomes that much harder to experience. Masses of travelers tend to leave in their wake the same hotels, souvenir shops, fast-food joints, Zaras, H&Ms, Starbucks—the "small monotonous world that everywhere shows us our own image," as tourism scholars have put it. Our relentless drive to ferret out and consume difference causes us to level the planet the way a too-large herd does a commons.

Into this scarcity step outfits that trade in a type of traveling—to war zones, political hot spots, dodgy locales—that is known as "adventure" or "disaster" tourism. Pick the right outfit, and you can go on a journey into North Korea or Iran. If that's not to your taste, you can go eat insects at the street carts Anthony Bourdain recommended. *Come,* the subliminal pitch goes, *discover locales that have managed to avoid the infectious monoculture of the contemporary world.* Never mind that, like explorers come bearing blankets, we can't help but introduce pathogens we've long since grown inured to.

Oh well—the market abhors a vacuum. Every place is in the process of becoming a someplace with a sterilized, commodified, and Instagrammable Cultural Experience to be had. Everyone is dreaming up and saving for that next trip, the contrails of our departing and arriving flights coiling tighter around the globe as we hunt down the last of its endangered difference.

As for Epcot—Epcot used to be different, but now it is not. Now its depictions of difference come across as dated, offensive, and ironically great. Think of it this way. If you were a disenchanted traveler who had trotted the globe twice over, why *not* go to the ground zero of the phenomenon, photograph yourself appreciating it like the world-weary connoisseur you are?

The gaucheness of the World Showcase—*real live Chinese are wearing queue braids and serving chop suey!*—is *so* cringey and clueless yet primitively earnest that it snakes back around into the realm of different and "authentic" experience. This postmodern ouroboros is a nightmare, I know. But one important to analyze if we are to comprehend the hell we have made for ourselves.

Almost all of the young people at Epcot had come to our same conclusion: Let's make a game out of despair. Around the World, as this diversion is called, is the most popular unofficial attraction at Disney. In it, you quaff a representative beverage at each of the eleven national pavilions. You douse your anxieties about having fun. You drown out the end-times tinnitus that hums: ". . . *the horizon of the transcendent has been evacuated . . . an unprecedented absence has appeared at the heart of human experience . . . the self has been progressively reduced to an isolated node of desire and will confronted by a universe of strictly immanent ends . . . secularist, relativist, materialist late modernity is a seamless garment, and our voluntarist culture of consumption and disposal is not merely accidentally associated with this "culture of death," but rather belongs to it essentially . . . and I, I am contributing to the incessant pollution of soil and water by the heavy metals and other toxins produced by the monstrous consumerist voracity of our way of life . . . local ecologies despoiled are impossible to recover, and the poor of the developing world constitute the vast majority of immediate victims . . . only a depraved moral imagination allied to a petrified heart could fail to see this . . .*"*

"Rod!" I said. "What's your poison? I'm buying."

"Beer, bro," Roddy said. "I'll take a beer."

---

* Adapted from the writings of David Bentley Hart.

Using his French, Glenn ordered four Fin du Monde ales at a kiosk in our first stop, "Canada."

"Bottoms up," Noah said. "Whoever makes it around the world without puking into his hands wins."

Following our stop at an Irish pub in "Great Britain," Roddy and I interweaved our arms round each other's shoulders. Onward to "France," where actual European children were swirling two fingers du vin alongside their grandmothers. We availed ourselves of Grand Marnier slushes in plastic martini glasses. We were having *fun,* goddamnit, and my massive debts were unrealer to me than the Eiffel Tower poking above this Potemkin arrondissement.

We stopped for Midori in "Morocco," got sake in "Japan." Roddy wanted to look at the weird anime crap in the Mitsukoshi department store; Noah offered to buy him a few packs of trading cards. Swimming through this bright abyss, the peace of my mind knew neither bottom nor surface.

Roddy, too, seemed at ease. With the camera's help, we got him to tell us how he was holding up. "Spiritually, man, I'm in a state of grace," he said, fanning his cards and thumbing through them. "I don't always feel it, but I'm feeling it now. I should have died so many times when I was using, guys. But He strengthens me so I can face my illness each day—and still being able to stay clean, you know? That's an incredible miracle!" Roddy withdrew one card in particular, a riot of green tentacles.

The exasperation of consciousness waned following slugs of limoncello in "Italy." I defeated Glenn in a bout of arm wrestling; this, he took poorly. With pokes and thwaps, he attempted to incite a slap fight every few dozen feet. As we were in Jesus' presence, I turned one cheek and then the other.

"What's you guys' deal?" Roddy asked. "Are you Christians? Have you made Jesus Christ your Lord and Savior?"

"I'm pretty sure somebody baptized me into something," Noah said.

"Papist," I said, raising an index finger.

"That's not *Christian* Christian, though," Roddy objected. "Did you know that the seven hills in Revelation, the end of days—there are seven hills in Rome?"

"Ah *ha* . . ." I said.

It wasn't until we pushed into "The American Adventure" after sundown that people started coming to Roddy for pictures. I suppose they took him for a part of the installation? I'm not sure. I'd just then guzzled a Jim Beam frozen lemonade; my field of vision was beginning to tip and sway like the horizon seen from the bow of a boat. There were taking place one or two more things than I could successfully process.

I *do* recall a fellow Around the World–er assuming Roddy was a kind of performance-art commentary. "Hypocrisy, yeah!" this drunk guy was saying, backslapping. Others, too, started to gather. Some lumbered like somnambulists; others wore the squint-eyed smiles of the soon-to-be horizontal. It was a bad scene there, man. I looked to my left and saw schnockered adults making out. Looked to my right: fully grown individuals leaving behind mis-deposits of barf. Or worse—they were dancing.

Roddy removed his cap, ran a hand through his hair. He closed his eyes and attempted to open up a line of communication with something else inside of him. I nudged Glenn, who slapped me back. "No, the *camera*," I whispered.

EXT. THE AMERICAN ADVENTURE—NIGHT

RODDY is pacing the pavilion like a shooting gallery bear, holding a revival for his audience of shitfaces. His demeanor: rampant and aglow. Words flood from him as though he has finally been allowed to write with his dominant hand.

RODDY

I died once. I died after I was shot. I went to the other side, where I was given a message with an androgynous voice. A bullet is still lodged under my tongue. I was released from the hospital a month later and went to stay with my mother in Atlanta, Georgia. Miracles happen every day. The point is that you have to look up and see them coming and catch them. Don't let them fall at your feet. You're living in the now, and now is where the future begins. On earth as a human being in your earth suit, there's a lot of fear.

Roddy downshifts his tone. He counterbalances this by throwing his shoulders and making rappy hand gestures. The crowd laughs, shouts affirmations, ebbs and flows.

RODDY (CONT'D)

People don't want to hear the word "God." They don't want to hear the word "Jesus." People who are in fear create their own fear, that's why I can say that I love my enemies, because my enemies show me things in myself that I need to change. Everyone's here for a purpose—the purpose is finding your own identity, your own purity, finding unconditional love, learning to forgive, accepting that you are a child of God. When you are in this place of learning and practice it every day, wonderful, amazing, beautiful things will happen to you.

A blue-shirted Disney security officer joins the crowd and mouths something into a walkie-talkie. Roddy doesn't notice. He holds his hands behind his back, pacing, while looks of frustration and then relief move like shadows across his face.

RODDY (CONT'D)

This came through me from Him: Your love inspires me to give you a fondue of my heart. A thankful position is the way to be in your own personal freedom, with your own personal power, that is thankful for everything you have been through, for everything you have done, everything you've failed at and everything you've accomplished. It's all okay. Everything's good. Your truth, which is undeniable, never fails. Power and freedom comes from your spirit. Spirit creates power, freedom, and truth, and power, freedom, and truth create love. And love is God.

A few more guards arrive. They see the three men filming Roddy and approach.

POTATO-FACED GUARD

This a friend of yours?

NOAH (O.S.)

We're just filming.

KENT (O.S.)

We're just making home movies.

RODDY

That's faith: Fantastic Adventures in Trusting Him. But some of you don't want to trust Him. You don't want to give up your vices. Your vices are the deepest thing you have. If I attack your vice, I attack your very being. And you can never forgive me for this. The devils who control you can't forgive me for wanting to destroy them in my way and not theirs.

The guards leave the men in order to position themselves around Roddy. Slowly, they move in.

GLENN (O.S.)

So should we . . .

NOAH (O.S.)

Free country, bro. He's free to do what he wants.

GLENN (O.S.)

We're not in America. We're in Disney.

KENT (O.S.)

We still got a few more countries to visit.

GLENN (O.S.)

(sighing)

Fine. If only to have a sense of accomplishment about something on this trip.

RODDY

That's truth: Taking Real Understanding to Heart. And that's trust: Talking Realistically, Understanding Sacred Truth.

FADE OUT

THEY CALL THEM "PRIVILEGED" FOR WHOM THE SYMBOLIC WORLD IS CONGRUENT WITH THEIR FANTASIES

Hungover and squinting in the gold-meshed sunlight, we pack our gear. We hit the road that once contained innumerable branching possibilities but has since been compartmentalized, made insular. Laden with our ill-shaped sacks of stuff, we accept again the yoke of Logistics.

We walked southwest and then west. We tracked the movements of clouds overhead with the enthusiasm of deadbeats at the race-track. We cheered our picks whenever they were poised to overtake the sun.

Either there's less stuff to notice now, or the road is pinching every last ounce of perceptivity out of me like toothpaste at the bottom of the tube.

"Keep an eye out for the big domestics," Noah advised. "Them's the elderly who are going to punch our cards."

Glenn remains unwilling to guerrilla-camp on any owned plots of land. To him, stealing a few hours of sleep on private property is as potentially deadly as poaching game on a lord's estate. I'm sure he's right. I'm sure we'd be blown away for our trespass. Still, having to find vacant lots or for-sale houses on the Zillow app most every night is a true pain in the ass.

Between Orlando and Tampa, suburbia gave way again to oaky scrubland, some of it developed but most of it in the process of being prepped for development. Wherever we could, we left the roadside to walk on wooden boardwalks laid down for earthmoving machinery. Soon, the sprawl stretching from the Gulf Coast and the sprawl stretching from the interior will meet here at the midpoint.

For a few days, I was able to forget my body while pushing my jogging stroller. My conscious mind bobbed above it all like a balloon stringed to a kid at the zoo. My body, however, refused to forget me. There was, for example, the plantar fasciitis I dealt with every morning. Though of course I didn't know that that's what it was. I self-diagnosed only after Googling: *terrible A.M. pain + feet feel like lumps of ground beef with bone chips in them??*

My original blisters have continued to heal, thanks to the frictionless shower sandals. Of new concern is the plantar wart on my right heel. I know it's a plantar wart because plantar warts used to pop up on the weight-bearing parts of my feet all the time when I was a kid. Somewhere along the roadside—or at Epcot, or a hotel bathroom, or a *gas station* bathroom, or?—human papillomavirus entered my right foot through one of my wounds, resulting in a crusty button of concentrated pain pressing into my sole. With each stride, it zaps me like I'm on the other side of a Milgram experiment. Glenn and Noah are treating this development as though it's a blight on my actual soul, something plague-like I contracted because of moral turpitude. They're terrified of communicability and upset that I've summoned this affliction into our camp.

But aside from all that, this stretch has been a peach. The sky: as blue and unpolluted as a baby's gaze. Herons frequently materialized out of it, drifting to earth as if weighted with the absent clouds' white. Dirtbag-looking scrub jays kicked up shindies in the live oaks. Meathead squirrels with well-defined trapezius muscles watched us from a distance while doing little squirrel push-ups, dallying like city joggers waiting for a stoplight to change.

Mostly what I did was drift into and out of the present and material *I* while making one with the road. Until Glenn stopped short in front of me, and I plowed the front wheel of Jog-a-bye directly into his Achilles tendon. He inhaled sharply but didn't otherwise react. He kept his head canted toward the phone in his hand. "Hey," he said. "Americans. You *do* realize the election is the day after tomorrow, yes?"

A better person, a person less certain of the position life has afforded him, would've used this long walk to foster . . . *some*thing. An awakening. A better understanding of this American Experiment. He'd've sought out the Native Americans from whom we obtained this very land. He'd've recorded the stories of the African Americans who continue to bear the brunt of state discrimination. He'd've advocated for the immigrants who are terrified of deportation. He'd've commiserated with the Experiment's human remainder, who find themselves ready to revolt against the fatuous leadership caste. He'd've reached out to that caste, who often mouth the right words about the common good but exist in a world insulated from (and frequently contemptuous of) the realities and beliefs of the remainder.

He'd've been fearless in the face of radical human brokenness. He'd've walked toward his fellow Americans, asked them without judgment about their lives, and with their cooperation and consent, he'd've made art. He'd've spoken truth to all with dignity. He'd've worked to show the world that the America they see on the nightly news is not the real America, or need not be.

A better person-slash-artist would've licked a finger, stuck it in the air, and recognized at once the apocalyptic tenor settling upon this land. The rough beast, its hour come round at last, slouches toward Bethlehem! He'd've fought that beast.

I, of course, am not that person. I ordered the three of us to a rental car agency.

⁓

Despite the temperature hovering in the mid-sixties on Election Day, we three began to perspire in the space of the twelve steps that separated our motel room and our rented Nissan Sentra. For once, the humidity was negligible; even so, the observable world felt as though it was on the verge of splitting open like an overripe peach.

The radio news informed us that every scenario in which Donald Trump captures 270 electoral votes and thus the presidency includes a win in Florida. He had to carry the Sunshine State, simple as that. According to the polls, he was close to doing so. He trailed Hillary Clinton by a single point.

Glenn was behind the wheel for our two-hour jaunt back to Gainesville, where Noah and I were still registered to vote. (Swing state, baby.) As soon as we hit the highway, distance reverted to time. It was remarkable. We were instantly upsized, like Super Mario eating a mushroom. Proportion returned to our world.

"It's almost giving me vertigo," Glenn said as we blew past covered territory at relative warp speed.

Noah grunted his assent while keeping his eyes on his phone. "You guys don't do Facebook, right?" Glenn and I said no. "Yeah, because it's not looking good. Everybody's swiftboating everybody. I got an uncle here linking to a post from something called USADaily Politics dot com. I got a cousin screaming at him in the comments. And he's screaming back about how it's no less reputable than the *Tallahassee Democrat*."

"The posttruth state," Glenn said. "It is upon you."

"There was a time when I might have celebrated the arrival of 'posttruth,'" I replied. "Now, not so much. Now, all facts have their alternatives, and feelings carry more weight than either. But, I mean—you dance with the devil, and . . ."

"'It's right there in the name!'" Noah said, exaggeratedly impersonating his uncle. "'The Tallahassee *Democrat!*'"

We rolled down our windows. The deafening rush of air helped to dry my sweat, temper my queasiness. Then I recalled the Trump premonition I'd had on the shrimp boat. A hot coil of unease rose in my throat.

And—look. I've talked to enough Trump supporters throughout this state. I understand that class division now manifests as geography. Rural, exurban, and suburban vs. urban, with all that that entails. I understand that Trump-forward partisans believe a nation should give preference to the interests of its current citizens over and against the interests of noncitizens, much as a corporation prioritizes the interests of its shareholders. Men like Noah and my father did not volunteer to fight on behalf of borderless nonjudgmentalism; they fought for the United States of America. I understand that.

Furthermore, I recognize that Donald Trump, like any demagogue worth his salt, reels off a moral inventory that is not entirely fraudulent. A lot of Americans *have* seen their economic prospects decimated, their communities hollowed out. Their religion deemed cruel and atavistic. Their yearning for a common culture (in which they recognize themselves as well as their ancestors and descendants) condemned as racist, sexist, a stumbling block to progress. Their desire for newcomers to assimilate to customs and procedures that may be alien to the newcomers' old ways of life—this does not seem like too great a burden to them, much less an injustice. If newcomers come to a place, it's because they hope to gain by doing so. Is it therefore unreasonable for the hosts to ask something in return?

I understand this. As well I understand that you cannot reason a man out of a position he was not reasoned into in the first place. Clearly, this Cold Civil War is going to seethe onward regardless of electoral outcome. The fake-news dismediation will continue apace. Cross-camp communication will become that much more difficult. The gyre'll widen. Things will continue to fall apart.

However, I cannot abide a leader who construes evil as a malignant, external thing, alien to himself and his people. I was going back to cast my vote against *that*.

⁓

The unimaginable is unimaginable until it happens. Then—like the fall of Rome, or the return of the undivided waters—the unimaginable reads as inevitable. But we're getting ahead of ourselves.

Noah's and my polling place was at the southwestern corner of the University of Florida campus. The students there steered very clear of our ghastly threesome, affording us the crescent berth you normally see New Yorkers grant to street people. Once in line, we had ample opportunities to consider ourselves in UF's shiny new surfaces. In spite of all the Circle K hot dogs, I have lost much weight—weight in my face, weight in my torso. All three of us, in fact, have shed many pounds of friendly fat. Our new, pointed selves appear to have been whittled out of something formerly benign, like prison shanks.

"I don't get it," Glenn said, turning to me. "If you're so adamant about how much you love this place, why did you leave to begin with?"

"The University of Florida is primarily a sciences school," I answered. "An engineering school. Most of its graduates go home and ply their trades there. Where was I supposed to go for writing except New York?"

"Fair," Glenn said.

But he had got me thinking. Back when I left, I'd thought I was leaving Florida for greener pastures. You know—the old saw about how the confined must run away in search of freedom, fulfillment. What I was actually doing, I realize now, was sending myself into exile. On a subconscious level I'd understood this, and wanted it. My vain hope was something akin to James Joyce's: that I could write in Zurich, Paris, or New York while nonetheless becoming more Floridian than ever, a dream cracker on the page. I don't think I could endorse that vain hope today. Months now of Florida's tangible air filling my lungs, pervading my blood—with each breath I feel I am becoming more fully myself.

Glenn filmed Noah and me before and after we cast our ballots. Defense of democracy done with, we interviewed some giddy first-time voters. At dusk, I drove us back to the rental car place in Lakeland.

"Can you imagine how great it would feel if this place were actually beautiful?" Glenn said while aiming his lens at the sped-by roadside.

Noah ducked his head back into the Sentra. "I'm just gonna float it again: the car con. We drive, we film like we're walking, no one's the wiser."

"We have to see this through," Glenn said. "We have to. For my sanity's sake."

To capture election night, we set up shop in an Applebee's that was squatting in the shadow of an I-4 interchange. No one around the square-shaped bar much cared that we were filming. A DJ— some balding schlub in jorts—scored the returns while other balding schlubs in jorts shrugged. I made eye contact with one across the bar as the combustive drum intro to Van Halen's "Hot for Teacher" started up. He saluted me with his glass, shouted: "Yeah! 'Runnin' with the Devil!' Hoo woo!"

Noah inhaled his tequila. "If these nitwits can't even keep their Van Halen straight," he said, "what the fuck are we doing entrusting our republic to them?"

According to the news, voter turnout in Florida was fairly high: 9.5 million votes cast, or about 74.2 percent of registered voters. Florida came to play—and the early results showed Trump building a sizable lead.

Glenn looked green. "Wait till South Florida gets counted," I encouraged. I was sure there'd be enough blue wrung out of Miami-Dade and Broward counties to quench the red engulfing the map. Trump dominated the Panhandle, as Noah had predicted. He also did better than expected in the medium-sized counties—Lee, Brevard, Pasco, Clay—scattered throughout the state. Hillary snagged Orlando, we saw. But it was looking like she'd win only nine of sixty-seven counties. Every place that wasn't a conurbation was falling to the Donald. This appeared to be the nationwide trend writ small.

The DJ played "Say It Ain't So" and "It Wasn't Me" and "The Final Countdown." I kept looking to see if he was trolling us, but he was always on his phone, never once checking the televisions. The other schlubs were collapsing into their full-back stools, no longer bothering to wipe their damp faces. Like almost-bankrupt gamblers who had risked their remaining fortunes on the turn of a card—and gotten their card—a hilarity was rising among them.

"The blue ones are where you go for when you wanna catch AIDS!" one balding schlub announced when the electoral map of Florida was broadcast.

With more and more whiskey I tried to dissolve the bolus of terror that was hardening in my stomach. I turned to appraise the rest of the establishment. The dining areas were operating more or less business as usual, with very few paying heed to the screens. I was overcome by paranoiac incredulity: *What is wrong with you people that you aren't freaking out right now?* The middle-aged couples, the youngish families around us—unperturbed.

"At least the crew of the *Cracker Style* isn't here to laugh in our faces," Noah pointed out.

Employees began to dismantle the decorative bunting before Florida had even been called for Trump. The DJ stopped spinning records. People filed out.

By this point, Glenn was nattering incessantly to himself. He swung from panic to mirth like a moviegoer at a horror flick. Behind him, a black family seated at a four-top traded I-told-you-sos. Noah read some of his uncle's triumphant Facebook posts to the camera. Disillusionment climbed from the well of my id and leered.

Glenn took me outside to film some impressions. I wanted to say, "This isn't the America I know." But wasn't it?

"Seems to me Donald Trump won the country by sowing doubt as to the veracity of received narratives," I said. "Doubt as to the veracity of received knowledge itself." Hell, through sheer single-minded assertion, Donald Trump managed to elevate fear, resentment, and gut feeling to the status of truth in the minds of his supporters.

Seems to me, I went on, they voted for a Trump administration because they felt a Trump administration would mean a return to the callous, heedless, retard-strong America that executed Manifest Destiny, overthrew Fascism and Communism, shot men to the moon. More than that, a Trump administration would serve as the yearned-for F-U to the sneering minority who revel in condescending to and/or demonizing the America where people go to church, send sons to war, work their asses off for less and less, fall further behind on mortgage payments.

Seems this way—but is it true? "Fuck you!" I told the camera. "Knowing's got nothing to do with it! Does any of this *feel* true? Then it *is* true." Trump admitted as much in his book *The Art of the Deal,* where he described his sales strategy as "truthful hyperbole." The real question is: Did the real estate developer manage to develop the truth into something you'd like to buy into?

"I would despair more," I said, "if this turn of events wasn't such a that's-so-funny-I-forgot-to-laugh example of the chickens coming home to roost." For more than half a century now, I explained, der kommissars of the arts & culture & entertainment & media & academic institutions in this country have worked to ensure that young and old alike get well drilled in the "axiomatic" principles of Gramsci, Foucault, Derrida, and the rest of the critical-theory chuckleheads.

(I know this because I myself was once an aspiring kommissar, media and academic divisions.) Call it what you like—relativism, postmodernism, deconstruction. The lesson is one and the same: The truth is not out there waiting to be objectively uncovered. The truth is *made*. Facts are fabricated as seen fit by the powers that be, and then consent for those facts is manufactured, enforced. The Dark Ages fantasy of a tabs-keeping sky daddy was an oppressive ruse of this caliber, sure; but no less so was the Enlightenment ideal of (white) man and his natural, neutral, unmediated, unbiased access to truth through reason.

Can you grasp the paradox? *There is no truth except this: There is no truth. And because there is no truth, there can be no ethics distinct from politics. No authority distinct from power. "Truth" has been subsumed under the form of war. Therefore, we must ask not whether a statement is true or false; we must ask, Who is stating it? And what does their side stand to gain by stating it?*

Each of us is a prisoner of language who *always* speaks our truth from a standpoint we owe to our background and biases. "As a straight white man, I think . . . As a native Floridian, I feel . . . As a practicing Catholic, I believe . . ." What I, you, or the person across the street holds as self-evident "truth"? Why, it's nothing more than the social construction we grew up with, or implicitly prefer, or were indoctrinated into.

Got that? To make the sociologists' and cultural anthropologists' point in more direct, Trumpian language: A lot of people are saying that fact is fiction, bigly. So why should I believe that lyin' [news media, advocacy organization, opposition party, member of any identity group I do not belong to] if what they're saying, I don't feel to be true?

LOL. Or so might croak the troll who appreciates *hubris* and the *nemesis* risen to meet it.

"Welcome to the Florida presidency," I concluded.

"The good news for you," Glenn said as we reentered Applebee's, "is people will be so fed up with Trump takes by the time this airs, they'll tune out your soft-cock pretension."

The three of us sat at the bar in our shared solitudes, sipping our drinks and widening our moats. It was official: This long, ugly, and immensely stupid election season had drawn to a close. The TV said

Trump had won Florida by some 119,673 votes while flipping a few other battleground states like Wisconsin and Michigan. Around the rest of the country, slightly more than half of voters went for Hillary. Unfortunately, this majority was improperly distributed, geographically speaking. And so, after having masterfully stoked culture-war resentments and peddled a nebulous program of populist economics and protectionism—all while simultaneously inaugurating our post-truth era—this confidence artist was awarded the presidency by the Electoral College.

"Only in America," Noah snorted. He licked salt from the length of his thumb like a man about to ship his parcel of consciousness around the world.

"I can't even fucking bother with this right now," Glenn said. Then his anger got the best of him, and he added: "You'd all sooner destroy the world than be made to feel uncomfortable. And *you*"—he elbowed me heavily. "Fucking, *you* . . ." He waved a hand. "Ehhhhh." He gagged himself with drink.

Donald Trump appeared onscreen to deliver his victory speech. His closed-mouthed smile seemed unusually taut, almost a grimace. His eyes appeared somewhat vacant, too, as though he was seeing past the present moment and into his future. Like he was realizing right this moment that, shit, those castles in the sky he'd been taking down payments on? He was now expected to *build them*.

I don't know. I could've been tipsily reading into it. But there and then I experienced something approaching . . . what? Not quite sympathy for the man. It was more a mixture of cringing nausea and vicarious shame. I had some small measure of pity for Donald Trump. From native son to adoptive one, I wanted to say: *You got too greedy, my dude. Sank in too deep. You should've begged off when the out presented itself, started that "reality" news network. There's no skipping town now. The marks have called your bluff.*

The few patrons remaining in the Applebee's applauded. One guy rebel-yelled. Then they went back to waving Bud Light bottles in the area of their mouths.

Like most Americans all of the time, they'd championed the guy who appeared to be Everyman and Superman at once. A quote-unquote self-made self-maker who had the attributes we respect (wealth; resiliency in creating wealth; a professed disregard for the opinions of others coupled with a crippling need to be liked), as well as the faults we not so secretly cherish (brusqueness; pride; malignant narcissism; pride; fuck you I won't do what you tell me–ism; pride).

"Christ Almighty," Glenn said. "What sorts of horrors have you just unleashed upon the world."

I didn't respond. Instead, I reached down and tugged on my right pinkie toe's dead squiggle of keratin. It stretched and snipped off like the tilde of translucent fat at the end of a piece of undercooked bacon.

I GOT NOTHING

The sun didn't come out. We walked to Plant City. We regretted all that we had done and all that we had failed to do.

Regret is memory on the offensive, I wrote.

SALUTATIONS! FROM DEATH'S FAVORITE STATE

We proceeded through blue-green strawberry fields on our way into the Tampa Bay area. My plantar wart broadened; the pain it summoned broadened, too. I convinced myself that the one great thing about a period of shocking decline is it lays everything bare. A period of shocking decline denudes a civilization; it pulls the stopper on the reservoir of mythos. Suddenly, everyone is able to see what had been hiding there all along.

While we shuffled, Glenn, Noah, and I repeated anecdotes and inside jokes (ending each with Captain Dale's trademark "uh-huh, yessir") as though checking the pilot light on our friendship, proving to ourselves that all was indeed well. And, indeed, Donald Trump's election *had* taught us some important lessons. Per our documentary, at least.

For one thing, we learned that practiced crudeness was a risky strategy, yes, but half crudeness was a certain one—certain to fail. For another: We received proof positive that nonsense can be talked into existence. No matter how outrageous the proposition, saps will trust you with their votes and their money if you purport to be letting them in on a little secret. Psst, here's the *real* story behind the true story.

Tampa is . . . fine. It's fine! Nothing much to say about it that hasn't been said elsewhere. White-sand beaches. An Air Force base. Couple of colleges. A historic Cuban district that houses a defunct cigar industry. A high concentration of Midwesterners, owing to the old Dixie Highway that connected the heartland to the Gulf Coast of Florida. (Whereas U.S. 1 ran from Maine down the Eastern Seaboard to Miami, funneling New York–New Jersey types to the Atlantic side of the state.)

Far more interesting is St. Petersburg, the peninsular city across the bay from Tampa proper, which happens also to be the first city to have hired a public relations director to convince the rest of the world that it was, it's true, a city. The PR flacks' first target: the elderly. St. Pete went after the elderly *hard* in the early 1900s. The "Sunshine City" sent them postcards featuring tourists and winter residents relaxing on the city's green benches whilst reading newspaper obituaries, drinking from dippers of Fountain of Youth water. The aged liked what they saw so much that they came and mimicked the advertisements. A *Fortune* magazine writer described the ensuing scene as "a bustling, cheery, thoroughly American sort of death." Another lampooned, "The old people sit like passengers in a motionless streetcar, without a destination." He added, "The grayness of age lies over them like a fine dust."

Success in attracting the elderly didn't stay localized in St. Pete. In the sixty years between 1940 and 2000, Florida went from a state numbering fewer than 2 million residents to a state with more than 2 million inhabitants over the age of seventy. A lot of factors went into this growth: the passage of the Social Security Act in 1935; the oversight of the Veterans Administration and the Federal Housing Administration; the world-historically robust economy that included guaranteed pensions; the democratization of the very idea of retirement and end-of-life leisure; the relative dearth of taxes and abundance of warm weather in Florida. Up north, promotions in Sunday supplements promised "retirement in Florida at $35 a month." The 1947 book *How to Retire in Florida* advised Middle Americans on how to do just that. In *The Truth About Florida,* a retiree promises that an elderly couple "can live comfortably, have a whale of a good time and save money on an income of about $40 per week."

These whiplashing developments were new and exciting, but they also bucked against millennia of conventional wisdom re: the elderly and what's best for them. Old people are *old*. They are frail. Often, they are senile. Why ever would they want to cut themselves off from their traditional communities, their families, their support networks?

For mother-loving *freedom,* that's why! Life expectancy shot up more than *thirty years* in the American Century. For the first time in human history, a society was faced with a surplus of aged citizens who were living longer, healthier, more active lives. Like everybody else postwar, these Americans wanted to test their new social, cultural, economic, and demographic privileges. They wanted to break out of the motionless stuffed rooms where they were objects to dust around but never to rearrange.

As for the long-standing belief that they were links in a chain of relationships? That they should thereby aspire to contribute to the common deposit that had been built by those who preceded them and would be maintained by those who followed? As for the idea that such chains bind together a shared social order which contains and conveys to succeeding generations the story of *place,* and how place may be lived in, sustainably tended, respected, loved, and under-stood? As for the truth that any place lacking in authentic local culture will be open to exploitation, and ultimately destruction, from the outside in?

"To live for the moment is the prevailing passion—to live for yourself, not for your predecessors or posterity. We are fast losing the sense of historical continuity, the sense of belonging to a succession of generations originating in the past and stretching into the future." Christopher Lasch wrote it in 1976. Those flocking to the Sunshine State lived it out. And thanks in part to them, Florida became a mega-state on par with California and Texas—yet, too, the state with the fewest native-born residents after Nevada.

By the early 1960s, a thousand retirees per week were arriving in Florida. By the 1990s, ten out of eleven of America's most senior counties, and fifteen of its top nineteen, were in Florida. The 2000 census revealed that the number of Floridians aged five to nineteen only slightly exceeded those aged sixty-five and older.

Senior living centers cropped up like mushrooms after rain. Sun City Center, Century Village, Kings Point, Sunrise Lakes, Hawaiian Gardens. "We give years to your life and life to your years," brochures promised. Most controversial was The Villages. Founder Harold Schwartz—whose ashes sit in a statue in the "town square"—came up with the idea while hawking mail-order swampland in Chicago: a pre-fabricated, elder-person Disney World. Schwartz purchased Orange Blossom Gardens, a trailer park off Highway 27, and converted it into a self-contained arcadia (about 130 miles north of Arcadia) where various snow peoples could enjoy all that the good life had to offer: polo fields, bowling alleys, microbreweries, a total and ruthlessly enforced embargo on children. Today extending across three counties, The Villages's 66,000-plus residents play out their strings at sixteen golf courses and four hundred social clubs where nary a whippersnapper is seen or heard. There's even a developer-run TV station and daily newspaper. The Villages is highly stratified by income and ethnicity; it is also wildly successful. "Still Booming with Retirees, The Villages Gives Trump, GOP Edge in Florida," the *Tampa Bay Times* proclaimed just recently.

The Villages is the prototypical community of tomorrow that Uncle Walt promised but never built, where (as one scholar put it): "The land uses are under control. The people in the neighborhoods are under control." *Everything* inside of The Villages's security perimeter was under the control of Schwartz and then Schwartz's son, H. Gary, until the latter's death in 2014. Now it is H. Gary's family who run things. (And whose refusal of filming privileges we were too scared to flout.) No mayor, no city council, no municipal elections in The Villages. Rather, Community Development Districts (ring a bell?) dictate how people live. The main one, the Village Center Community Development District, provides "water and sewer utility services, recreation, security services, and fire protection and paramedic services to the residents." It also taxes them without representation, funnily enough. The Villages, like Disney, promises not democracy but freedom from democracy.

The Villages is an extreme example of isolationism, certainly. But it's not as if the peregrine elderly have been embracing civic-spiritedness elsewhere in Florida. Senator Bob Graham dubbed this the "Cincinnati factor": Old people *physically* move to Florida, but emotionally they've never left Ohio. *Why raise my taxes to pay for schools, parks, roads?* they wonder. *These aren't my people. This isn't my home.* These recent immigrants have refused to assimilate, you could say.

"Florida," columnist John Rothchild wrote, "has not become a true home of those residents, but merely the penultimate resting place, a warm way station in which to relax and play golf, the blessed limbo between Cleveland and the Pearly Gates."

He's onto something. Florida's retirees have forbidden the past and future to bear on their present. They've snipped off today at both ends, like a coupon. They've abolished time in any form other than a flat collection or arbitrary sequence of moments. Their individual existences run like drag racers at a quarter-mile track: Florida → acceleration → death.

The idea of delay—especially delay of gratification—loses all meaning down here. What rules of thumb there *are,* are negative ones. Do not get too attached to this place; you are not long for it. Do not get too attached to the nice couple across the street; the less you invest in them, the less costly it will be when they (or you) go. In fact, do not think of your current resources as capital. What would be the point of fiscal responsibility in your last, golden years? You've got to rush to get rid of this foreign currency before your boarding number is called and it's time to depart.

When you get down to it, the retiree's rules of thumb are not much different from Florida Man's. Or the tourist's. The lot of them do what they do "in order to," and rarely if ever "because of."

OK? OK. This is acceptable, right? This is as it should be? The animating spirit of our great nation is, after all, a classically liberal one. Centuries ago, we decided to substitute the value of choice (as exercised by free and autonomous individuals) into the place formerly occupied by fealty to God or shared blood. We founded the first country in which the government arises *only* through the consent of the governed. We centered our political processes on the free choices of individuals; we venerated and defended the fragile institutions that make free choice possible. And, as a result, we Americans are expected to reject the past as a source of wisdom and counsel, of caution and limits. Every subsequent generation is made to understand that they must create the country anew through their choices. Who wants to receive or leave an inheritance? (A nonmonetary inheritance, that is.) The inherited is the unchosen. And the unchosen is anathema to America. Our only inheritance is the Constitution, and even *that* is perennially up for debate. Yes, yes.

These Yankee Strangers chose to leave an old world behind. It'd be un-American of me to fault them for that. What I *can* be upset about, I think, is the flip side of their animating spirit. What becomes of The Villages fifty years from now, after the current residents die out? Will it be sold off and torn down? Reimagined for contemporary tastes and chosen anew by a fresh batch of oldsters? What if Floridians like me never *chose* to come of age amid these plastic antiplaces, completely cut off from any history, community, or tradition I might like to know?

Even if I wanted to, I will never be able to gain admittance to the precursor heavens these strangers built. By the time I'm eligible for it, Social Security will have run out; the very mention of "retirement" will elicit wry smiles from my Chinese debt collectors and/or my robot overlords. The opportunity to do what these retirees have done—retreat from the world I made, ensconce myself in a secure zone of efficacy and intelligibility—I won't have it.

Most developments like The Villages are classified as belonging to an unincorporated area. This means a few things. It means the planners and residents chose not to attach themselves to any nearby municipality. Implicitly, they rejected the idea that towns and cities are where we maximize our collective potential to better solve current and future problems. Implicitly, they subscribed to a more Jeffersonian, a more neo-Lockean view of property and mutual responsibility. To them, an unincorporated area is a realm in which individuals just happen to exist proximate to one another. It is where those individuals (or the associations they choose to join) can live free and die decentralized, all while exercising their God-given right to develop their property as they see fit.

Very American. *Incredibly* Floridian: As early as the 1990 census, it was determined that more Floridians resided in unincorporated areas than incorporated ones. The trend has only accelerated.

And though it is the fourth most populous county in Florida— though at 1.5 million residents it is larger than ten American states—

Hillsborough County (county seat: Tampa) is largely unincorporated. The sprawl is such that Tampa's modest downtown housed fewer than one hundred residents until a few years ago, when a pair of towering condos went up. It needn't be said, but: Everyone here drives. Intentional pedestrians are hard to come by. What few there are get hit by cars at a rate only slightly behind Orlando's, earning Tampa the number 2 spot in terms of most dangerous places to walk in the country.

Fortunately, we made it through unincorporated Hillsborough in one piece. We kept our heads on swivels; we walked lengthy, shadeless streets full of identical houses. Our isolation was deep, and the residents' suspicion—palpable. Through smudged living-room windows, children kept their eyes trained on us while remaining still as things trapped under ice. Occasionally, a homeowner burst through their front door, strode to the edge of their lawn, and scrutinized us as though memorizing a description for the police.

Their reactions were not unjustifiable. During the housing bubble of the mid-2000s, a lot of these cookie-cutter homes around Tampa were gobbled up by people from elsewhere—by shady real estate firms, by drug dealers looking to launder money. Unscrupulous foreign investors moved many of these properties into and out of their portfolios at the speed of three-card monte dealers. For these flippers, the American Dream had nothing to do with stable home ownership; it had everything to do with trading disposable commodities the way horses were bought and sold along the frontier.

Banks didn't care either way. They were rubber-stamping loans without so much as glancing at the fine print. Mortgages couldn't be churned out fast enough for poor people with patchy credit histories. *Everybody* was getting well, from the day laborers and working-class tradespeople at the construction sites; to the lower-middle-class bank tellers; to the middle-class real estate agents, title insurance agents, and civil engineers; to the upper-middle-class land use attorneys and architects; to the crème de la crème developers.

You know what happened next. Money got too cheap. The sexy investment opportunity cooked up by whiz kid financiers in which high-yielding (yet completely safe!) assets were magically concocted out of pools of risky mortgages—investors finally started to wonder if these magical bundles of mortgages were really worth what they were supposed to be worth. Gradually and then suddenly, people doubted the reality of this perpetual-motion money machine.

When the bubble burst, a lot of unincorporated boomburgs transformed into foreclosed ghost towns. These came to be populated (if at all) by the desperate and the unsavory. By 2010, unemployment in Hillsborough had surpassed 12 percent. The residential housing market was dead. The commercial real estate market was shrinking. Formerly middle-class families were applying for what scant social services the county could provide. The less fortunate slept in cars. Growth came shuddering to a halt. It appeared as though the doomsday scenario had arrived for Tampa and the rest of the Ponzi State.

The solution offered by politicians and their real estate cronies was: double down. Hillsborough county commissioners slashed regulations and lowered impact fees in hopes of spurring new construction. Let there be more of the same! Give us helter-skelter development, or give us death!

The insane jury-rigging . . . worked. The market rebounded. Home buyers started trickling into town, lured by the Florida Dream. It was almost as if this perpetual-motion machine could never truly break.

The bad times—I guess we reminded some property holders of the bad times. For that reason, we stuck to the main drags whenever we could. There, we marched under billboards for home loans, car dealerships, accident attorneys, mortgage refinancing, cash-4-gold. We passed strips of vacant land. Countless strip malls with retail space available. Strip *clubs* as well. Oh so many strip clubs. Tampa is sultry like that, more debauched than the rest of North and Central Florida anytime outside of Spring Break. Its sex appeal isn't like South Florida's—spritzed with intrigue and jangly, rose-gold exoticism. Tampa's is more of a grunting, All-American, silk–Tommy Bahama–shirt-open-at-the-neck kind of sex appeal.

Ahead of the 2012 Republican National Convention held in Tampa, outlets like the New York *Daily News* hailed the city as the Strip Club Capital of America. It is not. That honor goes to New York City, or possibly Las Vegas by now. It just *feels* as though Tampa is the capital, because there are strip clubs packed into its incorporated and unincorporated areas alike. And to be fair, Tampa's not far off the lead: the forty-three clubs in its bay area place third in the United States per capita.

Name any tickle 'n' slap predilection you can think of, and the Tampa Bay area has got you covered. There are more than 120 erotic businesses within the incorporated city limits alone. Smut kings Seymore Butts and Dirty D call Hillsborough County home. Series like *Tampa Bukkake, Glory Hole Girlz,* and the ever-popular *Crack Whore Confessions* are shot here. The Magic Mike film franchise is set in Tampa for a reason: an XXX theater, swingers' bar, fetish club, massage parlor, or adult bookstore crouches in the corner of almost every stucco mini mall. It has been so since *Life* magazine dubbed the city the "Hell Hole of the Gulf Coast" in 1935. For the Midwesterners who settled Tampa, the unburdening of generations' worth of sexual prohibition, which had theretofore pickled their people like lutefisk brine, was apparently a big part of the appeal.

That, and Tampa boasts a legit pioneer: Joe Redner, the entrepreneur who "invented" the lap dance. "That's who you want," Noah told Glenn as we reached the Westshore business district long after nightfall. "Humble-beginnings-type mogul, always running for mayor. Sort of Tampa's answer to Donald Trump."

I agreed. It was settled. We found a Starbucks, and we set up shop, fronting like journalists.

~~~~~~

Glenn's going to be a dad!

We learned this while seated around our command center in Starbucks the other night. Glenn received a call from his wife, walked outside, walked back in with a hand to his forehead and a smeary smile on his face. "We're not sure yet," he cautioned. "Jess has had some negative tests before this positive one. So."

"*Ho-lee* shit!" Noah said. "Talk about 'from the annals of a dude not thinking through the timing of his actions.'"

Glenn kept his hand to his brow as if taking his own temperature. "I am having a Gainesville baby," he stated flatly. "I guess now I really do have to decide what I'm going to do with the rest of my life."

"And we're gonna have to get you home safely, homie!" Noah

added, brightening at the prospect of additional duty. "We're gonna have to deliver you through the gauntlet, like in the classic Clint Eastwood vehicle, *The Gauntlet*."

"This is the death throes of my youthful masculinity," Glenn said, looking to me. "How do you feel about that? You're getting the bachelor party of my prefatherhood."

"Some party," I deadpanned. I slid papers around the tabletop. "But as for the task at hand—you know, instead of waiting for his response, we could just go down to Redner's right now. Even if he doesn't want to talk then and there, we could still film some B-roll, right? Kill two birds?"

At thirty-five years old, Mons Venus is the oldest extant gentlemen's club in Tampa. Each year, a quarter million patrons pass through its doors. Some of those patrons are subscriber-connoisseurs of the Ultimate Strip Club List, which hails Mons as tops in the country. (Much lauded is the "major contact" with dancers.) Mons has been featured on the likes of *20/20*, *The Daily Show*, the documentary *Strip Club King: The Story of Joe Redner*, as well as Wyclef Jean's patron anthem "Perfect Gentleman." Truly, it is as close to a UNESCO site as these things go in Tampa: a windowless hut set back from a six-lane highway originating at MacDill Air Force Base, where U.S. Central Command carries out all of our Mideast adventures. Mons's small marquee (shaped vaguely like the female pubic mound the establishment is named after) is dwarfed by the signs of adjacent big-box stores.

Just as simple is its interior: The octagonal main stage is surrounded by chairs, padded booths, and the odd table or two. Low black lights, neon scrollwork accents, and a mirrored ceiling joined to mirrored walls combine to create a dizzying sense of lurid infinity. No booze—Tampa law prohibits alcohol in full-nude clubs. No DJ, either—the dancers play their own songs from a jukebox. Celebrities get no special treatment here, and Redner forbids any kind of champagne-room shenanigans.

"You couldn't put on closed-toed shoes, man?" Noah asked me as we paid our twenty-dollar entry fee. "You know that's the first thing they look at, right? To see who's got money?"

"Then I am doing them a favor," I said.

Mons's stable of dancers is hundreds strong, with eighty or so working most nights. Women come from all over the country to dance here, we learned. Some stay for more than a decade; many of those who leave for greener pastures return. This is because Mons is a libertarian's dream workplace. Laissez-faire as all hell. A dancer can work seven nights a week or just one. Whatever she wants; there is no fixed schedule. She can take a break for months or years and still come back, so long as Redner adjudges her to have kept up appearances. No advance notice is necessary—just stride on into the dressing room, slap on whatever accoutrements are necessary, and hop onstage when it's your turn. The rules are *there are no rules*. (Except: a three-hour minimum shift; no drugs on premises; no leaving the premises and then returning all coked out; and no probing of orifices, be they the customer's or the dancer's.)

We talked with the house madam at the front of the room. She informed us that Redner had left for the evening. Minutes later, though, Redner responded to Glenn's emails. Told us we were free to meet with him tomorrow, and that we could film in his club to our hearts' content, so long as we blurred the face of anyone who wanted the consideration.

Like the finely honed team we'd become, we deployed our cameras and mikes in two shakes. Only then did we allow our heads to bob about like birds', ninety degrees at a time, to take in the fatty excitement. We filmed what we could in the submarine gloom. Eros. Dust. Graying dads strumming the bodies of young women as though they were mere instruments. Glenn lined up artsy shots of mirrored surfaces and handsy reflections. I tried to keep my rawboned counterpart out of the frame.

That wasn't what Glenn intended. With an eye to the camera, he used his free arm to usher me forward like a parent guiding a child to the lip of a pool. He wanted me in the corners of these shots, he said. For the comedic dissonance.

It *was* funny, I gotta say. In the black light, I looked like a hobo's ghost. Quite the contrast to the lissome women whose faces went vacant the moment they took to the stage, or a man's lap. While Glenn arranged me, I watched them, and I couldn't keep from thinking: *Few of them could do this.* Could safely hit the road and chart their own pilgrim's progress. Through no fault of their own, I mean. It's just that the foremost narrative possibility our culture affords unaccompanied women on the side of the highway is not liberation, desire, *quest*—but rather rape, death, some combination of the two.

Glenn, Noah, and I don't worry too much about our presence "provoking" strangers. We are free to be obtuse. Rarely if ever do we fret about finding ourselves in a situation where we're, say, screaming into a man's palm. (Maybe Glenn does.) But deep inside Glenn, even, is the unshakable certitude that obstacles will melt if we white men but whistle. Each of us takes it for granted: *I am no one's prey.*

"I was just thinking about how many of my friends are just deep in it now," Glenn said, shouting into my ear to be heard over the music. "Fully jobbed up, one or two kids, a cottage they go to, savings in the bank."

"Well, that can be you soon enough," I shouted back.

"I used to have this desire to be, like, *'Sellouts!'* to those people. Like, 'You're too cowardly to be on the road!' When, in fact—the road sucks, dude! When, in fact—they're doing the far scarier thing."

"Good luck convincing *them* that after they've changed their ten thousandth diaper. Good luck telling *yourself* that," I said, giving him a nudge as if to say, *Look where we are.*

There were no distractions at Mons. No TVs, no food, no smoking, no drinking (though many patrons kept pinging between the parking lot and club, to partake of sneaked refreshment). The enterprise was free and pure: self-employed entrepreneurs willingly supplying a service for eager consumers. Rates for lap dances were negotiable—somewhere between twenty and thirty dollars per. Unlike many other clubs, which require a Mickey Mouse currency be used by customers and cashed out by strippers at the end of the night—Mons's transactions are one-to-one. Aside from a voluntary tip out, the dancers keep every dollar they make.

We learned much of this from Dakota, a slight blonde who was entirely nude apart from the hair extensions that extended to her butt. (In exchange for this information, she demanded a copy of the footage Glenn had shot of her contorting herself into cuneiform along the pole.) According to Dakota, a dancer can earn anywhere from five hundred to two thousand dollars a night. The house, meanwhile, collects its profit from cover charges plus whatever they make off the Red Bulls they sell. Money's good here, Dakota said, better than anyplace else—but most dancers tap out after seven years. "They go to school," she said of those who hang up their Lucite heels. "And then, if they want to, like, pay for a private preschool, they'll come back a few times for extra money."

I was reminded of why we were here. "Glenn!" I shouted. I pointed to a line of guys receiving lap dances. Smaller bodies were bobbing up and down against larger, stationary bodies; it looked like a strand of oil wells. "We're gonna need a volunteer."

Dakota took Glenn by the hand and led him to a booth. He complied sheepishly. I replaced him behind the camera. "Tarzan Boy" came over the sound system, per Noah's jukebox request. Dakota was as brisk and practiced as a nurse in her single-serving attention giving.

"One of my developing conclusions," Glenn called out while peering around Dakota's narrow shoulders, "is I'm ready for a salary. Just, an institution. Give me a ladder to climb."

"Sure," I said, zooming in on Glenn's apologetic expression. "Freedom qua freedom is never an adequate vision of the human good."

"*What?*" Glenn shouted.

"Problem is," I shouted back, "neither you nor me's got any skills."

"I'm saying it's a *realization*," Glenn hollered. "This realization opens up new problems."

Dakota returned Glenn by his elbow, geriatrically. You wouldn't know it to look at him—hunched to obscure his enthusiasm—but Glenn had been party to a crime. Technically, the "major contact" Mons is world-famous for is also illegal. Hillsborough County prohibits nude and topless dancers from performing within six feet of customers. The police could rush in at any moment and haul Dakota and Glenn off to the hoosegow. But as we'd soon discover, *nobody* wants to involve Joe Redner in a juridical dispute.

By making a show of paying for Glenn's go-round, I'd inadvertently chummed the water. Independent contractors came circling. They inveigled hard, pressuring us for dances with actual come-hither gestures. Glenn, the father-to-be, could not be made to relent a second time. Like an air-traffic controller, he directed dancers toward Noah using both of his arrowed hands. After each had finished with Noah, she was led to an empty booth by Glenn, where he and I interviewed her.

As we were doing so, a couple of sockless-loafer-ass goons approached. Upon their prompting, I recited our backstory with the speed of an auctioneer. "Huh," one said. "You boys wanna film something that'll really pack an audience?"

Absolutely not, I wished to say. *In fact, the last thing I want to do is talk with you, my russet sir, or film with you in your survivalist hidey-hole.* But instead I dissociated behind my professional facade, chewed my lip, and droned *Oh, wow!* when the man, inevitably, invited us to his sex party. He gave me a date next week as well as an address in Sarasota, an affluent town a little farther south along the Gulf Coast. Sarasota's where my father grew up; it's also where the Ringling Bros. Circus used to winter. Weird place. I told the goons we'd consider it.

A little later, Noah came by to check in with me. "We need more women in the film, that's for sure," he said. "But I don't know if, uh, strippers is gonna be the look."

"We can always come back down, film whatever we think we need," I reassured.

"We'll fix it in post!" Noah agreed, blurting our new mantra and turning away as though breaking huddle. Glenn slapped him an attaboy as he passed. Then he picked up the camera and tracked Noah in stride.

We closed down the club and joined a few dancers for a predawn breakfast at Waffle House. They showed us pictures of their kids, explained the majors they were studying at community college. Glenn filmed it all with dour professionalism. He was done celebrating; the full weight of his future was beginning to settle onto his shoulders. Sleepless, we made our way to Joe Redner.

What followed was the straitest-laced interview with a strip club kingpin you could imagine. We met Redner at his small office located within a larger warehouse complex—property he owned alongside a decent-sized portfolio of holdings around Tampa. The elderly, ponytailed impresario discussed his public-access television shows, his ongoing crusade for First Amendment rights, his many failed mayoral campaigns, his passion for social justice. We might as well have been shooting footage for a Chamber of Commerce jubilee. I had a hard time keeping my head from drooping.

Redner wore a T-shirt with Ray-Ban sunglasses hooked in the collar. His exposed skin managed to be at once tan and translucent-seeming; it appeared as brittle as an onionskin proclamation under glass. He spoke with a scratchy, adopted drawl and not infrequently referred to himself as a man "who is willing to stand up for the rights of those who are not even willing to stand up for their own rights." Nine times (and counting) he's campaigned for the mayoralty on a platform of sustainable development, high-speed rail, and healthier school lunches. He lamented that history will remember him only as the lap-dance king.

"And what makes a *you* and not a Donald Trump?" Glenn asked solemnly. I mouthed a yawn.

Redner gave us his rundown: Born in Summit, New Jersey, in 1940. Dad left when he was just a baby; mother relocated the family to Tampa. Quit school in the tenth grade, started drinking at sixteen. Worked with a carnival operator, where he learned all the classic cons. Later laid terrazzo floors, sold furniture, made tin cans in a factory. In between jobs he hustled pool in downtown Tampa dives. Eventually, he worked his way up to managing go-go bars. One night while driving home from the bar, Redner heard a bulletin on the radio that would change his life as well as the course of Tampa history: In the case of *Erznoznik v. City of Jacksonville,* the U.S. Supreme Court had ruled that a Florida drive-in theater could show movies that featured brief flashes of nudity. The justices deemed those flashes to be free speech protected under the First Amendment. Redner figured: "Dance is speech—ballet, the Indian war dances, dances in Africa. Nudity is the content of that speech, therefore it's got to be protected by the First Amendment. Christ, let's see if they really mean that." There was no law in Tampa *prohibiting* nude dancing—but no one had ever dared try it. Redner tried.

In order to combat all the legal challenges that came his way, Redner got sober and taught himself law. He pored over the books at

Hillsborough County's Law Library for six to ten hours a day, every day, for ten years. Stoking this effort was his unyielding contempt for politicians, ministers, anyone he considered a hypocrite. "They run my life, and they have no idea what they're doing," he said of these phonies. Redner scrutinized officeholders and prelates and, perceiving in not a single one of them any sign of undeniable rightness or superiority, returned to his own rationality as the most obvious and immediate source of truth. With retribution sounding a bugle call in his heart, Redner set himself over and against all that was sanctimonious in the world around him.

"I'm gay, I'm black, I'm an Indian, a Jew," he said, echoing the words he used when bringing a lawsuit against the Hillsborough County Commission after it passed an ordinance forbidding any acknowledgment of Gay Pride Month. "I'm everyone and anyone who has ever been oppressed for anything other than their bad character."

Redner and his lawyer prevailed in most every one of their cases. They also cohosted a weekly public-access call-in show called *First Freedom*. During the hour-long episodes, they discussed issues like censorship in rap music, the efficacy of the Department of Health and Rehabilitative Services, the immigration woes of professional hockey enforcer Bob Probert, the mistreatment of Haitian refugees, the legality of bungee jumping. Redner positioned himself as reformer and rebel, self-made man and defender of liberty—the Horatio Alger Americans profess to *want,* not the "real" one we ultimately received.

"Whenever I see injustice—my self-esteem is tied to it," Redner told the camera while idly running a finger over a copy of *Florida Jurisprudence: Building, Zoning, and Land Controls,* second edition, which lay open atop a highlighted printout of Instagram's decency guidelines. "My basic ethic is built around logic, reasonableness, and compassion. Don't lie, don't cheat, don't steal. And treat others like you would if the plane was going down—everyone has to put his mask on first, but then he can help others get theirs on after."

Redner could help because he's worth . . . fifty million dollars? Sixty million? He wasn't exactly sure. All he knew was he had enough lucre to stuff his cargo pants pockets with "help money," stacks of crisp blue hundreds still in their TD Bank wrappers. These, Redner dispensed to the needy on the street like a robber baron of yesteryear tossing silvers from his carriage.

While our local Larry Flynt detailed his charitable contributions, I eyeballed the books on the shelf behind him. I'd read many of them: Richard Dawkins, Christopher Hitchens, Eric Hoffer's *The True Believer: Thoughts on the Nature of Mass Movements*. There was some Tom Paine, too, and other works on the American Founding. A motley assortment, yet all of it was of a philosophical piece. All of it enjoined the reader to be free from authority, both the kind of authority that is nakedly coercive as well as the kind that operates through claims to knowledge. Redner's library argued in favor of the idea that freedom amounts to radical self-responsibility plus the primacy of noninterference. That is, freedom means letting each individual live and die as he or she desires, as though each individual had the luck to resemble no one, as if he or she were a blessed monster that came from nowhere and owed nothing to nada. Leave such monstrous individuals to themselves—this is the American Way. Seek betterment on their behalf, and you will be revenged.

"You a religious man, Joe?" I interrupted, despite knowing the answer. "Spiritual but not religious, maybe?"

When he screwed up his face, Redner looked like a sour babushka. "Minister put the cracker in my mouth, I sit there, they all chant this prayer," he said, explaining his childhood departure from the Methodist Church. "Didn't change a goddamn thing."

"How about a pillar of the community?" I asked. "Would you consider yourself one of modern Tampa's founding fathers?"

Again, he seemed taken aback. "No," Redner said. "Hell no. All those pillars of the community? They just want to tell people how to live."

He opened one of the accordion folders on his desk. He rifled through it for a filing pertaining to another embattled adult business. He gummed his lips as he did so, his mouth agitating like an old windfall apple be-wormed. "The courts," he said. "The court system is the only thing keeping us free."

Like all red-blooded patriots, Redner chooses to equate "liberty" with "license." Personal volition is *the* thing to be venerated and defended. "Bored Florida Man Uses Private Plane to Draw Giant

Radar Penis"—you do you, hero, so long as you aren't hurting anyone else in the process. Associate Supreme Court Justice Anthony Kennedy more or less codified this principle into law in a 1992 judgment: "At the heart of liberty is the right to define one's own concept of existence, of meaning, of the universe, and of the mystery of human life."

Neither political party would ever challenge this definition of liberty because neither political party quibbles with it. Individual, autonomous choice is the end-all be-all in the interpersonal realm (D), and it is likewise sacrosanct when it comes to economics (R). This is the American Dream, the Florida Dream, down to the gristle. This is what we have achieved with our experiment: the endpoint of modernity, where the freely choosing self finds meaning nowhere outside of itself.

As for those other models of liberty—the ones that came out of Athens and Jerusalem? The ones which hold that liberty is not the absence of constraint, but the exercise of self-limitation?

They can go to hell where they belong! With Redner's brand of liberty on offer, who is going to choose to adhere to some crusty, millennia-old metaphysics? Who will seek to cultivate the learned and practiced capacity to surmount self-defeating desire in order to become ever more fully what one *is*? Who's going to join hands with Aristotle and Aquinas and chant, *What makes a thing good? A thing is good when it attains the purpose for which it was created. How does a person attain it? By ordering oneself toward generous and generative relation to the Highest Good.*

Nerds and nobody, that's who! Not while "Florida Man Drinks Beer and Does Donuts on ATV as He Tells Sheriffs to 'Come and Get Me!'" Not while I can leave this room, walk a couple blocks, pay out two Hamiltons, and have a single mother grind her butt on my clothed boner at 11:00 a.m.—and then convince my heart I did a good thing because I added to her kid's college fund.

We wrapped for lunch. Redner took us to a nearby vegan joint, where in a couple weeks' time he'd be handing out Christmas "help money" to each member of the staff. Over mixed greens, he explained to Glenn, Noah, and me the particularities and loopholes of his newest legal venture: a challenge to the Florida Department of Health's rules barring individuals from growing cannabis for personal use.

"Oh, do we have ourselves a case," Redner assured us, baling quinoa with his fork.

"You ever think a day will come when filing another lawsuit—when having recourse to these lower courts—won't be enough to solve your problems?" I asked in good faith.

Redner looked at me as though I was from another dimension.

MILE 873 — GOLDEN GATE ESTATES

BARE IS THE BACK WITHOUT BROTHER BEHIND IT

Thanksgiving night, we reached Nokomis Community Park. The crickets sang, they stopped at our approach, they resumed singing when we'd passed. As we made for the park's farthest edge, we cut across a covered basketball court. In the deep shadow, we bumbled into three scabrous dudes. Glenn illuminated them with his phone light: Florida Men through and through, with tattered shorts, ponytails and beards, few teeth, rolling eyes. Each looked like a particular costume designer's idea of "Robinson Crusoe, except modern-day."

They had a certain something in a paper bag so rumpled it was velvety. At first they tried to hide this bag from us; then, reluctantly, they offered it. We demurred. They found this to be quite offensive. "When somebody's trying to hand you shit, you take it!" the head one was saying. "Nobody's handing you shit in life! You have a brain—use your brain! Don't be an idiot! God gave you a brain!" And so on.

We shrugged, moved along, made camp in a buggy copse next to some mangroves. In time, the shouting subsided. I checked my email in-box and was reminded that I am, in theory, an Ivy League professor. I wrote brief responses to the two students who were seeking letters of recommendation. I drifted off.

In the middle of the night, Glenn gave me a long, meaningful poke. I cracked an eye, saw that Glenn's own eyes were opened to a width meant to communicate alarm. I listened. The ten thousand sounds of night had hushed. Except—a rustle. A footfall. Then another. Glenn and I floated into ready positions. I felt around for the retractable baton, then remembered Noah had it last. I prayed that he, too, was getting ready to come out swinging.

"Fuck!" a voice shouted.

"Fuck! You!" a second voice added. A third voice sounded—a groan that rose to a keen. It was the Florida Men.

"God*damn*it," Noah sighed from his tent.

The lead Man began to fulminate against homosexuals. I won't relay the message. Suffice it to say that his hatefulness was raw and inventive, and left me with new gray hairs. His shadow paced our tent-front for all three minutes of his tirade. When he stopped, his shadow stopped. His silhouette just stood there, seemingly peering through the nylon.

Glenn and I held still. I glanced over at my friend. He glanced back. I half-believed that our high tension was causing our tent to light up like the glass bulb around a white-hot filament.

That's when the shadow moved for our flap. I'm pretty sure it moved for our flap. That's also when adrenaline picked me up and ushered me onward like a piece of heavy machinery caught in a storm surge. *Defend Yourself!* I thought. I burst through the flap, shrieking incoherently.

In front of me: Florida Man with the jerkied physique of an incorruptible saint. I took his ass *down*. I cinched his legs and drove him into the soft earth. As if waiting for my cue, Noah rushed from his tent, balls-ass naked and zeroing in on one of the Men who was rummaging through Jog-a-bye. With a flick of his wrist, Noah snapped open the baton. He raised it head-high and then brought it down like a large flyswatter, cracking the guy on his shoulder. The queasy *thwup*—it sounded like a wing being sheared off a raw chicken. The guy crumpled to the ground. Glenn emerged from our tent with a spotlight in one hand and his iPhone filming in the other. He ran up and gave the guy I was wrestling with a swift kick in the ribs. Then he gave him another. Seeing this, the third Man took off running. Noah took off after him.

"Fuck is you all's problem?" my guy coughed. He pushed himself

into a crouch, buried his head in his arms, and then decided to roll a couple of full revolutions away from Glenn and me. It was as though he was employing every safety maneuver he'd ever learned, one after another. "Fuck is wrong with you?" he asked again as he rolled. I could hear Noah administering a few swift kicks of his own.

"Don't touch our shit!" I screeched, still flooded with adrenaline. "Stay away from our fucking shit, man!" I made like I was gonna go after him again. The Man hopped to his feet and jogged backward.

"You all are fucked up, man!" he said as he retreated. "Wasn't touching your shit! Y'all are some fucking crazy asses, man. Fuckin', fucked up."

<hr />

We cleared a British Petroleum of its granola bars and protein snacks. We loaded up on water. "Our Boy Scout rations," Glenn called them. "All that's missing is a big Maglite and some porno," Noah agreed. The day was overcast and stale when we entered Golden Gate Estates via its one major road, Golden Gate Boulevard. There was no other avenue in or out.

Before it was Golden Gate Estates, this place was what it had always been: a muddy tract of ancient cypress and royal palms. Then two enterprising brothers, Leonard and Jack Rosen, laid eyes on it. Dollar signs danced across their field of vision. They saw an opportunity to spin swamp into gold once again, just as they'd done up the coast with Cape Coral, a 120-square-mile development adjacent to Fort Myers.

In the late fifties, the brothers had contracted dredges to drag straight lines through Cape Coral's muck, moving enough earth to fill a swimming pool every minute. This fill was then dumped and shaped into lots along the banks of the new "canals." Voilà—an instant maze of "waterfront" property! The brothers rebranded themselves the Gulf American Land Corporation, and they marketed Cape Coral as "a rich man's paradise, within the financial reach of everyone."

The Corporation dispatched high-intensity salesmen throughout the Northeast and Midwest. (The Rosen boys had experience with sales; prior to real estate, they had been in the door-to-door hair mousse game.) Their salesmen went about selling themselves as much as they sold parcels of Cape Coral. At churches' spaghetti dinners, at women's clubs' garden parties—everywhere everyone got the pitch: Put twenty dollars down now and pay twenty dollars a month, and then when you're ready to retire, lookit that! Your modern-day Venice (just south of Venice, Florida) will be waiting for you.

The Rosens expanded into television, got Bob Hope and Anita Bryant to shill for the Florida Dream. They gave away homes on *The Price Is Right*. They even expanded overseas, where Gulf American salesmen hawked the Sunshine State to very receptive audiences of Brits and Germans. Meanwhile, telemarketers did their best *Glengarry Glen Ross* impressions back home. They told prospective buyers that if they so desired, they could come on down to Cape Coral for a free stay at the company motel (where rooms were bugged so salesmen could learn how best to tailor their pitches). Prospective buyers could enjoy a steak dinner on Gulf American's dime (where paid plants at nearby tables yelled out things like "I just bought lot number eighteen!"). They could hop in one of five company Cessnas and pick out their home sites from the air à la Walt Disney, asking the accompanying salesman to drop a bag of flour onto the lot they liked (which was rarely the lot that ended up in their paperwork).

The Rosens' Cape Coral gambit was beautifully orchestrated and flawlessly executed. What it was *not* was on the level. It was a Ponzi scheme. The brothers took people's money, built shoddy houses, then showed off the fast-growing expanse of shoddy houses to new investors. The brothers took *those* people's money, built a yacht club, and the country's largest rose garden, and a dancing fountain known as the Waltzing Waters—then showed off the amenities to new investors. On and on it went with tier after tier of dupes.

The brothers never intended to build a *real* community. This, buyers discovered as soon as they moved in. There were no schools, churches, or hospitals to be found in Cape Coral. No water or sewer infrastructure, no direct access to the interstate, no pristine beaches. To this day, Cape Coral lacks for higher education, office space, a commercial tax base of any kind. It lacks for everything, really, except grids of stagnant canals and single-family homes.

And yet, and yet. Even when buyers realized they'd been played, they stayed put.

In confidence artistry, you call this "wizening the mark." You made a fool of another party, sure—but more importantly, you left them with a lesson. You showed them how readily they'd believed certain stories. Certain false narratives about the world; about themselves. After flattering them—*Only you are smart enough to act on this once-in-a-lifetime opportunity*—you unmasked their delusion and hypocrisy. After telling them exactly what they wanted to hear—*You deserve paradise, and you deserve it at little or no cost*—you exposed their calculative thinking for what it was: a selfish and transactional attitude toward the world.

You could say that in wizening the mark, you do the mark a kind of service. You send him or her back into the world a little less wide-eyed. A little more mature. The mark can now see past the surface of things. And some marks, having been so disabused—they come to take satisfaction in watching other people fall for the same scam.

Today, the Rosens' development boasts 154,305 residents. The Cape Coral–Fort Myers area has recorded America's most explosive population growth two years running, as well as a total of five years out of the last thirteen. Areas just like it—Deltona Lakes, developed between Orlando and Daytona Beach in 1962 by the Mackle brothers; as well as rat poison king Lee Ratner's Lehigh Acres; as well as razor-blade baron Abraham L. Mailman's Miramar—are expanding almost as quickly.

Having succeeded wildly once, the Gulf American Land Corporation expected to succeed wildly once again with Golden Gate Estates. The slapdashing brothers schemed even bigger this go-round, digging 183 miles of canal and paving 880 miles of road out of a Boston-sized chunk of the Fakahatchee Strand, the westernmost area of the present-day Everglades. "America's largest subdivision," they called it, envisioning a day when 500,000 marks would populate their 111,000 acres in the middle of nowhere. As per their MO, the Rosens built a few model units. They cajoled the first wave of visitors into believing that Golden Gate could be home.

This time, however, the Ponzi scheme stalled at the first stage. For you see, these unfortunate early investors bought their parcels during the winter, which is the Everglades's dry season. When they arrived during the spring, summer, and fall, they discovered that their parcels were literally underwater.

While nearby boomburgs boomed, Golden Gate moldered like the scum in its canals. Instead of investors, its most frequent visitors tended to be drug smugglers landing South American DC-3s on the development's desolate roads. Nowadays, the Estates is a ghost town haunted by abandoned houses, creeping swamp life, and the occasional meth syndicate. Otherwise known as: compelling documentary footage.

Branching off either side of the main boulevard were many empty lots as well as moldy old ranch homes with attached Quonset huts. Or: moldy ranch homes with big rigs in the yard; with a half dozen rusted-out Corvettes sprinkled around the property; with Mesozoic thistle bushes swallowing the garage and inground pool; with a family of unleashed Rottweilers on the prowl. An anti-Seaside, in other words, where there are no homeowners' associations and pretty much anything goes re: land use. Golden Gate Estates, we learned, is home to those who wish to drop off the grid, as well as those who can't afford anything else.

We stopped at the one shopping plaza amid the slippery landscape. We ate pizza at the Hungry Howie's, we filmed interviews in front of Fayard Hardware. *Why are you here?* "I'm a good ol' boy, man. This is it for me." *Did you know what you were getting into?* "No gas stations for miles, Walmart's an hour's drive, hospitals are another hour's drive. Yeah, I knew it. Not a bad place if you understand where you're living. I got two campers, and I'm not paying to put them in storage. I don't like somebody telling me how to do everything." *Do you know your neighbors?* "No way. In the Estates you need to respect others' land; everyone has guns and are waiting to use them. Going into someone's land or house is asking for a gunshot wound. And everyone knows that, so you're certain to know your land will also be respected."

Gingerly, very gingerly, we proceeded east and south into the underdeveloped development. We tallied the empty shotgun shells and syringes. We wondered how long the police response time would be. "Hour and fifteen, easy," Noah ventured. We choked on the cheesecloth atmosphere and were driven half-mad by the pulsing sound of insects.

"An ibis has been following along the canal next to us," I said. "Flies ahead, lands, waits, does it again. You been noticing this?"

"Yup," Noah said.

"You think it is auguring our doom?" Glenn asked.

"Yup," I said.

Here, we (gingerly) approached homeowners as they worked on their cars or did bench presses on their front lawns. We captured a kind of home ownership that felt true (or tru*er*) to contemporary American reality. These few citizens were recent immigrants, poor whites, and retirees whose status as property holders was unstable, to say the least. Their dwellings were continually encroached upon, constantly in danger of going under. (Dead fish were here and there washed up on the roads.) The swamp was coming at them from six sides. The banks were, too, in many cases. Nothing seemed to sleep here, much less dream.

And yet, and yet. Growth experts have been advising local politicians to expect several hundred *thousand* new Floridians to move into and around Golden Gate Estates in the next two decades, doubling the county's current population of 339,000. This despite the fact that life expectancy in the United States is falling, infant mortality is rising, the real median hourly income hasn't budged since 1971, more Americans die of drug overdoses each year than were lost in the Vietnam War, anxiety and depression are ubiquitous, social media are driving children to suicide, schoolteachers are considering bearing arms, real cooking is a luxury, personal fitness is a marker of class distinction, terms like "gig economy" and "precariously employed" not only exist *but are useful,* healthcare bankrupts anyone who isn't independently wealthy, the waters are marshaling offshore, Noah is out of work, Glenn is definitely going to drop his baby, and I am in debt up to my fucking eyeballs—despite all of this, the lure of Florida lives on.

It seems as though you don't even need to sell people on this unplanned, untenable boondoggle anymore. The spell now inheres in the place itself, is foundational, like a curse carved into an archway. ("All sense abandon ye who enter here.") If only the Rosen boys could've lived to see it. Their scam of a city proves William Jennings Bryan's maxim about Miami, which is really a maxim about Florida: "Miami is the only city in the world where you can tell a lie at breakfast that will come true by evening."

The green inferno was humid to the point of hindered exhalation. "It's December, and the sweat can't even leave my body," I announced. Noah kicked over a rotted mailbox. A fat man on a mufflerless Harley grumbled past, the uneven road causing his jowls to flap like the slack in a skydiver's jumpsuit. "Where could he possibly be going?" Glenn asked rhetorically.

Darkness descended. Like prehistoric hunter-gatherers, we became afraid. Hurriedly, we pushed through thickets, seeking one dry spot to camp. While bushwhacking, we chanced onto what appeared to be a foreclosed home. "Oh, Jesus, no," Glenn pleaded. "I don't even care about deportation anymore. I just don't want to die like this."

Yet he did not break stride while casing the joint with Noah and me. The house was a mustard-colored single-story; didn't look *that* desolate. We approached it from the rear, where we found a couple of shot-apart toilets. "In Golden Gate Estates," Noah half-joked, "no one can hear you scream." We came around front. Roofing tiles were heaped atop a cracked apron of cement that led into an open garage.

"So, what are we thinking?" I asked, pointing my chin at the open door in the corner of the garage. "Are we going to find runes on the walls painted with human blood? A pile of VHS snuff films?"

"Only one way," Noah said, charging ahead.

And, yeah, the house was full of junkie leavings. But it was shelter, so we took it. Outside, the extravagant prodigality of space winked to life. Inside, mosquitoes bounced against the ceiling like Ping-Pong balls in a lottery machine. Once or twice, animals squealed in the deep. A gun or two popped off in the distance.

We did not keep our ears perked for the alarming creak. In fact, we sank into sleep with as little resistance as bodies buried at sea. Fear, you know—fear begins and ends with the desire to be secure. I understand this now. Fear arises out of a yearning to be certain. Fear is me wanting to know for sure, once and for all, that I am on solid ground. And if there's one thing this place has taught me, it's how to make peace with fluidity.

As I rode theta waves into dreamless slumber, I smiled at the thought: *Imagine the delusions this land has absorbed.*

It swallowed the Spaniards' ambition. That much is certain. They reported to their king in 1570 that the South Florida saw grass marshland was "liable to overflow, and of no use." In 1845, the U.S. Treasury Department judged it "suitable only for the haunt of noxious vermin, or the resort of pestilential reptiles." Henry James took one look at the swamp in 1904 and declared it "Byronically foolish."

This is the mire I sprang from. The first Americans to spend much time in South Florida—the soldiers who chased the Seminoles into the Everglades in the 1830s—denounced the whole region as "hideous," "loathsome," "diabolical." It was "God-abandoned." "The poorest country that ever two people quarreled for," one army surgeon wrote. "It was the most dreary and pandemonium-like region I ever visited, nothing but barren wastes." Another officer pithily summed it up as "swampy, low, excessively hot, sickly and repulsive in all its features." Future president Zachary Taylor swore that he would not trade a square foot of Michigan or Ohio for a square mile of Florida.

The one reason South Florida remained so hellish and so empty for so long: water. Time was, the Everglades watershed began just south of Orlando with the Kissimmee River winding 103 miles to Lake Okeechobee. The lake then spilled water through seepage, springs, and overflow down the entirety of the southern peninsula, eventually passing into Florida Bay and the Gulf of Mexico. Couldn't much farm on that. Certainly couldn't build a lasting city.

The Glades appeared to be *useless,* malignantly so. This was a terrible affront to the tycoons and grifters who arrived in the nineteenth century. Some of these men had already made fortunes out of their refusal to accept the limits imposed by nature. Why should Florida's great southern swamp be any different?

"Land reclamation," they termed it. As in, reclaiming property that had been lost or stolen. In 1881, Hamilton Disston purchased 4 million acres of swampland with an eye toward draining them, *improving* them, transforming them into "the market garden of the earth." He failed. Governor Napoleon Bonaparte Broward also tried to establish an "Empire of the Everglades"—and failed. It wasn't until the middle of the American Century that the glaucous sheets of water began to recede. The technological wizards in the Army Corps of Engineers managed to build a thirty-foot-high dike around Lake Okeechobee. South of the dammed lake, they portioned the former

Everglades watershed into the Everglades Agricultural Area, which was planted with heavily subsidized, heavily pollutive sugarcane fields. East and south of the EAA were the euphemistically named Water Conservation Areas: hypersaline holding tanks compartmentalized by a maze of canals and levees that increased in total length from 440 miles in 1929 to around 1,500 miles in 2002. Water from these Areas is regularly pulsed out to sea in lieu of the gentle, rain-driven sheet flow that once sustained the ecosystem.

The Everglades used to be the actual world of South Florida. Now, the River of Grass is drained and paved and one-fifth its former size. Most of its remaining freshwater gets diverted to the sugar plantations and thirsty South Florida cities that displaced it. There's so little freshwater left that salt water is seeping through the underlying limestone, infiltrating the swamp. To combat this, Congress approved the largest-ever environmental restoration project back in 2000—but virtually no progress has been made in the intervening years.

What *has* happened is the Everglades got named a World Heritage Site, an International Biosphere Preserve, a Wetland of International Importance. Even as it is cut up, choked, and poisoned by man, the Everglades is labeled "wilderness," is declared a cherished island in the polluted sea of liquid modernity.

This weird dualistic tendency of ours—saying that *this* here is nature, but *that* over there is an overgrown lot—I believe to be most misguided. It alienates us from our surrounds and obscures our origins as animals, as collections of cells, as interconnected creatures. There is no primal state one can point to and call "nature." Nature is everything, or nature is nothing.

Marking off the Everglades with velvet ropes, treating it as though it were a precious museum piece—it puts nature and humanity at opposite ends of the spectrum. By imagining that the Everglades is something entirely separate from us, we forgive ourselves the world we inhabit around its edges. *It's not like my lawn is a rare hardwood hammock, so I'm going to go ahead and drain my radiator into it.* We become dismissive or even contemptuous of that which *isn't* designated "wilderness." Like the Romantics before us, we privilege certain parts at the expense of the whole—the mountaintop is more exalted than the marsh, the crashing cliffside is nearer to the godhead than the level plain. The shrinking swamp is more significant than the subdivisions carved out of it.

That is, *we* get to say when nature's "nature." (Indeed, when one retreats into the "nature" of Everglades National Park, one is retreating into a product of the human civilization one is seeking to escape.) In this way, we agree with René Descartes, the Founding Fathers' founding father, who believed that humans should "render ourselves the masters and possessors of nature." According to this instrumentalist view, nature is here to help us invent an "infinity of applications" which will not only enable us to enjoy the good life without effort, but will also emancipate us from "an infinitude of maladies both of body and mind." Someday, these "applications" will even allow us to transcend the limits of our own human nature, freeing us from "the infirmities of age" and "rendering men wiser and cleverer than they have hitherto been." As for the raw material that made it all possible, well—we have "dominion" over it, Descartes would say. If we want to grant a reprieve to certain portions of it, so be it. It's our call. We can let an area be useless "wilderness." We can grant it permission to become "nature."

My friend, we are all *of* nature, and we're in it, too. All the time. No matter what. It's a trite-seeming thing to say, but it stands reminding. The natural world is not over there, away from our human one, a pure but vanishing Eden. Nature's not civilization's opposite, a refuge or an antidote. Nature's not the name for the place where humans aren't.

So no, we don't save the swamp by isolating it. We save the Everglades (to say nothing of the state of Florida) by conforming our way of being to *it*. We repent in the old sense of the word: "turn away from." We about-face. Realize we've gone astray, and correct course. We accept that Florida is a wild place, and always will be.

~~~~~~~

We continued south and east for another day, filming as we went. I demanded more breaks than usual, as the plantar wart on my heel has spawned two lackey warts. Their triplicate pain is getting to be too much to bear. These warts bleed. They force me to alter my already comical posture and gait; this altered gait causes me to suffer new muscle and joint discomfort; this discomfort forces me to alter my posture and gait again; till here I am with ankles that have swelled to the circumference of Quaker Oats canisters.

"If I could just fly home, or die," Glenn said dreamily. "Either one would be acceptable at this point."

"Both're still on the table," Noah responded.

The empty grid of Golden Gate roads stretched into the Big Cypress Basin. Palms, pines, and oaks shagged either side of the crushed lime rock, lining up thin rails of jaundiced storm cloud overhead. Structures of any kind grew sparser and thus more sinister-seeming. The monotony was labyrinthine. It felt as though we were trapped in an endlessly rotating record groove. Or a subroutine that could not stop repeating its code because it had been programmed never to halt:

```
def florida ():
print ("Fuck you, Imma do me!")

print ("Can we base a society on nothing but atomized
individuals?")
florida ("Fuck you, Imma do me!")

print ("Can we base a society on atomized individuals asserting
nothing but their rights?")
florida ("Fuck you, Imma do me!")

print ("Can a society based on atomized individuals' rights
survive without corresponding duties?")
florida ("Fuck you, Imma do me!")

print ("How long before a society of atomized individuals
rightfully following only their desires, heedless of what they owe
others, destroys itself?")
florida ("Fuck you, Imma do me!")
```

Very suddenly in the early afternoon, rain fell with tropical force. Inside a minute or two, the water completely swamped the road. We tried to force our way into nearby foliage; this proved as difficult as trying to walk through a privacy hedge. Instead, we constructed a lean-to out of tarps and jackets. There we huddled watching fat drops hit standing water so hard that the ground appeared to be firing back at the sky. Glenn aimed the camera at me. "There he is, folks," he said. "The Grinch who stole my life." We laughed.

We waited out the frog strangler. All around us was a roiling cauldron until . . . it wasn't. The rain stopped as if a spigot had been turned. In rushed the voiceless hymn of silence, too seldom heard on this walk. We took a few moments to shake off our tarps.

I was wringing water from my mullet when Noah made another noise I didn't know he was capable of: a grotesque and immediate bating of his breath, something like if his heart had been stopped by thrombosis. Without turning to me, he grabbed the collar of my shirt. He twisted it around his fist. With his left hand, he pointed.

A Florida panther had materialized on the road and was padding toward us. I, too, gasped audibly. The endangered cat was sleek, golden, low to the ground. Like any luminary glimpsed in real life, it was both smaller than expected and more exaggerated in its features: steeply angled brows, neon-yellow eyes. The panther loped with protracted grace as though not subject to our laws of physics. I don't know what else to say. I was experiencing sheer existential surprise, which has shuddered through me once, maybe twice before—and both of those times I'd classify as religious experiences.

Paralyzing fullness. Intimate strangeness. One unambiguous touch lasting for one beat of my heart. I cannot speak to this occurrence directly, but at best analogously: Happening across this panther at this moment on this day was like being reminded of something rather than being informed. The world need not be as it is. It need not be at all. But it *is*, and that is a mystery to be contemplated with gladness and praise.

The panther veered off the road. It vanished as instantaneously as it had appeared. My revelation slipped away with it.

Snapped out of our trance, we fumbled for our gear. We were too late, but so what. We got to work resetting the scene for the dramatization.

We woke the next day to cashed batteries, which effectively ended our stay in Golden Gate Estates. We began the long double-back to the entrance. After some relatively quiet morning hours—"relatively" because the flora was seething like a kitchen timer counting down—we heard an all-terrain vehicle growling toward us a bit after noon. When it hove into view, we saw the ATV was being driven by a shirtless young white guy. Prison-tatted like our shrimp friend Wesley, this guy put me in mind of a Peter Matthiessen line: "Most of our old Glades pioneers was drifters and deserters from the War Between the States who never got the word that we was licked." This guy sped past while swiveling his head to keep eyes on us.

I shouted, "Where you going?"

"Runnin'!" he called back through the dust and fumes.

Did he catch up with us later? Oh yeah. Did he, after hearing our shpiel, invite us to his family's nearby property? Uh-huh. Did we accept his invitation less out of curiosity than out of a very strong desire to have all our shit loaded onto a Chevy Silverado and then driven to the entrance of the Estates? You bet.

On an unsignatured plot of swamp, his family had marked their X: cinder-block home with a dilapidated trailer out front. Out back: some old circular saw blades, earthmoving equipment, and a lean-to stacked with planed wood, all of it spread out like stations in a boxing gym. We kicked our way around the compound, running our hands along boards and testing our fingertips against the edges of honed tools. We saw some rows of vegetables, a shade house, and a decent-sized marijuana grow operation. Milling about that were a few more young adults who glowered like they might go for my floating rib if I made a false move. An older woman came out of the house, told them to relax, and they did.

Noah knew how best to play this particular instrument, so he did most of the talking. Thanks to him—and the lure of the recharged camera—we were joshing with everyone in no time. The older woman used to work on cattle ranches in Central Florida before retiring a few years ago. One of the men (no names, thank you) supplemented his modest drug income by diving for centuries-old cypress logs at certain spots along the Gulf Coast. "Places where, when there was a timber industry there, they used to load the logs, but then some of 'em would get jammed up and sink."

"So you salvage them?" I asked. "And it's finders keepers?"

"You think the state, the federal government, or the paper company is gonna go to the trouble—is gonna file all the licenses—to dredge this wood up?" the youngster scoffed.

The growers took turns monologuing into Glenn's camera. "See, what you do is," the ATV guy said, stepping between the others and the camera. "What you do is, after laying eggs, the turtle, you flip the turtle over. They can't even move. So you flip 'em over. Then you throw 'em in the truck. Then you drive down the beach to the next one."

"Sea cow, and the porpoise—you did it back then when you was young," the older woman explained. "Because that way, you had something to eat!"

"There's not a lot of meat in a turtle," a second grower said, putting a hand on the ATV guy's shoulder. He pulled himself level and then past the ATV guy on his way to the lens. "You'd think it's full of meat, but it's not."

"Like a little cone-shaped piece of meat," the ATV guy said, drawing nearer.

"Just the flippers, the neck, and the tail," the other said, pulling ahead.

"And that's it," ATV guy agreed, shouldering past the other grower, filling Glenn's frame completely.

"Rest of it's guts, yup," the other said, dropping his hand from the ATV guy's shoulder as though conceding defeat.

They continued in this vein for a while, rationalizing how they could love the things that made possible their economic and social freedom while simultaneously destroying those things through acts which (supposedly) revealed their love for them. I'd delve further into these rationalizations, as well as our time spent drinking their beers, riding their ATV, shooting their guns—but, c'mon. You've heard this song. The growers were Redner without the money and legal chutzpah. They were Cassadaga mediums without the emotional intelligence and flimflam aptitude. They're distantly related to Captain Dale, yessir, uh-huh. They're just some more Floridians, is what I mean.

We dealt with them not as subjects but as ends in themselves. It was nice. We listened to their many yarns about life in the Estates for no other reason than we wanted to. Which was incredible, they emphasized. Life in the Estates was incredible. True freedom. Could do whatever you wanted. Which was for the most part mudding, they emphasized. They loved to rip apart boggy vacant plots with their ATVs and trucks. That was the best part of life in the Estates, if you asked them. Though they needed new cameras for when they record themselves when they go. And they'd noticed me and Noah carrying around GoPros. Mightn't we be willing to trade?

Because we had been using our phones more and our GoPros less (and because I was the one who'd purchased them), I said OK, show us your wares.

Scrap, miscellany—their property was like a junk drawer mixed with a trailer park pawnshop. Scattered here and there were genuine bits of desiderata (read: knives) that Noah thought might aid us in our voyage into the Everglades. I, however, had eyes for but one thing: the mobility scooter in the garage.

She's all electric, the growers told me. Forty inches long, only twenty-seven inches wide. Three (3) pneumatic tires: a big sixteen-incher up front and two four-inch wheels in back. Baby looked something like a Big Wheel for the infirm. Rear-wheel drive, too, meaning it could scoot up to fifteen miles per hour. And range? She topped out at twenty-five miles on a single charge. Comes complete with handbrake. Front basket. Headlight. They'd even include the charging cable, they said, which is compatible with the standard electrical hookups provided throughout the Everglades' campgrounds.

"Hmm," I responded, pinching my chin and pretending as though I wasn't elated by the prospect of scooting across the swamp instead of fording it peg-legged like Ahab.

I pulled Noah aside. I hissed into his ear, *"Look, man, I know. But I am absolutely taking it."*

Because I am a master haggler in addition to an expert logistician, I convinced the growers to throw in a half ounce of the magic mushrooms I'd espied in a corner of their hothouse. "Unless you don't want the memory cards that're in the cameras?" I said. They handed over several baggies' worth. The caps weren't as gold as you'd like, and the stems weren't as bruised blue as you'd hope, but what can you do. I was now ready to tackle the squirming, yelping, rampant morass to the east.

We retrieved Glenn from the circle of swole pitbulls walk-hopping around him in the front yard. We loaded our gear plus the new addition into the growers' truck. A truck not too dissimilar from the one that almost sent us pinwheeling outside of Gainesville, Noah noticed. As we reversed out of the driveway, the older woman hollered, "Y'all so free!" She waved. "Don't you forget that. Hey, camera, make sure they don't forget that. Y'all so free!"

MILE 957 ⸺ THE EVERGLADES

WHERE HUNGER IS THE UNSTATED CORE,
AND DYING THE PROXIMATE REALITY

In a way, I thought as I throttled my mobility scooter, *we are what perfect agency looks like to a certain kind of despairing adult.*

I can see it in their faces when they drive by. They catch sight of us, they put two and two together, and they light up like they've just learned heaven is real. To these individuals, we represent a blessed state of being. A hereafter they might ascend to, God willing, once their obligations have been seen out or abandoned. Oh, to be an itinerant gadabout! An RVless RVer navigating a post-responsibility paradise where every day is novel and serendipitous. An unattached, uncommitted, unconfined, unconstrained, unimpeded, unobstructed, unregulated, untrammeled self walking the earth, meeting others face-to-face, getting into adventures along the way like Caine in *Kung Fu*. These despairing adults cheer to us and, in so doing, cheer to their own potentiality.

Then there's the *other* kind of despairing adults. To them, three flighty men, an eldercycle, and a jogging stroller full of film gear represents something else entirely: a condensed symbol of every last pathology that has spread throughout this nation as though vectored by the interstate highway system.

These other despairing adults *also* use their faces to communicate their feelings vis-à-vis us. As well their car horns, their hands, and their passengers' bare asses.

Glenn kicked a crispy snakeskin at me from the opposite shoulder of the Tamiami Trail. I came to.

"You know," I said. "Passing a, like, certified public accountant's office in a mini mall? I no longer think that's a sad thing. A sad, drab life."

"Wisdom from the scooter," Noah said, pushing Jog-a-bye behind me.

"No, I understand them now," I said. "Those lives seem remarkably sensible to me."

"They seem like reasonable lives that a person would want to live?" Glenn called out sarcastically. A sedan sped by while straddling the two lanes' dividing line, equidistant from us.

"Comfortable," Noah said. "Safe. Not along the side of the highway, where there are vipers."

"The offices don't seem like crypts for complacency or insufficient ambition," I explained. "Actually, they seem like monuments to love. You know? The small, thankless sacrifices that it takes to love and provide."

Noah made a raspberry. Glenn joked, "No, tell us more about love, you cretin."

"Fuck you guys," I said. "You know what I'm talking about."

"Yeah," Noah said.

"Yeah," Glenn said.

We lapsed into silence. We passed more Drive Carefully crosses planted in front of the guardrails that were holding back the swamp. Beyond them: lattices of mangroves drinking deeply from teak water. Golden saw grass prairie as far as the eye could see.

As its name suggests, the Tamiami Trail connects Tampa and Miami with 275 miles of L-shaped road. The north-south portion of the L was easy; the west-east, not so much. Prior to the completion of the Trail's Everglades leg in 1928, no road linked South Florida's coasts. Clearing crews had to slash through rank vegetation in order to lay rails for the drilling crews behind them. The drillers used sixteen-foot bits mounted on railway cars to bore deep holes along the proposed route. Blasting crews followed them, clearing out each hole with ten to forty sticks of dynamite. In the end, it took some 2,584,000 sticks of dynamite—thirty or forty boxes daily—to blast a way through the swamp. Dredging crews scooped this sludge in big metal dippers and piled it onto the Trail route, creating thoroughfare and canal simultaneously. The last workers in this procession were the road crews, who graded the Trail flat with tractors.

The two-lane highway was a huge success. It even brought the Seminole and Miccosukee Indians out of hiding. At first, they sold handicrafts along the roadside. In a few years' time, they became airboat pilots, alligator wrestlers—they became sideshow attractions. They built up tourist empires, they learned the ins and outs of politics, they mastered that grandest of American pastimes, governmental lobbying. In practically no time, they became the first Native tribes to win the right to run casinos. They grew fantastically wealthy—to the point where the Seminoles now own every last Hard Rock Cafe in the world.

As we walked, the mangroves chittered and the grasses stirred. Creatures ducked, hid, dove into the water. Alligators leapt from the Tamiami Trail's berm like swimmers off the starting block. If they were already in the drink, they slowly submerged.

"Smells like vaguely diluted diarrhea," Glenn said while tying a bandanna around his nose and mouth.

"That's probably not helping things," Noah responded, pointing to a fly-studded alligator decaying on the shoulder. The left half of its body had been crushed, most likely by a car traveling late at night, when the cold-blooded reptiles leave the water for the residual warmth of the asphalt. A swoosh of dried blood led from it to the middle of the highway.

"It really is just a soggy carousel of murder out here," Glenn noted.

Early December, and still the pitiless downpouring sun was lording over us. No reprieve on the way, either—the sky was empty of clouds. Occasionally a breeze flared up, and amid the waving blades of saw grass I could see the water's rocking reflection of blue. Off to the south of the Trail, a handful of buzzards were drifting down, down like flakes of stirred-up sediment.

Piloting the scooter took some getting used to. I don't know if the growers had tampered with the steering column or what, but the tiller on this baby was as responsive as a Formula 1 car's control yoke. I had to be extra careful when I felt a cough or sneeze coming on—one involuntary twitch to the right, and I went reeling across both lanes. Fortunately, I've spent months behind the bar of a shopping cart, a baby carriage, and a jogging stroller. The muscle memory is there. I can lean over these handlebars just the same, use my body weight to keep her steady as she goes.

I had excuses at the ready, but no police stopped us. The law enforcement presence in Everglades National Park is light; plus, officers patrol an area that is larger than Delaware. What's more, traffic on the Tamiami Trail is now a fraction of its former volume thanks to the "Alligator Alley" leg of Interstate 75, which was built out in the eighties. We saw more roseate spoonbills than Miccosukee PD cruisers.

"Did you know ninety percent of the wading bird population has disappeared in the last fifty years?" Glenn said, reading grim statistics from his phone. "Only two percent of the original Everglades ecosystem is truly intact."

Our shadows lengthened considerably. Magic hour had come for the Glades, and we were still a ways from the next campground. I led the charge past wet-black alligators lining the highway. They looked like close allies of geology. We avoided eye contact with these grinning dullards as though we'd ventured onto their gang territory. We focused instead on the bristling saw grass. Over there—a hardwood hammock floating between sky and tinseled water. Look right, and the ibises whitening a solitary tree took off in a single body. In doing so, one dropped a dead fish into our path. Its eye had been eaten out.

I'd like to call this beauty "otherworldly," but that would not be correct. This beauty was absolutely of this world. Of the *fundamentals* of this world. Heartbreaking beauty like this will remain long after there is no heart left to break for it.

⁓

When we broke camp at dawn, rags of fog were caught in cypress branches. Behind them in the Trailside canal, a flock of large birds could be heard taking off, fluttering a few dozen feet, alighting, taking off again. The sound made by the movement of their wings was something like oxygen being bellowed into a fire. Relative humidity: 97 percent.

The rising sun swatted away cloud cover as though it were a skein of cobwebs. We overtook a family of Miccosukee drifting in the canal. Subconsciously I reverted to stereotype, held up a "how" hand without (fortunately) saying "how." Noah and Glenn followed my lead for some reason. The father stood in the canoe, which tippled not at all, and asked, "Wanna buy some crabs?" "Nah, bro, thanks," Noah said.

An hour or two into the day's work, and we'd settled into our state of mindful no-mind like weavers at the loom. Blankly we stared into the future while advancing east toward Miami. Trucks rushed by, gusting mosquitoes off of us for a tail-swat's worth of time. Miles distant, powerful airboats sheared through prairie; as far away as they were, we could feel the vibrato of their engines in our ribs. Another mashed python had dragged itself under a guardrail to die. All we needed was a panther, and we'd have our Everglades roadkill bingo: gator, water moccasin, osprey, python, big cat.

Eyeing us sidewise from the tall grass as if from a pulpit were many gaunt wood storks, the bird world's reverend sirs. I was trying— honestly, I was—to unpucker my soul and allow the beauty of this place to pierce me once more.

Ergo, I scarfed two handfuls of 'shrooms.

I chewed them, holding the acrid cud on my tongue as long as I could stand. These doses I chased with swallows of half-evaporated spigot water from a crunched Zephyrhills bottle. Here I should mention that I'd stopped supping from our stash of protein bars. Likewise, I'd grown tired of Pemmican brand dehydrated meats. For all intents and purposes, I had been fasting these past couple of days.

Being no dummy, I pulled my scooter off the shoulder. I drove through the mown grass between road and guardrail. I asked Noah if he wouldn't mind keeping his mitts on or nearby the two push handles in back of my ride. He said he'd try his best to keep me from drifting into traffic. "We'll create a sacred space together, voyager," he deadpanned. He was grateful for the entertainment.

In the beginning was aesthetic experience. The swamp tilted slightly on its axis, as though shifting into an italicized version of *the Everglades.* Colors became more saturated: lush greens, golds like angel hair. I almost understood the prophet birds as they shrieked their messages and took to the air ahead of me. I found it difficult to remain seated. I had a strong desire to flee from anything made of plastic or rubber, and also to undress.

Time expanded, as if time had unbuttoned its pants after a long day. Half an hour, an hour passed. I remained firmly in control of my craft, so I gobbled a few more caps and stems. "Easy there, kemosabe," Glenn cautioned. I closed my eyes and saw his words streak past me like shooting stars. "You're filming this, right?" I asked. I opened my eyes and watched a Tercel inch toward me like a periwinkle fist in search of a bump. I understood on a subatomic level that I was living between immensities. For no more than a fraction of sidereal time. In a world that I—you—we did not make.

My duty, I saw, was to the present moment.

KENT

(over shoulder to Glenn)

You ready for a take?

GLENN (O.S.)

Hit me.

KENT

I feel really Floridian in this moment. I'm seeing only the present, having forgotten the past and taken care not to think about the future. The present. My duty is to the present.

GLENN (O.S.)

Nice. Got it.

I leaned my head back, stared into the gas-flame-blue sky. I could feel my coldness, my separateness melting away as though I were thawing out of a block of ice. I turned and nodded at a wake of vultures dotting a staff of power lines like musical notation.

KENT

It's crazy, right? These people, driving somewhere, like they're failing to realize what the whole *point* is.

NOAH

Oh boy.

KENT

The great mistake is thinking that one is alone. Uniquely alone. And that that condition is permanent.

The thin familiar film was peeling aside. A bell had been rung—was still ringing—and its waves of deep sonority were passing through me, reviving memories of a place well beyond. I tasted an internal and external harmony the likes of which Saint Francis is reputed to have achieved.

KENT

Every time we turn over the ignition or, like, take two extra ketchup packets—we are feeding quarters into a machine that kills us and—Hold on.

GLENN (O.S.)

Get more spiritual. Give me some God. Give me something like . . . the mushrooms are giving you *Koyaanisqatsi* pangs for the Gaia Mother.

I took Glenn's direction. For more than a few moments, I tried to collect my thoughts. It was as difficult as hugging water to my chest in the deep end of a pool.

KENT

—that kills us, profanes our dead, poisons our children-to-be. We're asserting our appetites without regard to the whole! And you or me asserting our appetites without regard to the whole—that is never not wrong. Confusing my self with the outside world—that is what we used to call sin.

I reclined on my scooter, pleased.

GLENN (O.S.)

Ehhh. You can do better.

I sighed. Minutes later, I bent forward and turned my head to the camera.

KENT

The stakes are real. Environmentally. Spiritually. There's mercury in our Lenten fish! Our moral and economic debt, having accumulated for quite a while now, is coming due. What yo—lee Jesus! Get that!

I was seeing, a dozen feet from the Trail, a pair of wings flapping on either side of an alligator's jaws. The long white wings went slack, and then they draggled like unmanned oars.

KENT (CONT'D)

That's there, right?

NOAH

Oh yeah. Real as hell.

GLENN (O.S.)

Try saying, "Real as climate change."

NOAH

Oh, yeah. Real as climate change.

GLENN (O.S.)

Well done.

NOAH

Eat shit, Julian.

I well know that drug-induced "spiritual" experiences are basically a kind of metaphysical pornography. A gross simulacrum of the real thing that, after you see it out, leaves you feeling emptier. And as is the case with pornography, an overreliance on drug-induced "spiritual" experiences can only result in a roaming unrest that ultimately despairs of and actually *resents* the real transcendence one is seeking. I get all that. This was a facsimile of positive emotion aroused without the encounter of a living person—the living *God* in this case. It's a type of psychedelic idolatry in which I was confusing a chemical form with the superform of God, who is not one being among many but *nothing;* that is, no-thing, *nada y todo,* the *very ground of all being,* whose presence can be revealed through material mediations but is not reducible to any material form, let alone a fucking fungus. Nothing short of a life given over to prayer and practiced virtue—along with a goodly dose of grace without reason—can dispose one to communication with the divine. Yes.

But, hey. Dostoevsky suffered from grand mal seizures, and *he* said of *those* neurological quickenings: "I feel complete harmony in myself and in the world, and this feeling is so strong and sweet that for several seconds of such bliss one would give ten years of one's life, indeed, perhaps one's whole life."

So I popped another toadstool.

KENT

My heart is a lump of wax in God's hands!

GLENN (O.S.)

Uh-huh. Listen, why don't we get you over to the Airboat Association of Florida while you're in this state. I read that beginning this year, no new licenses will be given—

I pointed to a dead gator floating on its back in the canal. Spread-eagled and inflated with the gases of decomposition, it looked like an overturned pool raft.

For some time, I watched my scooter rive the dense air like a prow through water. When I looked away from that, I found dragonflies composing cursive messages to me. Beyond them, the saw grass soughed in the breeze. Mangroves knitted their hands in prayer. The berm beside the Trail released its stored lightning in the form of a cottonmouth, which hissed as if asking me to shush and keep secret what I was seeing: the subjecthood of animal, vegetable, even mineral. Everything was kith and kin; everything returned my gaze. A dimension of intentional meaning was communicating itself. I perceived a creative intelligence in the fabric of it all. Presently, I made no formal distinction between nature and art. All was poetic achievement.

KENT

I'm still not positive the growers didn't sneak me moldy enokis.

NOAH

I'm sure it beats walking, whatever it's doing to you.

There was still an observing "I" here, yet it felt as though this consciousness was not burbling forth from my brain. "I" was simply a receptor of the consciousness being transmitted to me. And being transmitted to me then was: *This universe did not emerge as the result of arbitrary chance, a show of force, or a desire for self-assertion. Creation is of the order of love.*

Before me, two swallows whimmed across the Trail, whirling up mosquitoes and exulting.

And the business of any creator is not to bully his material medium or to escape it, but to serve it. Doing so, he will realize that its service is his perfect freedom. Service to the beloved gives form to liberty; liberty is actuated through duty to the beloved.

KENT

Eat shit, Juliiiiiaaaaaan!

My heart was flapping in my chest like well-trafficked saloon doors. I swiveled to admire Noah. Then to admire Glenn. I was sending out love and love was coming back to me, *such is the circuitousness of love—to receive it, you must give it freely.* In that moment, I realized: There was no Noah. No Glenn. Our souls had mingled and blended so completely that the seam joining them had been effaced.

Tears flooded from me. I wanted to address a thank-you note to each blade of saw grass, to the cloud luffing up above. To every individual who deigned to humor us along our way, or placed a grimy penny into our mendicant bowl.

> KENT
> (garbled)

. . . gratitude is happiness doubled by wonder . . .

> GLENN (O.S.)

Safe to say that Kent is officially gorked the fuck out.
> (to Noah)

You got him?

> NOAH
> (alongside Kent)

I got him.

> GLENN (O.S.)

I just don't want this to become Exhibit A in our involuntary manslaughter trial.

> KENT
> (garbled)

. . . maturity to rejoice in what you have and not weep for what you have lost, or never had. Where are we going? Home, always back home.

Gradually I descended from the heights of my short-circuited repentance. Selfhood seeped back in. By the time we reached the hokey, tourist-trap Miccosukee Indian Village, the sky had turned the color of watermelon juice, and I'd mellowed into a state of awed confusion. I guess I must have been still somewhat dilated when we talked with tribal representatives, because they denied us filming access and allowed us camping privileges only at the canalside turnoff to the Shark Valley loop road.

I slept soundly. So soundly, in fact, that I took no notice of the long, meaningful poke Glenn gave me in the wee hours. He had opened our tent flap onto the fifty-degree night in order to go pee, he told me later, but he reconsidered when his headlamp illuminated the eyes of alligators gathered on the warm asphalt around our tents. "I was too weary for panic," he explained. One more day of walking and we'd be out of the Glades. Glenn wasn't going to let some ticklish situation get in the way of that.

FADE IN:

EXT. CANALSIDE—AFTERNOON

The camera is back on its stroller-mounted setup, as Kent has abandoned his BATTERY-DRAINED MOBILITY SCOOTER in Shark Valley. Presently, the three friends are walking through the easternmost remnant of the Everglades. In stark contrast to the chaos at feast in the heart of the swamp, this cleared and drained region is eerily still.

>   GLENN
>
> We need to prep our denouement before we reach Miami.

>   NOAH
>
> Say what we've learned?

>   KENT
>   (grimacing)
>
> Give us an idea what you want.

>   GLENN
>
> In my case, I feel I have won a great and righteous loathing as to the obnoxious filigree with which other people adorn their self-indulgent lives.

>   KENT
>
> Hell yeah.

>   NOAH
>
> Fire flames.

>   GLENN
>
> For example, the bougie hipster-man shops that are everywhere in Toronto. Where they sell extremely expensive trinkety objects and

self-grooming kits. This kind of elevation of, like, self-care. I don't know if I'll be able to take it when I get home.

KENT

The phrase "self-care" in general makes me want to shoot the person saying it in the stomach with a Civil War revolver.

GLENN

I guess I always found it obnoxious. Now, it's abhorrent.

KENT

(exaggerated narrator voice)

"Having walked a thousand miles, the friends realize there is a level of disdain which is the appropriate response to much that exists in the world."

GLENN

It's banal. But that's supposed to be one of the tentpoles of this genre, right?

NOAH

(unflattering impersonation)

"I walked, and I walked, and now I'll never look at the world the same way again!"

KENT

Or actually, no—it's like the human-scaled fantasy of the Grand March. History is supposed to be this splendid progressive march inching nearer to the more perfect world of happiness and justice. If you're moving forward, you're getting better. Why would a walk be any different? When it ended, you'd *have* to be better from when you started.

NOAH

"And if you do like me, then you too will come home enlightened!"
Like you're going hiking to receive a reverse lobotomy or
something.

KENT

When in fact it's like, *Fuck outta here, that's not how this works at
all.* Have a little humility. Understand human nature. If anything,
walking like this makes me realize how much *more* difficult
nonwalking life is.

GLENN

There's definitely, you could argue, a nugget of useful wisdom to
take from realizing that expecting a sudden transformation while on
a journey is itself juvenile and counterproductive.

GLENN (CONT'D)

This is all banal, too. But we're talking about the consumerist
salvational dream, where if I can just find that one product that
eludes me, or trip that eludes me, or *experience*—upon purchase and
consumption of *that,* finally, I'll be whole.

KENT

Suburban "seekers" of the world—unite!

GLENN

Don't get me wrong. This trip has made me want to give back. To
the people who were kind enough to film with us, but to the world at
large, too. I know I should become a participant in the gift economy.
Or whatever you call it.

GLENN (CONT'D)

It's just that I *also* know I'm going to promptly forget this upon
my reintegration into the rhythms of my narcissistic life. Like, as
soon as I go to buy deodorant, which will be my archway back into

normalcy, and a pharmacy cashier is rude to me, forget it. Out the
window.

KENT

NOAH

Do I think I'm going to go home and automatically be a more
conscientious husband? Fuck, I hope so. I want to be. But I know
I'm also gonna be the same dickwad I left as. For the most part.
Same dickwad, but with stronger calves and less patience for people
who aren't as honed as this made me. Yeah. No magic bullet.

KENT

The thousands of little actions that being decent entails. Everyday
decisions that have to be made. *Steps to be taken*—if you want a
metaphor, there you go.

KENT (CONT'D)

This trip has made it that much clearer to me that virtue and
goodness and . . . fucking . . . *peace of mind*—these aren't things you
just happen across on your travels. You have to choose to cultivate
these things. Opt in and work toward them.

GLENN

Simply just staying the course. Not picking up and moving on in
pursuit of something else that I think will make me happier.

The three men nod without noticing one another nodding.

KENT

The end of this *does* kinda feel like rending the veil a little bit. Like,
yeah—now I know how far I am from being a fundamentally decent
person.

GLENN

Having to be in a completely codependent relationship with people
other than my wife for the first time in, like, twelve years—building

that from the ground up—has forced me to understand what the mechanics of that are. Again. And what's required to make the mechanics work.

NOAH

Maybe it'll be like staring at the sun, but in a life sense. Where you can't blink that shit away, or not for a while you can't. You see the afterimage of it over everything else.

NOAH (CONT'D)

Yeah. Exercise patience. Move on from the grievances.

KENT

And, like—put in a small act of generosity where it's not required.

GLENN

Try to be an active agent in communal success. Banal again, but it *is* true. I've thought about it *a lot* on this trip.

Again, they stare ahead while nodding.

GLENN (CONT'D)

That's the thing about this place. If *you* do you, and *I* do me, then I have to wonder: How are we going to do *us*? We have to do us! We have no choice!

KENT

Florida: People existing for themselves, by themselves.

GLENN

Florida: Don't ask of me, and I will not ask of you.

KENT

Florida: You had a choice, and you chose this.

NOAH

(pointing at road shoulder)

There's another fork sharpened into a shiv. What is that, three today?

GLENN

All of this is getting fixed in post . . .

FADE OUT

IN THE END, WE ARRIVE AT THE FUTURE

We emerged from the swamp bare-chested, our shirts spun over our heads like helicopter rotors. Miami! We'd made it! Like the original Marathon Man, we came bearing a message of victory. Or, barring that, a message of our arrival. To passing motorists, we likely appeared to have come bearing news of some imminent calamity.

A small joy spasmed us. We'd proved that *we could,* which is the animus behind climbing mountains, having children—all your more popular forms of demonstrative suicide. We'd wrung every last drop of effort from ourselves. We'd done what peripatetic heroes are *supposed* to do: reminded ourselves we exist.

"So we're not going to the Keys, then?" Glenn asked.

"Only if we're going by Jet Ski," Noah said.

That settled, we left the shoulder of the road for the last time. We ramped onto pink sidewalk as we pierced the high-density sprawlburbs of West Kendall and Sweetwater, where the uniformity of desire was on full display. Though I didn't want to jinx it, it was looking more and more like we'd made it through the most dangerous pedestrian state without getting pizzaed. We filmed some triumphal scenes of us waving our shirts yet again.

"Who's got it better than us?" I asked, practically skipping along toward my birthplace.

"Nobody," Glenn said. "Maybe everybody."

With the camera rolling, I soliloquized: Proto-Miami was a muddy, malarial nightmare. One soldier garrisoned here during the Spanish-American War wrote to his parents: "If I owned both Miami and Hell, I'd sell Miami and go to live in Hell." Now, though, it is our dynamo of perpetual motion and ceaseless self-reinvention. It is our bleeding edge.

KENT

If Florida is Hothouse America, a microcosm or synecdoche of the larger nation, then Miami is *that* once more again. Miami is the concentration of the concentrate.

Perfect, Glenn said, swapping camera batteries.

Miami's been intractable since it rose out of the sea. Its constant wetness and nursery heat make it so. The Tequesta hunted and gathered around the present-day city but didn't stay year-round; the mosquitoes were too much. The Spanish dream of a sugar colony was kaputted by the monsoon seasons and heat that blanks the brain. The South acquired it late, but for cotton it was unsuitable.

Neither Spanish nor Southern, and with trainloads of Yankee Strangers several decades away, Miami for a long time was the center of nothing. It wasn't a frontier marketplace, it wasn't a transportation hub. It didn't attract industrial capital, and it didn't produce anything anyone wanted to buy.

Really, the main reason Miami exists is because a widow from Cleveland decided it should. In 1895, Julia Tuttle sent a bouquet of orange blossoms to Henry Flagler to prove to him that this sodden outpost had gone unscathed by an otherwise statewide frost. They worked out a deal: Tuttle would give Flagler free plots for a hotel and a railroad station, and then half of her land on top of that; in return, Flagler would extend his railroad, build a palace of a hotel, but also pave streets and dig sewers. Tuttle wanted a real first-class city, not a southernmore iteration of Flagler's baroque Franken-island, Palm Beach.

Miami had only a few hundred inhabitants at the time of its incorporation. Tuttle went into debt waiting for more people to show up and buy in. Flagler—he was able to bide his time. He developed his holdings with what remained of his Standard Oil wealth, though he believed that Tuttle was fundamentally nuts: "[Civilizing Miami] would be silly," he said. "This place will never be anything more than a fishing village for my hotel guests!"

To raise cash, Tuttle sold off property, which drove down the prices of her remaining land. Flagler tarried while demand caught up with what he had supplied. When, hounded by creditors shortly before her death, a bankrupt Tuttle appealed to Flagler, he wrote back: "I do not want you to suffer but I cannot accept the responsibility of your suffering."

KENT

This is why Flagler and not Tuttle is remembered. And why Miami's endowment is his and not hers. Down here, the inevitable would be moneyed.

Compared to contemporaries like Chicago, Pittsburgh, and Cincinnati, Miami's early social organization and civic leadership was a travesty. Recent arrivals didn't want to consider bond issues; they'd left home to get away from bond issues. They wanted to enjoy the weird trees, unwholesome sunshine, and liquid land market.

By 1900, Dade County (then constituting the future Broward, Palm Beach, and Martin counties) could claim 4,955 inhabitants. Land then boomed, but in 1926, a hurricane came along and spoiled the fun, leveling the burgeoning city. It killed hundreds and left more homeless. It was the costliest storm ever, equivalent to two Katrinas. Redevelopment, though, didn't take long.

There was no business but the real estate business. Until 1949, any twenty-five property-holding registered voters could establish a municipal corporation around Miami. If they chose to do so, they were then granted the powers of taxation and regulation by the state. Money lured many to damn the larger community and found their own cities. This is why metropolitan Miami today is a two-thousand-square-mile ganglion of almost thirty municipalities. Miami begat

Homestead in 1913 and Florida City in 1914, both of which were stops along the new branch of Flagler's Florida East Coast Railway. After that, rich-as-Croesus real estate families incorporated Miami Beach (1915) and Coral Gables (1925). Opa-Locka (1926) was the Scheherazade fever dream of aviation pioneer Glenn Curtiss, who hoped his city would become the "Baghdad of America." (Oh, man, did it ever, except not in the way Curtiss had hoped.) Subsequently came Miami Springs, South Miami, and North Miami. The Great Depression gummed up the gears but could not break them. Five more cities were created during the thirties: Miami Shores, Biscayne Park, El Portal, Indian Creek Village, and Surfside. The last pulse came in the 1940s with the incorporation of Sweetwater, Bal Harbour, Bay Harbor Islands, Virginia Gardens, Hialeah Gardens, and Medley.

In 1959, Havana's upper and middle classes fled Fidel Castro's revolution, and the process of contemporary Miami becoming what it is was begun. Miami for the Cuban bourgeoisie had been a vacation destination, a day trip. As such, it was the only place that made sense to muster themselves in exile. The lower strata of their social pyramid arrived periodically thereafter. Hot on their heels came all the major refugee streams of the Western Hemisphere: Nicaraguan, Haitian, Panamanian, Colombian, Honduran.

KENT

Right as the peninsula's tourism industry was being swallowed whole by Orlando, Miami received this newly impoverished if also highly trained and motivated labor force. The cheesy old hotels and restaurants gave way to international finance, insurance. Real estate, of course. Suddenly, Miami was a real place, with resources unique to the country. "Capital of the Caribbean," "Capital of Latin America"—

Kent steps lively around a car rolling through a red light into a right-hand turn. Salsa shines through its cracked window like a line of light under a door.

GLENN (O.S.)

I have never had such a palpable sense of everyone being on their phone.

KENT

Eyes on the prize here. Take two. Ahem.

KENT (CONT'D)

Miami grew unplanned, as if not needing to be sown. Like the land couldn't help it.

Planes banked low overhead on their final approach to Miami International. Noah noticed that a shopping cart had been parked at every covered bus stop we passed.

"Where's the, uh, opulence?" he asked. "I was expecting, y'know, zeppelin titties. And for there to be, like, oligarch yachts sliding through intersections like this was *Speed 2: Cruise Control.*" He gestured at the surrounding metropolis stretching on low and vast like a used-car lot.

I tried to explain the special Miami combination of arriviste decadence and abject poverty. Promise v. reality. That we're perennially ranked worst or second-worst in terms of inequality, gun violence—yet one out of every ten of us is a millionaire, if you account for homes, stocks, and cars. "The grit keeps us from being a bigger, shittier Palm Beach," I said, "and the glitz hides the fact that we're not *too* too different from most Sunbelt cities on the make."

But Noah and Glenn weren't listening. They were debating as to which restaurant should serve us our first post-PowerBar meal.

So we weighed our options at a three-tiered strip mall before settling on El Palacio de los Jugos. Glenn and Noah were rebuffed by the Spanish-only *mamis* awork behind the sneeze guard. It was glorious to watch—though my kitchen Spanish has left me, and I could not help them. Nor could I any longer summon the Miami accent—that rubbery locution honed here by the children of immigrants. (The shibboleth is the word "like," which when enunciated in the Miami accent is very tongue-forward, sounding almost candied, *lllllllllaike* the curved gloss on a bauble.) The Miami accent shoehorns English into Spanish cadences and pronunciation rules. Words are molded on the lips and given much forward thrust, ticking higher in pitch and tempo as they're spoken. The Miami accent is often mistaken for a Latin accent by Americans, but the Miami accent affects Spanish, too. Monolingual Spanish speakers consider the inflection of Miami Spanish to be a variation of the *gringo* accent. What a strange way to be apprehended. A few degrees from foreign in either direction.

While a rouged grandma holding a ladle full of black beans shook her head no at Glenn, he surmised: "No concession to whites. It's great. There's a little bit of this in L.A., but not at this level."

And he's right. When the first Cuban exiles began to arrive, the original Miami power brokers (tourist-oriented fellers who referred to the place as "My-ammuh" like Captain Dale) were concerned largely with preserving their own good-ol'-boy prestige and way of life. They were doomed, of course. The Cuban exiles had the power of the federal government behind them. A most important ally in the struggle against Communism and its spread in the Americas had literally washed up on our nation's shore. For geopolitical reasons, Uncle Sam could never allow the Cubans to be just another ethnic group. They had to become the "most successful immigrant story of all time."

The 1966 Cuban Adjustment Act ensured that these exiles would qualify for permanent residency and then citizenship only one year after arriving in-country. They would be exempt from immigration quotas as well as requirements that their family members enter the United States through a legal port of entry. (Contrast this with the treatment of Haitian refugees, who were shown exactly zero sympathy.) And if after receiving their leg up these exiles threatened to displace "Anglo" (i.e., white American) hegemony in Miami? *Así es la vida* . . .

That's a vital distinction to keep in mind: The first wave of Cubans, the doctors and lawyers and landowners, did not *immigrate* to Miami. They exiled themselves following a revolution. They came here with no intention of assimilating. Instead, they brought with them the heirloom seeds of bourgeois Havana and cultivated them in an amenable clime. Oh, they underwent the trials of the immigrant, same as everyone else. But as they strived and prospered, the Cubans opted not to enlist in prevailing American organizations. Rather than join the Greater Miami Chamber of Commerce, they participated in the Cámara de Comercio Latino. Instead of petitioning for entry into the Builders Association of South Florida, they created the Latin Builders Association. In lieu of the American Cancer Society, they supported La Liga Contra el Cancer. As they waited daily for Fidel to topple, they nourished a community separate from provincial Anglo Miami. More and more exiles (plus *marielitos*) arrived, and distractedly they built a metropolis.

Meanwhile, the dwindling Anglo elite preached the old standard to the newcomers: learn English, soften your strange ways, get in back of the ethnic queue like the Germans, Irish, and Italians before you. This inspired little enthusiasm. The Cubans—at least the pre–Mariel Boatlift Cubans—were not tired, nor weak, nor huddling. They were professionals who'd been forced out of their home. They did not fawn; they ran for local office. They gained seats, and standing. They consolidated power.

Before the Anglos could know what had hit them, the *Cubans* became the ones enforcing cultural standards and effecting others' assimilation. Anglos now had to bargain in a sociopolitical arena in which white men no longer occupied the center of gravity (as is still the case in New York, L.A., et al.). Their city had ceased to be *just* a vacation destination like those other Flagler whistle-stops along the coast. Miami became a less relaxed, more complex place thanks to the exiles and subsequent immigrant groups. In jockeying with one another and bringing down the old order, Miami's various communities produced a unique urban experiment long before, say, Houston began undergoing something similar.

De facto pluralism was—is—the norm in Miami. It's the only city in the world where more than half of the citizenry is made up of immigrants who arrived within the past fifty years. Sixty percent of Miamians are of Cuban extraction, 18 percent are black, 12 percent are white, and 10 percent are Venezuelan-, Nicaraguan-, Mexican-, Puerto Rican–, Colombian-, Brazilian-, Haitian-, Russian-, Israeli-, et cetera–American. This overlap of languages, customs, institutions, and social systems gives rise to acculturation in reverse. That is, *newcomers* don't conform themselves to Miami; *Miami* morphs to fit them. Crucially, this means that Miamians have no common frame of reference. Everybody lives in a different Miami—their own Miami.

Everyday events get filtered through interpretive frameworks that are different to the point of near unintelligibility.

KENT

(through mouthful of ropa vieja)

This is tomorrow's America, today!

"I can't believe this place made you," Glenn said to me as we passed more stucco apartment houses crumbling next to luxe new high-rises, with riotous vegetable growth grouting the space in between. "That is the mystery," he added.

While we walked, the Tamiami Trail became regular old Eight Street. Calle Ocho. My smile could not stop widening. We were into Little Havana now—98 percent Latino, though the original Cuban exiles moved to the 'burbs long ago. Around us: actual street life. We watched as a "Safari Tours" bus pulled up to bustling Domino Park. Alabaster Germans disembarked, thrust cameras into the faces of ancient *jugadores.* They tried to look stoic, these *jugadores,* but their flaring nostrils betrayed just how tired of this shit they were. We joined the Germans and filmed B-roll of their clinking ivory tiles.

The *jugadores* drove their words with gestures, practically shooed them away in cycles of bickering and flirtation. They made for far more compelling footage than the adjacent body shops, tire marts, muffler stores, and car dealerships. I tried to calculate the car dealership per square mile ratio for Little Havana, West Flagler, Flagami, Westchester—basically, for the length of Calle Ocho between Biscayne Bay and the Everglades—but I couldn't do it. I'm certain there are more car dealerships here, proportionally, than anywhere in the United States. Someone smarter than me should be writing a thesis on the historical impact of car dealing on South Florida.

The sun was by now leaving its post, but its setting was overshadowed by black-lined cumulonimbus. In every sewer grate we passed: high water smelling of gasoline. Rain began to fall, fat slugs of water warm as though fired from a gun. We ducked into a Burger King and waited out the storm among teenagers, *abuelas* in floral nightgowns, and the old Cubanasos whose ball caps were perched tip-top like cockscombs. Outside, the rain lashed the boughs of a tall ceiba tree; the Santeria offerings cradled in its roots remained dry.

Not long after it had started, the rain stopped, allowing lurid nighttime to descend. The puddles paved our final miles in neon. The sulfide lamps lining our approach into Downtown Miami could barely vault the night, and the yellow they threw off was thin, salty, and seemingly ready to go out, like flare light. "What are we going to *do* with ourselves when we wake up and don't have any forward momentum?" Glenn asked. There was more than a little solemnity in his voice.

We wandered through Miami's ever-expanding skyline in pursuit of Bayfront Park. Over here: the thickset SunTrust building, where I worked in the mail room during college breaks. There: the Metromover, a glass van that rolls on donut tires along an elevated track. Hovering above like puppeteers' hands: so many construction cranes. Idle for the moment, they'd soon be back to supplying the demand for Miami's record-setting condo boom. Some 230 condominiums are currently under construction, and their thirty thousand new units are more than any other U.S. city's. Moving into these luxury boxes will be more brokers and financiers, impresarios and dignitaries. Trailing them like sharks behind a shrimp boat will be the hustlers and shysters who come to scam the world-industrial con men. The circuit is rather beautiful in its symmetry. It ensures that metropolitan Miami leads or comes close to leading the nation in every conceivable form of white-collar crime, from mortgage fraud to Medicare fraud, income tax fraud to insurance fraud, identity theft, loan fraud—shall we just say *fraud*. Miami is the fraud nexus of the Western Hemisphere.

But let us not overlook our industry-leading creativity in other fields: fake lotteries, telemarketing scams, sham marriages, seafood double-dealing, unlicensed butt implants.

KENT

Miami is so false, cruel, and beautiful, man. The concept of due diligence is nigh on inconceivable. It's like we had it decreed: *Never shall there be anything written, built, or said in the direction of "Wouldn't you like to reconsider?"*

Miami excites the imagination. But more than that, Miami excites avarice. I'd be remiss if I didn't mention that while the Cubans were reshaping Miami, it was the drug dealers who were financing the skyscrapers, yachts, luxury malls, and Lamborghinis. Miami was reconstructed with their flight capital. It was sold and resold depending on the street price of cocaine, the exchange rates in Central America, who was in power where. Consider the six years between 1977 and 1983: Miami went from having zero foreign banks to having more than 130. At that time, my father, a feeder fish in the real estate ecosystem, was paid for services rendered with cash-stuffed duffels. He bought our house at auction off a jailed "importer/exporter." My high school's prom king was the son of the actor who played Rico Tubbs on *Miami Vice*. One of my neighborhood pals lived under an assumed identity because *his* father was a Noriega coke lieutenant who'd snitched. ("Blanco" being maybe not the choicest of pseudonymous surnames in his case.) Two of my best friends growing up had been coke dealers, and an even higher percentage of my less intimate friends were involved in the trade. Everyone was, as they say, getting well.

Drug money, transfer payments, life savings. Condominiums, vacation rentals, retirement homes. This is the sloshing liquidity on which Miami floats. Even in their most hallucinatory fever dreams, the conquistadores never could have imagined it. Five centuries after their first Florida missteps, there's finally a Spanish-speaking metropolis here, a true world capital shimmering like a mirage between the swamp and the breakers. And how stranger-than-fiction is it that the whole enterprise *still* runs on convincing others to bring and invest and squander the wealth they made elsewhere?

Before fording the narrow Miami River, Glenn, Noah, and I had to ford a brand-new, billion-dollar, semienclosed plaza of luxury retail, office space, and private apartments known as Brickell City Centre. Conceived during the real estate bubble of the mid-aughts, abandoned during the subsequent crash, revived in 2012, constructed right next to the goddamned water, and opened just the other month as if *no, no this is not a metaphor for anything,* City Centre was packed with visitors. They were entering two and two unto this ark of late capitalism via escalators from the street.

There's a question near the end of Homer's *Odyssey* that gets me every time. After having yearned for home for two decades, Odysseus finally reaches Ithaca. But he's been away so long that he can't believe his lying eyes. "And tell me this," Odysseus says, "I must be absolutely sure. This place I've reached, is it truly Ithaca?" That's how I was feeling. In my youth, the Greater Downtown area was nowhere you wanted to be after dark. Come the end of the workday, cars streamed out of bank offices and law firms like ants abandoning the colony. This, now—it's truly home?

"Mmuh," Glenn said, suckling from the tentacle of his hydration pack while simultaneously staring into his phone. He spat out the hose, let it drop to his side. "It's built by a Hong Kong outfit," he said.

We skedaddled before security could round on us. As we crested the drawbridge over the Miami River, I looked back at the shoppers and tourists swarming the mall—so many in, so few out—and I thought again of ants. Ants entering a liquid trap and getting mired to death in the stuff they'd come to take home with them.

NOAH (O.S.)

Is that from *Zen and the Art of Motorcycle Maintenance,* you undergrad slap dick?

I sigh.

GLENN (O.S.)

Say something about how, like, the storm is obviously coming for this place. But even so, for you to be wringing your hands and quoting NASA reports about sea-level rise here—it'd be a jeremiad for no one.

KENT

Something something disbelief, unreality. Willing self-deception.

GLENN (O.S.)

Winner winner.

I take a few moments to think.

Beneath the din of stalled traffic, the incoming tide is splashing against pilings. The resulting sound is a lip-smacking one, like that of an aficionado who has tasted the wine and is anticipating the rest of the bottle.

KENT (CONT'D)

There's a story about how, right before Hurricane Andrew hit Miami in 1992, these exotic animal dealers, their new stormproof warehouse wasn't ready, so they rented an old greenhouse and loaded it with their latest shipment of spiders and frogs and snakes and plants. Then Andrew blew the greenhouse off the earth, and the creatures fell with the rain. It's probably not entirely true. But it serves as a decent creation myth in terms of how Miami came to be populated by so many invasive species. Brown tree snakes, Asian carp, Burmese pythons. The giant African land snail most recently. These species get here, they find Florida to be a lively surrogate with niches they can fill. They join the competition. And they thrive.

PASSING MOTORIST

Get a car! *¡Carajo!*

KENT (CONT'D)

Of all Florida's invasive species, the most successful has been optimism. Ineradicable optimism. It has taken over like a fast-growing strangling vine. Not hope, mind you, but optimism.

The optimist believes in progress. To him, the past is nothing but a record of inferiority, both moral and technical. No sense sifting those ashes. *Anyway,* the optimist says, *the steady accumulation of scientific discovery and ethical betterment means I am on the spear tip of history.*

Because of his belief in progress, the optimist does not make intelligent use of the past. He practices a kind of deliberate forgetting. *How can history repeat itself if the future is always a straight shot forward?*

And since he doesn't really give a hey about how he got here—and since the world to come can't help but be better than this one—the optimist has no desire to make provisions for the future. Why would he? If everything is continually getting better and smarter and more perfect, then whatever problems we face now will surely pose no challenge to those strange and superlative tomorrow people?

Hope, on the other hand, does not require that you treat history as though its stages were drop-away boosters to be jettisoned on our upshot to the moon. Hope sees a continuity between past, passing, and to come. As such, hope perpetuates its name, its origin, its glory, its virtues. Because more than anything, hope is a belief in justice. Past wrongs will be righted. The wicked will be punished. Suffering is not endured in vain.

Hope, then, requires a trust—a *faith,* you could say—that comes across as absurd to those who don't share in it. Those who do share in it? Maybe things will get better, probably they won't—in the end, what we trust in is the fullness of time.

We footed into Bayfront Park, a beautifully manicured greenspace where a man once tried to murder FDR. (He missed and killed Chicago's mayor instead.) When I was a kid, Bayfront Park was still considered an ideal place to get shot. This night, though—young professionals jogged and businesspeople strolled about shaping ice cream cones with their tongues. The three of us were very much out of place. We wanted to do anything but go straight to where we were.

We reached the waterside railing. Beyond it was Dodge Island, where one kind of freight is unloaded at the Port of Miami and another is loaded at the Carnival cruise terminal. Beyond that: Miami Beach, and the deep blue sea.

KENT

Carl Fisher, you know—the first thing he prohibited after he'd summoned Miami Beach out of the water? Cemeteries. Cemeteries wouldn't be allowed on his island. No lie.

~~~~~~

FADE IN:

INT. BASEMENT OFFICE—AFTERNOON

Behind his desk in a subterranean, cinder-block cell at the University of Miami sits DR. HAROLD WANLESS, a slumped elderly man whose droopy mustache is the color of wastewater. The chair of the Department of Geological Sciences, WANLESS speaks like a man who understands the future all too well—which is to say, he speaks in a flat, Eeyoreish monotone. Wanless has been giving this same interview to government officials and newspaper reporters for decades at this point.

WANLESS

It's nice that you three still talk to one another.

GLENN (O.S.)

Yes, well. It's been something. The walk has definitely been some thing. But, Dr. Wanless—you're known as the Paul Revere of sea-level rise. Is that fair to say?

WANLESS

It's hilarious. Sort of sadly hilarious.

Wanless removes his glasses, rubs the bridge of his nose.

WANLESS (CONT'D)

Can I explain what global warming is?

KENT

(half-joking)

As quickly as possible.

WANLESS

As quickly as . . . OK. Only 7 percent of the heat being trapped by greenhouse gases is stored in the atmosphere. Do you know where the other 93 percent lives? Of all the heat that's been produced by the extra greenhouse gases we've put into the atmosphere since the beginning of the Industrial Revolution or maybe before—93 percent of that heat has been transferred to the oceans. So, global warming is really heating up the oceans. The warming atmosphere is for centuries going to continue to warm the oceans. That's now what's starting to melt ice. And once that sinks in, you realize we're screwed.

Wanless delved into his practiced presentation. The Intergovernmental Panel on Climate Change predicts that sea levels could rise by more than three feet by the end of this century, he said. The Army Corps of Engineers projects as much as five feet. The National Oceanic and Atmospheric Administration thinks up to six and a half feet. According to Wanless, however, all these worst-case scenarios are too conservative; they don't account for how exponential the glacier and ice-sheet melt will be in the decades to come. Wanless described it as being like a positive feedback loop: Water on the melting ice surface absorbs more heat, accelerating surface melt. Meltwater then percolates through the ice, resulting in more extensive fracturing. Still more warmed water seeps into these fractures, softening the ice and further accelerating melt. Round and round she goes, faster and faster.

WANLESS

We're just seeing the beginning of what we know becomes a rapid ice disintegration. We've really kicked over the bucket, as far as something that we really didn't want to mess with. It's not something that's if we behave, it's going to go away. We're in for it. Even if we stopped burning fossil fuels tomorrow, the greenhouse gases will keep warming the atmosphere for at least another thirty years.

Wanless points to a JAR OF WATER on a shelf.

WANLESS (CONT'D)

This used to be ice in Greenland. There's more where this came from.

KENT

(hastily)

And what does this mean for the state of Florida?

WANLESS

At six feet, more than half of Miami will be submerged. Miami Beach will be gone. Miami, as we know it today, is doomed. It's not a question of if. It's a question of when.

Miami is second only to Guangzhou in terms of world cities most imperiled by rising seas, Wanless droned on. Be that as it may, no help is forthcoming from the state and federal governments. And, anyhow, Miamians are still building like there's no tomorrow. Which there isn't. Forget levees or dikes. What works for New Orleans and the Netherlands can't work here, because the underlying limestone and sand substrate is too porous, too permeable. Water will come from the east, yes, and west from the Everglades, too—but the big problem is that it will burble *underfoot* at the same time.

As little as twelve inches of rise will bring salt water into the aquifer that sustains 5.5 million South Floridians. It'll also wreak havoc on the sewage system that keeps this megalopolis somewhat sanitary. Insurance and mortgage rates will shoot through the roof. People will stop coming; the ones who are already here will try (and likely fail) to sell their properties before cutting and running. Tax bases will plummet. There won't be enough money to fund infrastructural upgrades, to say nothing of the salaries of police officers, garbage collectors, and firefighters. And that's before the rising sea reaches the core of the Turkey Point nuclear plant twenty-four miles south of Miami.

Bye-bye, tourists. Adios, flight capital.

WANLESS

This is the kind of Ponzi scheme you'd want to invest in. This is a sure thing. In the maps we have of Miami-Dade County, the elevation maps—there's about 44 percent of the land left after a six-foot rise in sea level. But three-quarters of what looks like dry land is less than two feet above the new sea level. So we're really down to like 11 percent of what we started with that is habitable in any sense of the word. And then if you go on up to 10 feet, which is where we're headed and beyond—it's less than 10 percent.

I perked up.

KENT

Can we see those maps?

Wanless brings up satellite images and computer projections. One shows that at four feet of rise, Miami Beach, Key Biscayne, and Virginia Key will be swamped. Wanless clicks over to six feet, and the Keys are gone.

KENT
(pointing)

Huh. It looks like northwest Miami is actually going to be fine.

WANLESS

Yeah, there's some nasty business going on there with developers coming in and talking inner-city people into selling cheap. Because the inner city, a lot of that is up on the higher ground.

KENT

I . . . see.

While Wanless answered Noah's question about increased mosquito populations and the threat of disease, I used my phone to search out properties for sale in the northwest region of the city. The way I figured it, we could slip the family some cash, get them to go along with a scene in which we appear to hornswoggle them out of future beachfront property. *Gold,* I thought. And, hey—maybe their price would be reasonable?

WANLESS

We're on our way. This isn't just a trivial little experiment humankind tried. Mine the coal. Suck the oil out. It's a massive effort. And it's been very successful, unfortunately. We won't give up our comforts now. We won't go back to hunting whales for lamp oil. We'll be controlling our climate by the end of this century, I'm sure. But. That's not going to change rising sea level. That's not going to change aridification. To undo the sea change . . . I believe that's out of our grasp. Just massive. And let's put it this way: It's out of our grasp to undo it *right.* We always try to engineer things, and they always end up causing horrible side effects that we didn't anticipate.

Wanless shrugs, palms up.

WANLESS (CONT'D)

This is what humans have done to themselves. This is what *we* have done to ourselves. Some of us believe we see it clearly enough that we have a responsibility to share it.

GLENN (O.S.)

Speaking of abdicating moral responsibility—what do you make of the recent political developments as they pertain to climate change?

WANLESS

I certainly hope that Donald Trump is going to understand the seriousness of this. He, uh, maybe he can do a few other things like . . . we *do* have too many regulations and things. Drives people crazy. We've had Democrats and Republicans, and they haven't really done a lot. What they have done, they did as decrees. Which the next president can undo. It's time we get a leader that's willing to . . . to gut these things. Maybe overgut them, so they can be rebuilt as needed.

KENT
(stifling laughter)

NOAH (O.S.)
How about that.

GLENN (O.S.)
I mean . . . but . . . surely. Surely you have to be skeptical of Trump's picks to lead environmental posts?

WANLESS
OK. Here's my sense. I think Hillary was a consummate liar. She would've said anything to get elected. I just hope that . . . Trump said he's not a liar. And if he becomes a true denier . . . then he's a liar. He has so many properties that are so vulnerable, though. I've looked at the elevations of all of them . . .

HARD CUT

IF THERE WERE NO FLORIDA,
WE SHOULD HAVE TO INVENT IT

We kicked sand along South Beach. Huge new condo buildings towered over us to our left. In the shadows behind them across Ocean Drive, older bungalows were shuttered, gutted, and getting ready to become condos themselves.

Growing up, I rarely came to this place. Miami and Miami Beach are not the same thing, tourist misperceptions notwithstanding. Miami Beach is a separate city dredged out of the bay and removed from the landed part of the metropolis by a causeway. It's as if Miami were holding Miami Beach at arm's length. Proffering it.

Miami Beach is for the uninitiated, for them to come and have their expectation of "Miami" confirmed without encountering the starker, obverse side. Every now and then my family would visit, go to Joe's Stone Crab following a wedding or something. When I got old enough, my friends and I held prom after-parties in the sleazier boutique hotels. We'd pool our money, sleep thirty to a room, rent a carpet shampooer from Publix the next day. Generally, though, we didn't hang around here any more than Caribbean islanders with nothing to hawk hang around the bright, kempt area cruise ships disgorge at.

Carl Fisher would have approved. A Hoosier born in the latter part of the nineteenth century, Fisher made his name manufacturing auto parts and operating the world's first car dealership. He also thought up the idea of the Indianapolis 500 and spearheaded the early push for national highways. Was one of the founders of the Dixie Highway Association, touting "your favorite route to and from Florida." Fisher retired to Miami to live out his fortune, but like Henry Flagler before him, he grew restless here. He found himself drawn to a strip of mangroves just off the coast. There, a guy by the name of John Collins grew avocados but had a hard time transporting them to market. Fisher lent him money to build a bridge; Collins gave him two hundred acres of land in return. Fisher purchased another two hundred acres and declared his intention to build "the prettiest little city in the world right here." The spittle of dreams was in his eyes. Friends feared for his sanity.

He brought in men, machinery, two elephants even. Fisher's work crews blasted, drained, filled in the mangrove swamp and adjacent barrier islands, which had hitherto been Miami's buffer against hurricanes. Giant steam shovels dredged Biscayne Bay. They dumped shell and muck into new middens. The middens were graded level. Abracadabra! *Tabula rasa ex nihilo!*

The ribbon was cut in 1915. Not long after, a Florida land boom hit—thanks in part to the Dixie Highway Fisher had lobbied for. With Barnumesque flair, he lured prospective buyers to Miami Beach with beauty pageants, polo and sport-fishing tournaments, and the blandishments of President-elect Warren G. Harding for some reason. Society people settled in and planned manors of their own. Fisher had built it, and the people were coming.

Then the Great Miami Hurricane of 1926 hit, killing the land boom and kicking off the Depression in Florida. Fisher lost practically everything in the crash. Penniless, he spent his last years wandering up and down the white sand beach he'd contrived.

In the decades that followed, Miami Beach cycled through just as many downturns and reinventions as the mainland. Servicemen and -women filled the island in the forties. The fifties and sixties were a gilded age: The Beatles came to frolic, and the Fontainebleau served as a backdrop to Rat Pack movies. The seventies were less sunny; the original infrastructure was deteriorating at the same rate as the initial crop of Jewish retirees. The early eighties were terrifying—Miami's cocaine-cowboy violence spilled across the causeway. Then came the

Beach's *Birdcage*-era gentrification in the late eighties and early nineties. Art Basel and its traveling circus of courtiers, *millonarios,* and charlatans trailed along after.

The three of us filmed in hotel lobbies done up like white-marble movie palaces. We shot B-roll of curvilinear staircases and indoor/outdoor lounges abillow with white drapery. Glenn tried to capture the absolute tyranny of white. White buildings that looked like refrigerators, white buildings that looked like ice cube trays on edge. White shorts everywhere, poolside especially, where their wearers went shoulder to shoulder with white sculptures that were imitations of late Renaissance imitations of Greek and Roman statuary.

We wrapped in front of a new white condo tower anchoring the just-invented "Faena District," which will include a Rem Koolhaas–designed arts center as well as a high-end shopping mall meant to invoke a "modern-day souk." On the ocean-facing side of the development stood a glass-encased woolly mammoth skeleton that had been coated in twenty-four-karat gold by the artist Damien Hirst. Title: *Gone but Not Forgotten.* Meanwhile, above us, propeller planes pulled banners for DJs performing at irony-free nightclubs which did not exist on the Beach prior to *Miami Vice* suggesting that such clubs should exist.

"The restaurants, pools, cabanas," Glenn said, wincing at the plane, whose engine noise was ruining his shot. "But especially these condos that get flipped . . . fucking . . . what? Three years after purchase? Before the boom goes bust? Everything here feels fuck-adjacent. You're preparing to fuck, you're taking an intermission from fucking. You are getting financially fucked."

"Or financially fucking another," Noah added, wiping his sweat-wet brow. "Jesus hell. A week till Christmas?"

The sun dominated the horizon like a searchlight. Tourists were cramming the beach beneath it, to be serviced by it. With the camera rolling again, I bent down to palm a handful of crystalline sand. I nodded thoughtfully while letting the broken crockery of once-living things run through my fingers.

KENT

You know, the only state that has more coastline than Florida is Alaska.

I did not mention that half of Florida's 1,350 miles of coastline are designated as "critically eroding" by the state's Department of Environmental Protection.

KENT

This sand qualifies as "fine" sand, since each grain is smaller than the ball in a ballpoint pen.

Why bother viewers with the truth of the matter: These grains were imported from a plant in Moore Haven, where engineers dredge sand from deepening ponds. Recently, Miami Beach paid about $12 million for their top-shelf product in order to patch three thousand feet of shore. This is a perennial undertaking, since the waves are forever sawing at the coastline, picking up sand and depositing it elsewhere. Miami Beach *could* dredge its sand from Biscayne Bay, like Fisher did when he sucked up 6 million cubic yards for his original version. Or like the city did four decades ago, when another 14 million cubic yards of sand—four times what was used to build the Great Pyramids—was dredged to rejuvenate the beach. But this Biscayne sand, it is . . . less than Instagrammable, let's say. Bay-bottom muck hardly fits today's preferred aesthetic.

KENT

Gorgeous. You just want to come down and make sand angels in it.

The city engineer in charge of implementing Miami Beach's antisea-rise measures, BRUCE MOWRY, is a round and ruddy man who resembles nothing so much as an apple dressed up as a comptroller for Halloween. He is gesturing excitedly at a hulking pump house built into one of Miami Beach's raised streets.

MOWRY

Right now a lot of people are spreading false information on social media about flood insurance and Miami Beach, saying they're not getting covered because the raised streets mean that a shop at street level is classified as a basement now. Not true!

Mowry straightens his red tie, waves the men onward to more construction sites.

> MOWRY (CONT'D)
> (over shoulder)

This is a step forward, you see? Is it going to be enough? No, probably not. Are we making mistakes? Yes. But what we're doing is taking a step forward.

The three friends zig and zag through the traffic backed up around the sites.

> NOAH (O.S.)
> (to Mowry)
>
> (half out of breath)

When you pump the floodwater back out, do you do anything about, like, the dog shit and oil it's picked up? Do you treat it?

> MOWRY
> (shouting over jackhammer)

That could be a problem. Sure! Could be! But consequences like that, we could worry about them and not do anything. Or we could take action. It takes thirty years to implement solutions, so we'd better start implementing them now! This is one of the few places in the country if not the world where we're actually trying to be proactive about sea-level rise.

Like a taxi driver attempting to confuse a fare, Mowry kept doubling us back to Sunset Harbour on the west side of the island. This is where the worst flooding occurs. Especially so when there is a full moon and a high tide—then, salt water spurts through sidewalk cracks. Storm drains transform into an irrigation system, sluicing brine across the narrow island. Pedestrians splash past garbage cans bobbing like buoys. Homeowners have to put up No Wake signs in their yards.

MOWRY
(over shoulder)

You see, flooding had been accepted as a way of life to a point where people came in and said, Why are we continuing accepting this issue of our streets flooding? And so we had politicians listen—Philip Levine, that's what he campaigned on—and they ran and got elected by these people.

Miami Beach's current mayor, Philip Levine, won office on the promise of combating sea-level rise; that much is true. How he's gone about combating sea-level rise is . . . by embracing more and bigger development. But before you chortle despairingly, friend, remember that Florida's government does not officially recognize climate change. Even if it *wanted* to take action, the state lacks the power to levy income taxes to pay for improvements. So cities like Miami Beach are on their own. And the only real way for the Beach to raise funds for defenses is through real estate taxes, hotel taxes. If Miami Beach wants more of those, it has to keep slapping together luxury resorts with the planned obsolescence built right into them. Each one increases the magnitude of risk, sure—but what other recourse does the city have? What was once a choice is that no longer. Miami Beach *has to* front like it is unconcerned with reality. If it stops fabricating itself—and its property values stop rising—and investors and tourists get spooked—it takes on more water. If it doesn't continue to build itself up—it slips beneath the waves.

Before we met with Mowry, Glenn had mentioned a newspaper story he'd read. In this story, it was reported that Mayor Levine had declared a state of emergency and waived competitive bidding requirements in order to sign an $11 million contract to build three

storm pumps in this area, Sunset Harbour. This area where, coinci-
dentally, Mayor Levine owns real estate.

The three of us confabbed while walking, wondering if we should
ask about it. Noah, canting the boom, said: "We're gonna start expo-
séing *now?*"

I said, "Well, maybe at least we should—"

KENT

(to Mowry)

The idea that you have to keep spinning the ball on your finger,
you have to do enough to keep the real estate and tourism viable
so that you can continue to generate cash for a potential solution,
as well as all the stopgaps you have in place—of course, not a lot
of communities can do this. Very, very few, in fact. A place like
Pinecrest saw that it'd cost them $40 million to fight sea-level rise,
and they really can't afford that. They don't have the tax base. You
do because . . . you don't mention the risks to investors? Or they
don't care about them?

Mowry stopped. He waved the camera down. He said, "Uhh, if I
answered that question, I probably wouldn't be the city engineer for
Miami Beach!" He laughed. We laughed.

MOWRY

We need to always make sure that when visitors and investors
come they feel welcome, they feel like they're at a place they want
to be. That's what we're working for. To maintain that culture,
that environment. We're implementing $500 million in elevating
30 percent of streets, heightening seawalls, installing pump stations,
improving drains and sewers. We're working for iterative-type
solutions.

Mowry ended our tour at a small bayside park where his men were
raising the seawall and replanting mangroves. He thought Glenn
might like to get shots of the birds and the fish tentatively inhabiting
the root system.

MOWRY

(gesturing at Miami across water behind him)

Iterative-type solutions! Nothing is impossible. It may just take a little longer to implement a solution. The City of Miami Beach will be here in a hundred years because it wants to be here. Sea-level rise won't kill a city if it wants to live.

Glenn tried to make something of this visual anticlimax. A smell like soiled diapers was emanating from the drains the workmen were installing new grates over. Noah did the googling. Tonight was a full moon.

MOWRY (CONT'D)

The key question here, gentlemen, that we're talking about here, is that we're in a life of change. We're not like you build it now and a hundred years from now it'll be exactly the same. What we're saying is you'll continue to have to adapt, change. Look at this. This is what this country is built on. The solutions we're implementing today are solutions to be built on. Many people think we're wasting a lot of money putting in pumps for a city they believe we should just abandon and retreat from. The word "retreat" is not in our vocabulary, gentlemen!

Mowry continued like this for some time, waxing hydrological about other "iterative solutions." A resin that could be injected into the limestone, sealing the interstices? Why not! Waterproof shields underneath new buildings, similar to the tarps under our tents? Who could rule it out! Ever the optimist, Mowry was certain that technological mastery was not merely a guiding principle but our one convincing model of truth.

He closed by repeating a line I'd heard him give other audiences.

MOWRY

If we can put a man on the moon, then we can figure out a way to keep Miami Beach dry. You know, I came up through school that we didn't even have calculators. Isn't it crazy? If you would have told me we'd have iPhones, iPads, I wouldn't have believed you. Can you imagine what iterative solutions we'll have in thirty or forty years?

And the obligation of stewardship? I wondered. *Thoughtfulness as to the impact of our actions upon the future, based upon our knowledge of the past?*

God, could you imagine if I'd actually asked that? The uncomprehending look on Mowry's face? Or even the disgust? I think I would prefer disgust. Since what I'd probably get instead is a whole lot of cant and synergy-speak about how stewardship *really* means full trust in the market. It means making sure we don't set up any hurdles or red tape which might hinder tomorrowland imagineers when they're dealing iteratively with the costs and consequences of our self-interest today.

Future generations: Go easy on us. Forgive us our sins. You will not be ruled by desire, as we were, but by circumstance—particularly the circumstances resulting from scarcity, devastation, and chaos. When or if you find these postcards amid the quagmire we've bequeathed, please try to sympathize. Had you been lucky enough to live here and now, you might have made the same mistakes. You, too, might have rejected out of hand the truth that human appetite is insatiable and the world limited. You, too, might have known how *good* it feels, living wastefully at your leisure. Understand, please—we weren't monsters. We were all too human.

And we who must die demand a miracle. We beseech our god of progress: Send unto your people the environmental messiah! For us and for our salvation, may he come down from somewhere, soon, and deliver us from ourselves.

MOWRY

How was that?

KENT (O.S.)

Perfecto, Bruce.

FAKING IT TILL WE'VE MADE IT

I had one last stop to make. Prodigal son that I am, I needed to return to my father's address.

After our meeting with Mowry, we left Miami Beach and headed for Coconut Grove, one of Miami's constituent neighborhoods that happens to be older than the city itself. The Grove, as its name suggests, is an exceptionally vegetal place. Whatever the Spaniards were trying to connote when they dubbed this state *La Florida*—those connotations reside in Coconut Grove. Here you have thick, high canopies crosshatched with sunlight; swaying palms nearer at hand; hanging vines everywhere. Tunnels of verdancy, really, and all of them connected. Along with fragrant hibiscus, inkwell water, peacocks sashaying across driveways. It is a garden, truly. As we walked through it, our steps released rasps of decomposition—a few degrees past the death smell; more akin to the pleasing hint of indole that perfumers add to their bouquets—from the dried leaves and crushed berries underfoot.

The thing about paradise is you can't recognize it as paradise until you're forced to leave it. Returned now to Coconut Grove, I realized: This is paradise. Sadly, though, I saw there were new condos here, too. It looked as though the Grove was becoming a leafy alternative to Miami Beach for the international set. Like mausoleums stacked with empty, prepurchased niches, these towers had something of the grave about them.

We walked south and then east and got to my old street, a big cul-de-sac that branches off of Main Highway. Our progress was halted when we discovered that the residents had put up a guardhouse. Not a wooden-arm gate or a buzz-in intercom but an actual air-conditioned hut, within which sat a guy clearly grateful for the job. He admitted car after car but told us to stay put. While doing so, we considered our reflections in the hut's smoked glass. We appeared to have about us the coiled intensity of the fugitive. We looked, in a word, insane. The tableau caused Noah to crack up. Glenn and I followed suit.

Even after I showed the guard my old driver's license, which listed this street as my address, he refused to let us in. He kept repeating, "You don't want me to lose my job."

Which gave me an idea—

KENT

There's a back way in. An amphibious landing along the seawall. We'll need to buy one of those pool rafts with the plastic oars, is all. And then wait for the tide to come in.

So that's what we did. After purchasing our inflatable raft for a cool fifty dollars (Christmas discount), Glenn suggested we pass the time by filming some extra exit interviews. I pointed us to the Bayshore Landing Marina, where we had our choice of backdrop: bobbing cutters, bobbing yachts, or bobbing megayachts. We took a long five to compose our denouements. Then we workshopped them with one another. Noah went first.

Noah plops onto a bench wearing, as per usual, a preemptively aggrieved expression.

GLENN (O.S.)

Try smiling, eh? Like you've reached an epiphany and are glad.

Noah widens his eyes and smile as suddenly as an agoraphobe wrenching heavy drapes apart.

KENT (O.S.)

Eeeee.

GLENN (O.S.)

Just, at ease.

Noah clears his throat.

NOAH

No, but now I know I gotta commit. To *something*. Like I mentioned before—a child, maybe. A house. Here on out, I'm having my adventures in my mind. I'd rather go to prison for five years than have to do this again. This was it for me. The last hurrah. Last stand at the Dumbshit Alamo.

Noah exhales out of the corner of his mouth.

NOAH (CONT'D)

That being said, it doesn't mean I'm ready for this to end.

I took Glenn's spot behind the camera while Noah moved off-screen.

GLENN

I will say a few things. Number one: I feel like this trip was worth it at least in the sense that I am going home with a really lucid vision of my self. My derangements. Just what rock bottom is. Number two: I am never coming back to Florida. Number three: Plundering Florida for our personal, creative, and financial fortunes like so many before us—I definitely don't think that is going to work out. I definitely don't think that is going to happen. What I've learned is that what Florida is uniquely good at is taking people's capital and sinking it into the swamp.

GLENN (CONT'D)

Do I have some small glimmer of hope that this film can still be something? Yes. Do I think it's going to be a smash hit? No. I think it is going to be a first film. With plenty of mistakes. Lots of shitty cinematography. Some scenes where the sound is terrible. It is going to be a first film.

KENT (O.S.)

You think there's gonna be some charm in that?

GLENN

What else does it have?

I took my turn.

KENT

Yessir. To piggyback on what Noah was saying: I, uh, understand that I am not an excellent dude.

NOAH (O.S.)

Stop the presses.

KENT

The good that I desire is not the good that I do. Though maybe what I've learned is that there is a good person gestating inside of me? Waiting to be born?

I let the tape roll for a bit, blinked a few times. I checked the notes in my lap.

KENT (CONT'D)

More importantly, now I *know*. Now I can tell a person, whenever I hear them shitting on Florida: "What you are actually shitting on is the Republic itself." For what is Florida but an ahistorical sanctuary for the exiled and vagabond? What is it but an experimental home for all those who lost or hated home?

We portaged the raft to an unguarded street paralleling my own. At the end of it, pavement gave way to spinifex grasses and a mucky littoral zone. "Are you kidding me?" Glenn sighed. He pointed to a yellow, diamond-shaped sign planted near some mangroves. "WARNING: CROCODILES." "Huh," I said. "That's a new one." Salt-water crocs never swam this far north when I was a kid.

We took a few minutes to duct-tape garbage bags around the vulnerable parts of our equipment. As we did so, the furnace grate of mangrove roots fired sweat from our noses and fingertips. Off in Biscayne Bay, a speedboat blasting "Holly Jolly Christmas" thudded against the chop.

I brushed back my wet mullet, put my hands on my hips, and listened to the water. I thought of noting in my notebook: *Death is a grinding down of obdurate surfaces, a pulverization of even silica's will*. But why bother with that now?

"I'll see you on the beach," Noah joked, and we three wedged into the raft knees to spines. I navigated at the bow, Glenn filmed from the stern, and Noah manned the oarlocks in between. We paddled northwest on a soft parabola that took us some hundred yards into the bay. Glenn secured the camera in front of his face with all the intensity of a possession receiver catching a fourth-down buttonhook. Otherwise he was calm despite the possibility of our losing everything. Noah grunted with effort—the oars were short and hollow—yet he seemed to be enjoying the view. Shoreward, multitiered *alcázares* hugged the coast as it curved toward the downtown skyline, which stood glinting in the late-afternoon sunlight like ice stalagmites beginning to melt. Seaward, powerboats and windsurfers plied the mint-jelly-green waters between Key Biscayne and the mainland. Sitting there amid the swing and sway of the tide, spritzes of oar water tickling my cheeks as if from an aspergillum, I had a feeling of my real life being past, and my posthumous existence just beginning.

We arced toward my street, which was connected to the bay through a narrow canal. That canal had been deepened considerably, to accommodate the pleasure crafts hoisted above it in boat lifts. The seawalls, too, had been raised a few extra feet. Lining both sides now were huge Italianate mansions, most likely the fruits of permissible criminality. Part of me wanted to say to my friends: *You shoulda seen this place back when!* But I knew better.

I told Noah to lift his oars out of the water. I wanted to shoot a scene. Delicately, I turned in the raft.

KENT

(gesturing to canal sides)

Being American has always meant being in headlong flight from the world you have made. Being American has always meant trying to outrun the past, outrun history, in order to find someplace new to experiment with the idea of the good. And where, pray tell, has America turned last to run to?

We tied the raft to a dock ladder. As he took his turn climbing out of the boat basin, Glenn said, "You know how it takes eight minutes for sunlight to reach the earth? And how if the sun stopped exploding, we wouldn't know for eight minutes?" Noah passed him a bag of gear. "I feel like this place is living in those eight minutes."

Ashore, I could hardly recognize the neighborhood. Gone were the sagging old Grove homes, the raised wooden ones built to catch and funnel sea breezes. Every second house was some garish architectural portmanteau. Palms had been planted; the seepage improved; the scrub cleared. It appeared as if the members of the neighborhood association had agreed (if they agreed on anything) that "unrepentant" was the only way to go out.

"Hey!" I said as we toured the neighborhood. "They drained the field where one of my neighbors got stabbed to death by his lover!"

And of course Glenn is right. Of course time's up. The light is dying, as it must. And yet. As always—yet. Hobbling around this gilded cul-de-sac—blue-and-gold macaws crowing overhead—the salt of the rising tide recalling the taste of blood and tears—I'm home. I'm home, where I have no lasting home. The light is dying—and yet this is the light by which I see everything else.

I backpedaled, my arms thrown wide.

I am radiating the calm and unconscious double movement of love, taking it in and giving it away in turn. I am inspired.

We reached the plot of land that used to contain my house. My folks sold it a few years ago when they themselves got the hell out of Miami. They didn't need Wanless's maps to apprise them of what decades' worth of flash floods and storm surges had already made clear. They dealt to our next-door neighbors, Yankee Strangers who lorded over a high, fortified keep they'd built atop an old orange grove. Upon closing, those neighbors promptly demolished our hurricane-damaged home.

And did little with the lot in the intervening years, I saw. It was, in fact, the only vacant lot remaining in the neighborhood. The pool had been filled in. Tasteful vegetation imported and planted. Judging from the sculptures, cocktail tables, and strings of vintage bulbs threaded through the big oak that once sheltered the driveway, those neighbors had turned my childhood home into spillover space for their many soirees. *They fundraise for the Clintons, you know,* my dad used to whisper while peeping through parted blinds. I didn't believe him then, but I guess I do now.

I took this as an affront at first, standing there, my soul aching like an old wound in bad weather. *My history has been razed so that moneyed others could have their walled garden?*

While Glenn and Noah trespassed to get poignant B-roll, I stewed. But the more I stewed, the more ambivalent I came to feel. *At least there's no parvenu Versailles here, right?*

I check the TILTING STONE MAILBOX in front of the lot. Stuffed inside is faded, water-bloated mail, some of it for me.

ME
(to self)

I am absolutely telling the Internal Revenue Service that this is my new address.

ME (CONT'D)

(to Glenn, Noah, and camera)

In the Land of Good Living, let's call it. It'll be half *Let Us Now Praise Famous Men,* half *American Movie.* It will capture the state that swung the presidential election. It will capture the swamp of self-creation that, for better or worse, leads the nation the way a jutting thermometer leads the infirm.

ME (CONT'D)

There will be unintentional humor. Oh, yes. Laugh at us all you want. There will also be wistfulness, fabulism, history. There needs to be history. But it will not be history for history's sake. It will be history that makes clear Florida isn't just *Weird America*—it is *Impending America.* The further south we walk, the further along the United States' narrative arc we travel. We move from the stagnant Panhandle, where the worst fears of antebellum whites still obtain. We pass through Central Florida, where there is sprawling modern "civilization," of a kind. We wind up in majority-minority, wildly unequal, hilariously corrupt, vapid, gorgeous, climate-change-doomed South Florida, where the shallowness serves to reflect the future like a scrying glass.

ME (CONT'D)

There will of course be set pieces. Quote, unquote *colorful* characters. There will also be philosophical digressions. On, like, Publix supermarket sandwiches. Alligators and plume birds. The bankrupt tradition of Romantic walking narratives. The nature and destiny of Man.

GLENN (O.S.)

On freedom. The state of freedom! Because who's freer than us?

ME

Now you're getting it. It seems to me not unimaginable but inevitable that the next great American novel won't be about America, exactly, and won't exactly be a novel, either.

I took my friends to my favorite stretch of seawall along the bay, where the sun was primed to set. Fifty yards distant, birds were diving and skipjacks flitting out of the water. While prepping for our next shot, I scribbled a note: *I am feeling homesick at home, and this is the feeling that marks me as a Floridian, and an American, and a human being on this earth.*

We stared out at the sea dazzle. The sky went striated with lines of pink, purple, white, and blue.

"I guess this is it," Noah said.

"I think it is safe to say that we failed in making a documentary that lived up to the one we envisioned," Glenn said. "The stresses of actually walking everywhere proved too difficult."

Noah picked up and frisbeed a leftover terra-cotta tile into the bay.

I take a few theatrically deep breaths, hold them, exhale them slowly.

ME

And yet. *What if.* What if instead we chose to say *Fuck that!* and pushed on anyway?

NOAH
(voice-over voice)

Florida: You have one choice—don't choose this.

The light smoldered along the horizon line. We watched it while standing on grass from Bermuda, in the deepening shade of a Brazilian peppertree hung with Mexican vine. Off in the distance: the man-made fantasy island of Miami Beach, where the condos are built with flight capital and the white sand regularly trucked in from quarries. Whatever the real once was—it has been superseded.

Most everything on this peninsula is destined to reappear as simulation. That's our lone industry: transforming Florida into "Florida." Make-believe—we do it to survive down here. We think up novel ways to excite cupidity and incite belief. Make *you* believe; make each other believe; make ourselves believe. Like the very best marketers and confidence artists, we work to destroy the distance between the fantasy and the person who might consume the fantasy. Friend.

That's the thing about the Florida Dream. That's what greases the grift: Its inherent dishonesty and exploitative nature indict you, too. There are no innocents here. Only individuals who wanted waterfront property for pennies on the dollar. Who wanted a consequenceless good time in the sunshine. Who wanted, what? A second home, a retirement paradise, a tax shelter. A duty-free getaway, a noplace without a no, a blank canvas for the unencumbered will.

You can't cheat an honest man, as the confidence artist says. The wizened mark—the Floridian—understands this.

"You know," I said. "Those used cars in Little Havana were, what—five hundred bucks?"

"The car, bro," Noah said. "I *been* telling you."

"Think about it," I said. "It's all fresh right now. We know what we need to go and do. To make it what we wished it was in the first place."

"We're already here," Glenn said, warming to the idea. "We won't have to buy you a mullet wig like we will in six months' time."

"A fucking do-over," Noah said.

"Print this—"

ME

You gotta understand: Florida exists in the future continuous tense. Florida *will be* a personal paradise, yours to own as soon as we fill in this hellish bog. Florida *will be* growing in perpetuity, so long as we keep persuading suckers to move here. Florida *will be* saved from the water by the same selfish, manipulative energies that made her, God willing.

I shake my hair onto my shoulders as I turn to look past the lens.

ME

So how do we tell the true Florida story? By revising it. Continuously. Unscrupulously.

"Let's get out of here before the crocodiles or the cops come," Noah suggested.

We got moving once again.

"History repeats itself, eh?" Glenn said, throwing his arms around Noah and me. "First as tragedy, then as travesty." Holding us for a few steps, he added, "My wife is going to murder me."

"You and me both, brother," Noah said.

In the last of the light, I got Glenn to roll film one more time as we approached the guardhouse.

ME

What if, for the log line, we go with something like . . .

ME (CONT'D)

"If you're willing to suspend your disbelief—"

ME (CONT'D)

No. How about: "If you're willing to disregard the sober investment—"

ME (CONT'D)

"—in favor of the hyperbolic, the hypothetical, the too good to be true—"

ME (CONT'D)

"—well then, friend. I've got a swampland to sell you."

ME (CONT'D)

No, wait, better still—

Time to get fast and loose with the truth.

Author's Note

To the question, "Is this book one hundred percent factual, down to the last syllable?" I answer: This book is about Florida. To write a hundred percent factual book about Florida would be like writing an on-the-level guide to fraud.

So: some names have been changed. Some chronologies and dialogues have been tweaked. An unreliable narrator has gone somewhere and experienced some things. The preceding is as Florida as can be: the real story built upon the true story.

Acknowledgments

Thank you to everyone who sheltered us, humored us, and avoided us with your car. We're lucky, and we know it. Thank you to Jim Rutman, Jordan Pavlin, Nicholas Thomson, and all of the fine folks at Knopf.

Printed in the United States
by Baker & Taylor Publisher Services